In this book, Randall D. Germain explores the international organization of credit in a changing world-economy. At the center of his analysis is the construction of successive international organizations of credit, built around principal financial centers and constituted by overlapping networks of credit institutions, mainly investment, commercial, and central banks. A critical historical approach to international political economy allows Germain to stress both the multiple roles of finance within the world-economy and the centrality of financial practices and networks for the construction of monetary order. He argues that the private global credit system which has replaced Bretton Woods is anchored unevenly across the world's three principal financial centers: New York, London, and Tokyo. This new balance of power is fragmented with respect to relations between states and ambiguous in terms of how power is exercised between public authorities and private financial institutions. Germain's analysis thus suggests that we are living through a period of fragile international monetary order.

CAMBRIDGE STUDIES IN INTERNATIONAL RELATIONS: 57

The international organization of credit

Cambridge Studies in International Relations is a joint initiative of Cambridge University Press and the British International Studies Association (BISA). The series will include a wide range of material, from undergraduate textbooks and surveys to research-based monographs and collaborative volumes. The aim of the series is to publish the best new scholarship in International Studies from Europe, North America and the rest of the world.

CAMBRIDGE STUDIES IN INTERNATIONAL RELATIONS

Series list continues after index

The international organization of credit

States and global finance in the world-economy

Randall D. Germain
University of Newcastle upon Tyne

CAMBRIDGE UNIVERSITY PRESS

PUBLISHED BY THE PRESS SYNDICATE OF THE UNIVERSITY OF CAMBRIDGE
The Pitt Building, Trumpington Street, Cambridge CB2 1RP, United Kingdom

CAMBRIDGE UNIVERSITY PRESS
The Edinburgh Building, Cambridge CB2 2RU, United Kingdom
40 West 20th Street, New York, NY 10011–4211, USA
10 Stamford Road, Oakleigh, Melbourne 3166, Australia

First published 1997

Printed in the United Kingdom at the University Press, Cambridge

Typeset in 10/12½ pt Palatino [CE]

A catalogue record for this book is available from the British Library

Library of Congress cataloguing in publication data

Germain, Randall D., 1961–
States and global finance in the world-economy / Randall D. Germain.
    p.   cm. – (Cambridge studies in international relations : 57)
Includes bibliographical references (p.   ) and index.
ISBN 0 521 59142 2
1. International economic relations.
2. International finance.
I. Title.   II. Series.
HF1359.G476   1997
332'.042–dc21   97–1195   CIP

ISBN 0 521 59142 2 hardback
ISBN 0 521 59851 6 paperback

This book is dedicated with thanks and love to my mother, Helga, my wife, Cindy, and my daughters Elyse, Bronte, Rowen, and Kyla.

Contents

Figures and tables

Preface

International political economy (IPE) is today both too narrow and too broad an intellectual enterprise. Its narrowness derives largely from the rigidities imposed by economics and political science as its primary intellectual mentors. Economics and political science each think of international political economy as a natural part of their academic universe, a distinct solar system perhaps, but one inhabiting a familiar galaxy of thought. Its broadness, on the other hand, is often due to the imperial pretentions harbored by those who identify themselves as international political economists. Few subjects fall outside their intellectual purview: the world is their oyster and they are keen to analyze it as such. As a result, IPE offers something to nearly everyone. It is a field with few boundaries and more than its share of questionable concepts and definitions.

Contrary to many excursions into this new and wide open field, my purpose in the following pages is to alternately broaden and narrow IPE as an intellectual discipline. I wish to broaden its narrowness by looking beyond politics and economics as its principal intellectual inspirations, in this case towards history and the development of an historical mode of thought about IPE that is capable of breaking down intellectual barriers rooted in disciplinary prejudices. At the same time, I seek to narrow IPE's broadness by arguing that there is a particular subject matter at the heart of IPE which should guide its major lines of inquiry. This subject matter is what Fernand Braudel calls the *world-economy*, and explicating the meaning of this term and showing how its precepts can guide our inquiries is a central goal of this study. IPE, in other words, must both broaden its intellectual horizons and narrow its field of inquiry if it is to develop into a coherent and reflective discipline, capable of providing critical reflections about the way in which the world is organized. For in the end, I believe that such critical reflection is the chief promise of IPE, and if this work moves us along that path then it will have realized a good deal of what I set out to do.

This project has travelled a long path since its inception as a doctoral dissertation at York University in Toronto, Canada. York University in the late 1980s was a place of considerable intellectual ferment, and it provided a challenging environment in which to pose the question of international monetary order from an IPE perspective. For their support, encouragement, and critical comments on various parts of the manuscript, I wish particularly to thank David Leyton Brown, Stephen Gill, Paul Evans, Keith Krause, and Jennifer Milliken among the faculty members, and Grant Littke, Geoff Martin, Robert O'Brien, Timothy Sinclair, and Deborah Stienstra among my student cohort. Lou Pauly from the University of Toronto also provided helpful comments on an early draft. At the University of Sheffield in England, where I held my first academic post at the Political Economy Research Centre, I found a congenial environment in which to reflect on the larger project, undertake new research on the regional organization of finance, and then transform the dissertation into a book. In addition to many enjoyable conversations with Sylvia McColm about the idiosyncrasies of British life, my work benefitted from exposure to the critical insights of Michael Dietrich, Andrew Gamble, Ian Hardin, Ankie Hoogvelt, Ian Kearns, Michael Kenny, David Marquand, Tony Payne, Jonathan Perraton, Andrew Tylecote, and especially Ngai-Ling Sum, a wayward soulmate on the intellectual odyssey known as academia. The assistance of a group of bright young postgraduate students – Dominic Kelly, Gavin Kelly, and Peter Wells – in the reassessment of my ideas on the organization of finance was also invaluable. Without implicating any of these individuals in the arguments of this book, I would like to thank each of them for their time and engagement with the ideas presented here.

Funding for this research has come from several sources. In Canada, my doctoral work was supported by scholarships from the Social Sciences and Humanities Research Council of Canada and the Ontario Government. In the United Kingdom, further research on the regional organization of finance has been supported by the University of Sheffield, the Nuffield Foundation, and the Political Economy Research Centre. This research in turn has influenced my thinking on the international organization of credit. Finally, the Department of

Politics at the University of Newcastle, where I have recently taken up a lectureship, has kindly provided funds to compile the index, a task which Paul Langley has efficiently executed. I take much pleasure in acknowledging the support which these institutions have offered this project.

I would also like to express my thanks to Roger Tooze, John Haslam, and Barbara Docherty at Cambridge University Press. Roger's initial enthusiasm for this project placed the time I took to do the revisions into a helpful perspective, while John and Barbara's efficiency in the production process was very much appreciated by this first-time author.

There are three individuals whose contributions to this project and to my own academic career over the years warrant special acknowledgment. I have counted on the intellectual companionship and honest friendship of Michael Williams for a good number of years now, and can think of no better way of expressing this than by implicating him, however remotely, in one of the products of that friendship. Although he and I practice our crafts in different fields, I have always thought that he would have made a good international political economist if only he could have left the field of security studies to its just desserts. I have also taken my association with Robert Cox, from my earliest days at York University, to be one of those rare treasures that life occasionally and inexplicably bestows upon us. Not only has his work left an indelible impression on my own, but he has, through his generosity of spirit, consummate professionalism, and profound sense of integrity, confirmed for me that humane individuals can also make first-class academics. And my father-in-law, Dr Iserdeo Jainarain, through his unstinting belief in the rewards of higher education (including his constant encouragement thereof) and his indefatigable penchant for engaging in critical conversation, has imparted to me an admiration for the life-long process of learning which I hope never to exhaust.

Finally, more than most young academics today, I owe a debt to my wife and family that cannot be repaid in mere words. My mother has always understood and supported the difficult decisions which eventually took me from my home in Canada's Yukon Territory to a city on the coast of north-east England. My wife (and first friend) has continually encouraged me in my work, even as the opportunities for career advancement took us further and further away from family and friends. Together with our children, she has ensured that the process of becoming an academic has not eclipsed a healthy perspective on life itself. Our first child was born on the day in 1990 when the outline of what eventually became *The International Organization of Credit* was due to be delivered to my doctoral supervisor, and the imminent arrival of our last child in 1995 sped the process of completing the revisions far more effectively than any publisher's deadline. My family is as intimately bound up with this work as are the comments and ideas of my many academic colleagues, and it is therefore to them that this book is dedicated.

Randall Germain
Newcastle upon Tyne

Note on figures and tables

The use throughout the figures and tables in the book of "net long-term capital movements" is an attempt to separate these capital movements from both short-term capital movements and movements of reserve funds, whether destined for public or private monetary institutions. It is these funds which are most likely to be used for investment purposes, rather than the funds which are issued, bought, and sold in order to shore up liquidity positions. An attempt to identify them, therefore, is an attempt to arrive at a picture of the movement of those funds most important to the functioning of the world-economy.

Net long-term capital movements are derived from the items in the IMF *Balance of Payments Yearbook* identifying unrequited transfers, long-term private assets and liabilities, and official long-term assets and liabilities. The latter two are included as "non-monetary" capital movements by the *Yearbook*, in order to distinguish them from movements of capital related to reserve requirements of public and private monetary institutions. These categories have changed over the years in their form of presentation, but every effort has been made to be consistent in what is included in these figures.

The main intention of using the data presented in this way is to begin thinking about monetary order in terms of productive investment, capital recycling, and the organization of credit. In order to do this, it is necessary to know about the extent of long-term capital movement; its composition (securities, equities, or direct investment); and its source, i.e., whether it is public or private. These figures and tables are a first attempt at making these distinctions.

All figures are in US dollars, and have been converted at end-of-year exchange rates. Unless otherwise indicated, the source used in the construction of these tables is the IMF *Balance of Payments Yearbook* (various issues).

Glossary

BIS   Bank for International Settlements
EMS   European Monetary System
EPU   European Payments Union
FDI   foreign direct investment
Fed   Federal Reserve Bank (US)
GATT General Agreement on Tariffs and Trade
IBRD International Bank for Reconstruction and Development
IMF   International Monetary Fund
IMS   international monetary system
IOSCO International Organization of Securities Commissions
IPE   international political economy
IR   international relations
MNC   multinational corporation
NATO North Atlantic Treaty Organization
OEEC Organization for European Economic Cooperation
OPEC Organization of Petroleum Exporting Countries
PFC   principal financial center
TNC   transnational corporation

1 Routes to international political economy: accounting for international monetary order

Towards an interdisciplinary international political economy

The renaissance of international political economy (IPE) scholarship on the international monetary system (IMS) is now twenty years old. It crystallized in 1977 with the publication of Benjamin Cohen's *Organizing the World's Money* and Fred Block's *The Origins of International Economic Disorder*, both of which reflected a growing belief among a small band of scholars that the disciplines of economics and politics could no longer credibly uphold their claims to being the monopolistic heirs of knowledge on monetary issues.[1] As IPE coalesced as a field of inquiry in the late 1970s and early 1980s, other studies picked up and extended the themes that have come to mark the core of its analysis of the IMS.[2] With the publication over the last ten years of work as diverse as Susan Strange's *Casino Capitalism* and Ethan Kapstein's *Governing the Global Economy*, IPE must now be considered one of the central avenues of inquiry through which the

---

[1] In charting their way, Cohen and Block were able to draw on the pioneering work of a handful of scholars who had themselves begun fashioning a political economy approach to international economic and/or monetary relations, among them Feis (1930/1964), Brown (1940/1970), Polanyi (1944/1957), Triffin (1960), Hirsch (1967), Clarke (1967), Cooper (1968), Gardner (1969), Meyer (1970), Strange (1971) Kindleberger (1973/1986), and de Cecco (1974). The monetary crisis of the mid-1970s prompted the publication of further analyses, including Rowland (1976), Strange (1976), and Hirsch *et al.* (1977), all of whose points of departure reflected the gathering strength of IPE as an approach to monetary relations.

[2] These studies include Crough (1979), Gilbert (1980), Calleo (1982), Lombra and Witte (1982), Odell (1982), Zysman (1983), Spindler (1984), and Kindleberger (1984/1993).

organization of the IMS is explored.[3] This renaissance has been driven in part by the way in which IPE both cuts across disciplinary boundaries and seeks to understand the totality of its subject matter, free from the intellectual chains of a single, entrenched discipline. More by accident than design, IPE has begun to emerge as a discipline in its own right.

Despite the claims of many IPE scholars, however, two significant hurdles stand in the way of developing IPE as a more self-conscious or reflexive field of social inquiry.[4] The first hurdle is the imperial pretensions which both politics and economics harbor towards their erstwhile progeny. Indeed, there is a discernible trend in contemporary scholarship which views IPE as the logical outgrowth of each discipline's natural arc of inquiry. In economics, this tendency is best exemplified in the public choice approach to the interaction between economies and polities. Its hallmark is the use of neo-classical economic techniques, principally the application of rational choice analysis, to understand decision-making at the international level (Frey, 1984; Frey and Serna, 1995). While this type of analysis has advanced our understanding of how to frame the costs and benefits to states of adopting particular economic strategies, it should not obscure the imperial pretensions represented by this view, namely the emergence of an economic theory of international politics.

Such intellectual imperialism is replicated in the appropriation of IPE by political science. It is best captured in the title of a popular IPE textbook first published in the late 1970s, Joan Spero's *The Politics of International Economic Relations* (1977/1990). Spero's goal was to subject economic processes to a political logic in a mirror image of the economists' attempt to subject political processes to an economic logic. Although both of these imperial routes have yielded intellectual dividends for their respective disciplines, they have also constrained the emergence of a dialogue which might allow IPE to move in an interdisciplinary direction. Trying to establish *international political economy* as a truly distinct field of inquiry from the starting point of

---

[3] In addition to the work of Strange and Kapstein, we may count Frieden (1987), Hawley (1987), Pauly (1988), Eichengreen (1990, 1992), O'Brien (1992), Goodman (1992), Walter (1993), Porter (1993), Helleiner (1994), Sobel (1994), and Kirshner (1995) as part of this growing field.

[4] I am using "reflexive" here in the sense of its use by those international relations (IR) theorists who consider the development of theory to be integrally linked to the capacity to understand its origins and account for its own development. See for example Walker (1987), Hoffman (1987), Lapid (1987), and Neufeld (1995).

2

either politics or economics appears to be the scholarly equivalent of mixing oil and water.

The second hurdle IPE faces in its bid to become a self-conscious field of social inquiry is the problem of defining its central object of inquiry. Many scholars have looked to states and their national economies as the principal objects of inquiry for IPE.[5] Following Stephen Krasner (1976), they have argued that the international economy is the creation of state practices in so far as states, and the national economies they govern, provide the foundations or preferences which make international transactions possible.[6] Others have chosen to consider IPE as a methodology or an approach that promises a more comprehensive analysis of contemporary political–economic problems than either discipline can offer on its own. What both groups of scholars share, however, is an underlying conception of the international economy as the cumulative product of economic exchange between national economies.[7] Jeffry Frieden nicely captures this conception of the international economy when he asserts (1987: 4) that: "there is, after all, no international economy in the abstract . . . The international economy is simply the sum of many national economies, and each national economy is subject to powerful domestic pressures."

This consensus regarding the central object of inquiry for IPE is clearly evident in scholarship on the IMS. Despite very different theoretical starting points, Barry Eichengreen's definition of the IMS as "a set of rules or conventions governing the economic policies of nations" (1990: 271), for example, corresponds precisely to Fred Block's formulation of the IMS as "simply the sum of all of the devices by which nations organize their international economic relations"

---

[5] This focus on national economies has led to a large literature in IPE on the role of particular states in the international economy, especially the United States. With reference to monetary scholarship, examples include Odell (1982), Gowa (1983), Cohen (1986), Hawley (1987), and Frieden (1987).

[6] Even where international economic structures are the primary unit of consideration, the national basis of this international economic structure is clear. Thus David Lake can argue that "the IES [international economic structure] is defined by the two dimensions of relative size and relative productivity . . . relative size will be measured by a *nation's* proportion of world trade. Relative productivity will be measured by a *nation's* output per man-hour relative to average output per man-hour in the other middle and large sized nations" (1984: 146, emphasis added).

[7] See for example Gilpin (1987: 9), Calleo (1982: 79–84), Cohen (1977: 2–8), and Block (1977: 1).

3

(1977: 1).[8] While under some circumstances this consensus on the object of study might conceivably promote disciplinary cross-fertilization, for IPE it has meant that scholars rooted in each discipline have little incentive to adopt a less imperial approach to IPE: each discipline can continue to claim that it provides an authoritative account of its perceived domain by virtue of applying a discipline-specific logic to the phenomena under study. Since a crucial test to decide between the two accounts is not available to those working in the social sciences, the actual amount of interdisciplinary learning is limited.[9] Such an apparently low level of interdisciplinary learning between politics and economics is a significant brake on the development of IPE as a robust area of social inquiry.

If IPE is to develop into a self-conscious and reflexive field of study, it will have to loosen the grip of economics and politics as its principal intellectual guardians, and advance a conception of its central object of inquiry that invites genuine interdisciplinary exploration. To do this, it will need to advance in two directions. The first direction must broaden the disciplines used to inform IPE analysis beyond the standard refrain of politics and economics. The second direction must advance a conception of IPE's central object of inquiry that is able to provide a theoretical and empirical anchor against which competing claims of knowledge can be framed, explored, and assessed. In other words, IPE scholars must be able to define clearly the international political economy as a distinctive social sphere in which a multiplicity of tools can be used for analysis. This study aims to contribute towards the establishment of these new directions for IPE, and in the process to further the self-conscious identity of IPE as an area of inquiry in its own right. While some may see in this privileging of subject matter over methodology the spectre of closure, it is argued here that the attempt to provide IPE with a clear and broad focus of inquiry is in fact necessary if it is to remain open to more than one disciplinary or methodological approach. Providing IPE with a distinctive subject matter that cuts across established disciplinary bound-

---

[8] This understanding of the IMS is widely shared by IPE scholars from either side of the politics–economics divide. See for example Cohen (1977: 3), and Cooper (1987: 7).

[9] A good example of the problem of interdisciplinary learning can be found in the laudable and innovative analysis of regionalism in the Asia-Pacific region edited by Frankel and Kahler (1993). Especially illuminating are the comments by Gilpin and Hoshi.

aries is one important strategy for maintaining the openness which many of its practitioners so rightly prize.

To accomplish this task I proceed along three fronts. First, I draw upon the work of a small number of scholars who have similarly sought to straddle the politics–economics divide, in order to establish the intellectual foundations for considering IPE along the lines proposed here. Second, I develop a particular structural understanding of IPE, informed by what I call the historical mode of thought, as one avenue through which the study of IPE may be pursued. And finally, I turn to history, and in particular to economic and business history, as the chief means by which successive structural orderings of the international political economy can be traced. I call this the world-economy approach to IPE, and argue that it provides an historical–institutional future for the discipline which both relaxes its current disciplinary barriers and articulates a conception of the international political economy as a distinct social sphere of inquiry. The medium through which this study proceeds is an argument about how we should account for international monetary order, with a special focus on what I call the international organization of credit.

Accounting for international monetary order

Most attempts within the IPE tradition to explain the construction or erosion of monetary order emphasize one of two related arguments. The first and most common argument is that monetary order is created by states, and that the aims, interests, and powers of major states are the principal moving forces to investigate. This argument has been most forcefully explored in a number of works associated with the interwar period, which take as their theoretical point of departure some version of hegemonic stability theory. Charles Kindleberger provides one of the earliest and strongest forms of this argument when he argues, with reference to the interwar period, that the United States was unwilling and Britain unable to take the necessary steps to confront the problems of war reparations, inter-allied loans and lender-of-last resort requirements at the beginning of the depression in 1929. He maintains that the post-1919 leadership vacuum exacerbated the monetary problems of the interwar period and ensured that the depression was longer and more scarring than it needed to be. Such claims are echoed by virtually all scholars who dwell at any length on monetary aspects of interwar history.[10] This view also informs several recent studies of global finance which suggest that, contrary to common perceptions of the origins of integration and globalization in the IMS over the past twenty years, states in fact have been in the vanguard of these developments.[11] Without embracing hegemonic stability theory, this scholarship argues that the foundation of the IMS remains a political creation, and that transnational processes are always and everywhere mediated by specific state structures. While states may operate within clear constraints that are more severe for some than others, it is nevertheless states which in the end choose to allow financial markets to operate with any particular degree of openness. National and international markets are always socially and politically embedded; thus politics and the exercise of sovereign authority cannot be absent from any account of the foundations of international monetary order (Underhill, 1995).

A second and often related argument centers on the effects of economic efficiency on monetary order. Here the basic claim is that efficient markets lead to a stable IMS while inefficient markets lead to an unstable IMS. This argument, whether from scholars of a more liberal persuasion (such as Richard Rosecrance [1986]), or of a more mercantilist bent (such as Robert Gilpin [1987]), sees the erosion of efficiency as inevitably leading to a reduction in the capacity of a dominant economy to generate wealth and power. As national economic efficiencies wax and wane, growth becomes uneven, leading to the international redistribution of wealth and power – the natural by-product of uneven growth in this reading (Gilpin, 1987; Kennedy, 1987). In the monetary field, for example, Gilpin argues that the inability of hegemons to fund growing expenditures over time, due to flagging growth rates and escalating imperial costs, results in an increasing debt load that leads almost of necessity to economic decline and the abdication of hegemonic responsibilities (1987: 339–40). When directly linked to the paramount role of the state, changes in national economic efficiency help to account for the political foundation of monetary order. Taking account of the role of

[10] Similar arguments, albeit with different emphases, have been made with respect to the interwar period by Block (1977: 19), Calleo (1976c: 237–46), Cohen (1977: 83–9), Eichengreen (1990: 271–311), Gill and Law (1988: 129–36), Rowland (1976), and Strange (1988: 100–1).

[11] For example, see Frieden (1987), Goodman and Pauly (1993), Helleiner (1994), Schwartz (1994), and Strange (1986, 1989).

economic efficiency is therefore critical to a political economy understanding of monetary order.

In the case of the postwar period, these two general arguments
provide the basic framework through which the creation and demise
of Bretton Woods as a fixed exchange rate system is understood. In
this reading, the question of maintaining monetary order in the
postwar period became embroiled with the attempt to sustain the
exchange rate regime under conditions of increasing financial and
political uncertainty (Volcker and Gyohten, 1992). This uncertainty
was most closely associated with the creation and distribution of
international liquidity, defined as those assets which governments can
readily use to support their currencies and run balance of payments
deficits. The financial dimension was accurately identified by Robert
Triffin (1960) shortly after the assumption of full currency convertibility by western European governments in 1958. He argued that
continued US balance of payments deficits would create a dollar
overhang that must inevitably outgrow US gold stocks and prompt a
crisis in the fixed value of the dollar related to gold. The solution to
this problem became known as the "Triffin Dilemma," on the basis
that any attempt to narrow or eradicate the US balance of payments
deficit would necessarily compromise the provision of credit to the
international economy. Europe was especially vulnerable, since at this
time it depended on US deficits for additions to its official reserves.
The problem of monetary order thus became bound up with the
question of how to increase official liquidity without undermining the
fixed exchange rate regime. For liberal scholars in particular, this came
to define the problem of the postwar IMS.[12]

It was of course a difficult problem to solve because of the emerging
uncertainty surrounding the political commitment of the United
States to live within the rules of Bretton Woods as its own economic
position evolved through these years. This political commitment was
itself dependent on maintaining Bretton Woods as a creditor-biased
system, from which the United States derived significant privileges.
There were two main aspects to this bias. First, the adjustment
mechanism built into the Bretton Woods Agreements placed the brunt
of adjustment costs onto economies in deficit on their current account.
These economies had generally to borrow abroad to finance their

---

[12] This formulation of the problem was central to the investigations of Gilbert (1980),
Cohen (1977), Cooper (1968), and Gardner (1969).

deficits, thus bestowing a privileged position onto the surplus economies which financed these deficits.[13] This privileged position ensured that change in the system became a matter for negotiation among creditor countries alone. Second, by linking the parities of all currencies to gold through the US dollar, the exchange rate regime allowed for only one source of credit growth in the system: US balance of payments deficits.[14] Increases in international liquidity were thus entirely the prerogative of the US government and economy, providing American authorities with unparalleled choice in determining how much credit was created, and an exorbitant influence over the purposes to which this credit could (or could not) be put within the international economy. Unsurprisingly, this proved to be a privilege the United States was reluctant to abandon. The political uncertainty which came to dominate Bretton Woods in its later years thus became almost entirely a question of American management of the monetary system.

Those accounts which choose not to emphasize the related arguments of state power and economic efficiency in the construction and erosion of monetary order take as their starting point the institutions of finance and their interaction with political authority. Porter (1993), for example, explores the effectiveness of selected international institutions (the Basle Committee on Banking Supervision and IOSCO) within the context of the relationship between inter-state regimes and the structure of the industries they regulate. He concludes that the strength of these regimes – an important dimension of monetary order – is directly dependent upon industrial structure: highly competitive industries are open to the development of strong inter-state regimes under certain circumstances, and oligopolistic industries less so. Another recent analysis has argued that hegemonic stability theory is rarely able to explain the construction and erosion of monetary order. It contends that "hegemony is certainly not a sufficient condition for international monetary stability and there seems to be no strong *a priori* arguments that it is even a necessary condition" (Walter, 1993:

[13] Domestic alternatives to borrowing abroad to finance deficits included raising taxes and printing money. If the former was everywhere politically unpalatable, the latter ultimately led to an increase in inflation, thereby placing downward pressure on the currency and returning policy-makers to the original dilemma of how to maintain a fixed parity in the face of a payments imbalance.

[14] While increases in world gold stocks could also theoretically increase global liquidity, there was no practical way to ensure that increases in gold stocks could keep pace with the demands of international trade.

79). Rather, order within the IMS is much more firmly linked to the durability of social consensus within national economies and to the balance of international transactions which this consensus is able to support.

Such conclusions are supported by the work of other scholars who focus on factors within the financial system itself which tend towards stability and/or instability.[15] Their common point of reference is the close attention paid to the economic and financial dimensions of monetary order, and especially to the fragile institutional artifice commonly identified as "finance." In particular, they view the mechanisms by which networks of monetary agents transfer wealth throughout the international economy as central to the way in which order is constructed within an IMS. Thus, while some scholars have attempted to explain the operation of the IMS in the early twentieth century with reference to a world credit system centered around cities acting as international clearing centers (Brown, 1940/1970), others point to the way in which London absorbed overseas balances, especially those of Britain's colonial crown jewel, India, as the chief means by which the pre-1914 gold standard achieved its much-vaunted stability (de Cecco, 1974). This sensitivity to institutional factors is embraced by others whose work explores the wider structural parameters of the international economy. Cox, for example, points to the changing nature of social relations as a key attribute of the structural transformation of the postwar period. In his analysis of the Bretton Woods era, global finance became the preeminent agency of conformity to world order, and as such a principal institution of the *Pax Americana* (Cox, 1987: 267). Cox argues that the subsequent unravelling of Bretton Woods has placed the role of global finance in a precarious position: it might be strengthened or weakened depending upon whether a state-capitalist or hyper-liberal state emerges as a principal structural characteristic of the emerging world order.[16] The utility of these approaches lies in both embedding the IMS into the structural foundations of the international economy and in exploring the institutional basis (public and private) of its organizational form.

Others have reflected on the wider institutional basis of the IMS to argue that monetary order in the postwar period exhibits a remarkable

[15] See for example Eichengreen (1990), de Cecco (1974), Brown (1940/1970), and Feis (1930/1964).

[16] This general conclusion finds echoes in the work of Gill and Law (1988), and Ruggie (1982).

degree of continuity despite the widespread perception of fundamental change. For example, neither Palloix (1975) nor Andreff (1984) see a "breakdown" in monetary order occurring in 1971. Their focus on class relations and the restructuring of economic life leads them to conclude that global finance has emerged from the crisis of the 1970s stronger and more privileged than ever. Susan Strange and Charles Kindleberger, iconoclasts from within their respective disciplines, have arrived at substantially similar conclusions. Strange sees 1971 as an important date because it marks the extraordinary power of the United States unilaterally both to change the rules of the game and to reduce systematically the scale of public control over the activities of private financial firms (1986/1989: chapter 2; 1982: 79–82). Kindleberger, on the other hand, while conceding that 1971 is an important date, points out that the perceived root cause of monetary instability – the American balance of payments deficit – was in actuality nothing more than the efficient performance by New York of international financial mediation, borrowing short to lend long (1969/1981: 43–5). And finally, Walter argues that "the image of the 'breakdown' of Bretton Woods . . . is most misleading because it underestimates the *continuity* in the evolution of the international monetary system since the late 1950s" (1993: 190, emphasis in original). The utility of this broad spectrum of scholarship lies precisely in its treatment of the way in which private financial institutions are organized within the IMS. Whether framed in terms of class relations, market operations, or institutional structure, this sensitivity to how social forces are organized provides the starting point in reconsidering the foundations of international monetary order.

From money to finance: reconsidering the IMS

In general, the renaissance of political economy scholarship on the IMS shares several common traits with regard to the question of how international monetary order is constructed. First, there is a common understanding of the IMS as the set of rules governing the policies nations adopt in the course of carrying out their international economic transactions. Second, there is common agreement on the central issues under study: monetary order within the IMS is the result of an adequate provision of liquidity, the establishment of stable exchange rates, and the smooth operation of an adjustment mechanism working through appropriate levels of capital mobility.

Finally, the principal focus of monetary scholarship is the way in which the monetary policies of the major states contribute to the achievement of a stable monetary order. Taken together, these characteristics define a broad consensus within IPE regarding what constitutes legitimate scholarly inquiry into the IMS. Such inquiry examines in the first instance the public institutional framework within which international monetary issues emerge, and through which the monetary policies of states are pursued. This framework places international governance firmly within the public domain and links it to the actions and policies of states as they facilitate the achievement of monetary order.

There are strong reasons for this consensus to exist. Both politics and economics have a long-standing concern with public policy. This concern is reinforced by historical practices associated with the organization of wealth and power around the twin poles of the sovereign state and the national economy. It is also clear that the key issues of the IMS are directly connected with the outcomes of public policy initiatives. While they may be at times heavily influenced by the operations of private agents acting through market systems, it is only through concerted public action that the problems associated with these issues can be addressed. In short, the principal strength behind the consensus on monetary scholarship is the practical relevance which government policy has for the creation and maintenance of the public institutional framework of the IMS, and hence for the construction of international monetary order.

As powerful as these reasons are, three related arguments suggest that the complete acceptance of this consensus is an inadequate basis for a comprehensive understanding of order within the IMS. The first argument is that the concentration on public power, authority, and policy clouds the growing role of private monetary agents within the IMS. Despite being active within markets that are established and maintained by public authority, private monetary agents have enjoyed a growing sway over the organization and operation of the IMS during the last twenty-five years. Thus, their role must be brought to the center of our understanding of order within the IMS.[17]

---

[17] Over the past decade, the role and regulation of banks in the IMS has received increasing attention. See for example Crough (1979), Moffitt (1983), Spindler (1984), Moran (1986), Cohen (1981, 1986), Strange (1986/1989), Frieden (1987), Pauly (1988), Porter (1993), Kapstein (1994), and Sobel (1994). This study extends and builds on the work of these authors.

The second argument cautioning against complete acceptance of the consensus on monetary issues concerns the role played by the system of international clearance in maintaining a steady and predictable flow of international payments. This system, although partly monetary in the sense of being involved in the exchange of currencies, is more importantly considered part of the credit system on the grounds that it is the only means whereby the exchange of claims and obligations that arise out of international transactions can be realized. The clearance system is also the prime mechanism through which risk is transmitted internationally. Since risk and the exchange of claim and obligation lie at the heart of any definition of credit, the way in which international clearance is organized must also be included as a central dimension of our analysis.

Finally, the dominance of the monetary consensus can be questioned on the grounds that it adequately explores neither the way in which long-term credit is made available to actors within the international economy nor the impact which particular forms of long-term credit have on how the international political economy is organized. The common focus on liquidity, exchange rates, and adjustment is most often set within the context of capital movements of short-term duration, the "hot" money of every policy-maker's bad dreams. It remains the case, however, that long-term credit is one of the most significant determinants of expansion in the levels of production in goods, services, and technology or knowledge throughout the international economy. Considering the way in which long-term credit is made available to the international economy is thus crucial for any understanding of the foundations of international monetary order. Together, these arguments suggest that we must broaden our approach to the question of order within the IMS to capture the full implications of having credit organized in a particular way. They reinforce Benjamin Cohen's recent call (1996: 296) to "take more serious account of alternative and potentially complementary conceptualizations of rule and dominion in the modern world" in order to understand the reasons for the risen phoenix of global finance. Shifting the burden of analysis from money to finance is the indispensible starting point for the consideration of monetary order offered below.

The international organization of credit
The world-economy approach

Accounting for monetary order from the perspective of the international organization of credit begins with a reconceptualization of IPE's core object of inquiry, the international economy. In contrast to the dominant conception of the "international economy" signaled above, alternative understandings have been advanced by scholars ranging from economic historians to world-systems theorists to those working loosely within the tradition of historical materialism. These views begin not with the entire scope of economic activity evident on a global basis, but with a bounded social totality marked by distinct boundaries, clear centers of public power, a particular division of labor, and a coherent set of recognizable social practices. I will follow Fernand Braudel in calling this a *world-economy*, a term which he carefully distinguishes from the more widely-used term "world economy" (1979/1984: 22). Whereas the "world economy" is a grand description of the linkages of exchange which extend across the entire world at a given point in time, the more cautiously considered notion of a "world-economy" attempts to focus attention upon only a specific set of economic and related practices evident across a part of the world.[18] These practices are considered in terms of a bounded social totality that has an objective foundation and an inter-subjective unity linking together its seemingly disparate parts, and broad temporal boundaries that mark off one world-economy from another. By embracing a definition of the international economy that is in the first instance social rather than narrowly political or economic, Braudel helps to provide the theoretical framework whereby the insights provided by these two disciplines can be incorporated into a broader understanding of particular social orders over given periods of time. I will call this approach to IPE the world-economy approach.[19]

Although the world-economy approach takes its lead from Braudel, he is not the only scholar to consider the "international economy" in these terms. Immanuel Wallerstein, for example, identi-

---

[18] A world-economy is "a fragment of the world, an economically autonomous section of the planet able to provide for most of its own needs, a section to which its internal links and exchanges give a certain organic unity" (Braudel, 1979/1984: 22).

[19] Helleiner (1990) and Germain (1996a) offer concise introductions to Braudel's work from an IPE perspective, while Overbeek (1988), Arrighi (1994), and Germain (1996b, 1996c) demonstrate how Braudelian categories can be applied.

fies a single world-system in existence since the long sixteenth century, including a single international division of labor (1974: 347–57). His work has been taken up and refined by subsequent world-systems theorists like Christopher Chase-Dunn (1989) and Peter Taylor (1996), who have insisted that the deep structures of global capitalism must be theorized on an interdisciplinary basis. Charles Albert Michalet points to a transnational production structure operating outside of the traditional international economy, where the "integrated and planned area of MNCs is gradually taking over from that of the international economy" (1982: 43). Charles Kindleberger hints at the problems associated with thinking about the international economy in terms of standard national accounts when he argues that US balance of payments deficits in the 1960s should be considered more as an example of efficient international financial intermediation performed by New York rather than the root cause of postwar international monetary instability (1969/1981: 43–5). Robert Cox argues that the internationalization of both production and the state serves to invalidate conventional political and economic categories (1987: 1–11), while Stephen Gill points to the emergence of a transnational liberal economic order as eclipsing the international economy of the postwar period (1990: 84 and chapter 5; cf. Gill and Law, 1988: 146–55). Finally, Susan Strange sees the international economy as a single global social and economic system that coexists with a series of national societies (1988: 18), and John Agnew and Stuart Corbridge are among a growing band of geographers who insist that the international economy is more properly apprehended in terms of a single geopolitical order (1995: 3–7). Although these alternative approaches to the "international economy" may diverge methodologically, they are united in their attempt to apprehend what they believe to be a different object of inquiry as compared with the dominant consensus. My elaboration of the world-economy approach builds on this common strand evident in their work.

Following Braudel, a world-economy may be defined as the set of relationships and practices that binds together a social totality realized in the first instance through the creation of a certain kind of wealth.[20]

---

[20] This kind of wealth Braudel preferred to call "capital," wealth which sought to reproduce itself. Defined as such, "capital" was present only in those spheres of the economy where the possibility of its reproduction existed (1979/1982: 232–9). In this sense a world-economy may be identified by the logic of its most powerful wealth-producing agents.

This totality is given a structural coherence by virtue of its boundaries, its division into particular realms, and its temporal experience. Historically, for example, world-economies have had clear boundaries that change only slowly, and have been marked by the dominance of a single city acting as their central logistical center. This dominant city is connected to the various zones of a world-economy through political and economic means, and powerfully shapes the way exchange relations develop throughout these zones.[21] It is within these central cities that a concentration of rulers, merchants, and intellectuals develops, able to impart to their world-economy a distinctive form of enterprise and a recognizable coherence centered around the flows of information, credit, merchandise, ideas, and power contained within their established institutional networks. These are the practices and relationships that allow a world-economy to be defined.

At the same time, a world-economy does not subsume all economic activity within its particular space to one primary dynamic. One of the chief innovations of Braudel's notion of world-economy is to incorporate into it a variegated notion of space as consisting of three inter-related and yet partially autonomous realms of social activity: material life, the market economy, and capitalism.[22] The realm of material life is largely concerned with the activities of everyday living: repeated actions and processes which are handed down from generation to generation. Their evolution is slow, often imperceptible, and embedded in our consciousness as "common sense." The realm of the market economy is characterized by routine exchange that is transparent in its motivations and whose consequences are well understood from common experience. It is the realm in which analytical certainties derived from observation are most likely to be applicable. The final realm is that of capitalism, the preserve of speculators and others whose primary motivation is the accumulation of capital on a massive scale. Here both certainty and "common sense" are difficult to achieve because of the lack of transparency surrounding the activities of "capitalists," which encourages multiple and often contradictory interpretations of events. While these three realms all coexist

---

[21] Schwartz (1994) has argued that these zones can be conceptualized as von Thünen zones, after the nineteenth-century German economist. Schwartz's use of von Thünen is similar in some aspects to Braudel's considerations of economic space.

[22] Braudel considers these realms from different perspectives in all of his major works. See for example (1967/1973: ix-xv; 1977: 39-75; 1979/1982: 455-7; 1979/1984: 619-32).

within a single world-economy, they are not differentiated primarily along geopolitical lines as world-systems theorists or geographers insist (cf. Wallerstein, 1974; Agnew and Corbridge, 1995). Rather, these realms are differentiated by the types of activities which occur within them. They are dominated by particular types of activities that are informed by different motivational expectations and built around contending sets of environmental pressures. They are, in other words, social realms.

These motivations and pressures are framed against the temporal rhythms that mark the final dimension of Braudel's conceptualization of the world-economy. The dominant practices of each realm experience the temporal rhythms that are most strongly associated with its own particular set of motivating forces, although variations are of course not absent (Braudel, 1958/1980). Where large profits are to be made on the basis of exploiting information differentials, time is experienced as *histoire événementielle*, a rapid sequence of directly connected events whose trajectory is nevertheless uncertain and subject to high levels of contingency. Where exchange is more routine, based perhaps on agricultural production synchronized to the rhythms of the seasons or perhaps on the slow expansion of arable land, time moves more slowly, in cycles of measurable proportions. These are the *conjunctures* that are between about ten and fifty years duration, and which provide the backdrop to the events of *histoire événementielle*. Finally, Braudel alerts us to the movement of the *longue durée*, those slow and undulating rhythms that so dominate the realm of material life. Here the *mentalité*, or mental framework of inter-subjective ideas, provides the key that allows individuals to fix their collective relationship to the realities which intrude upon and constrain their everyday lives, and which can remain in force over several hundred years. Ultimately, understanding the coherence of a world-economy directs us to examine the complex and multi-level interactions between its boundaries, realms, and temporal rhythms.

Outlining the framework

We can put into effect the movement from money to finance in our consideration of the IMS by initially focusing on the role of private monetary agents, the system of international clearance, and the availability of long-term credit as the critical foundations around which the international organization of credit is constructed. Crucial

16

to this movement is the capacity to distinguish clearly between money and finance. I shall follow Susan Strange in her analytical distinction between money and finance, where money is considered as the determination of currency values together with the system used to exchange currencies, while finance is the system whereby credit is created, bought, and sold (1990: 259; Stopford and Strange, 1991: 40). Although they are not without their overlapping practical connections, within the world-economy money and finance are often associated with different end-purposes, and it is these which provide the basis for considering money and finance to be analytically distinct.

How, then, should we define finance? I prefer to use the term "credit," because the key question of finance is gaining access to credit. For our purposes, the idea of credit represents a social invention in which fungible assets are exchanged for future promises to pay. Credit here is a resource which people, firms, and governments have access to at the discretion of others, and at a cost established by others: it is both a material resource and a set of social practices associated with realizing it. In other words credit is more than a social convention, it is also an actual network of institutions whose business is precisely to provide access to the value represented by this social convention. As a material resource, credit can exist in several forms: as cash, bank balances, lines of credit, or as an enforced right (e.g., to tax or to compel the purchase of future promises to pay). In this sense credit either arises out of economic activity in the form of savings or profits, or it can be created by public and private monetary authorities through the manipulation of the banking system, what is sometimes called fictitious credit.[23] Credit, however, must also be mobilized or realized if it is to have any effect upon economic actors, and therefore we must also consider it as a set of social practices through which a particular kind of material resource passes. In this sense credit is a closely knit yet intensely competitive network of institutional agents who control the access of others to the resources which they either own themselves or have access to. The social and political implications of credit thus concern who controls the access of others to credit, who is privileged by access to credit, and who reaps the competitive advantage which access to adequate credit imparts. As Strange main-

---

[23] Guttmann notes (1994: 42) that the key characteristic of fictitious capital is its formation in terms of "credit circuits and security values that are relatively divorced from the accumulation of industrial capital, [which] enables individual financial institutions to expand without being directly tied to industry."

tains (1988: 88), "the power to create credit implies the power to allow or to deny other people the possibility of spending today and paying back tomorrow, the power to let them exercise purchasing power and thus influence markets for production, and also the power to manage or mismanage the currency in which credit is denominated."

Because of these social and political dimensions, the phrase "international organization of credit" is used here in a very precise way. The term "international" carries a dual meaning. It serves to denote both the specific realm within the world-economy to which this analysis applies, namely the realm of capitalism as Braudel would understand it, and the boundary-crossing practices associated with the institutions of that realm, whether public or private. Our analysis thus largely focuses on those authorities, institutions, practices, and resources which cross boundaries. The term "organization" is used in preference to the term "system" in order to avoid the rigidity and over-determination with which the latter term has become associated. The way in which credit is organized has an elasticity contingent on its historical character which systemic analyses such as those undertaken by world-systems theory tend to obscure.[24] Finally, the term "credit" represents a financial resource that actors can gain access to only through networks of specialized monetary agents. In other words some kind of a social mechanism must be in operation before credit can be realized as a material resource. The "international organization of credit" can therefore be defined as the network of private and public monetary institutions which realize and mobilize access to internationally mobile financial resources. This definition may be contrasted with more standard definitions of global finance that focus upon particular types of cross-border financial transactions and the way in which these transactions encourage the broad integration of national markets.[25]

---

[24] World-systems theory, as a body of scholarship, owes far more to the late Marx than to the eclectic strands of historical materialism that inform this inquiry. In terms of Braudel's work, for example, the attempt by world-systems theorists to abandon the elasticity and indeterminacy of his approach means that in the end they abandon the historicity that is one of its cardinal strengths. Braudel (1979/1984: 70) applied such a criticism to Wallerstein's work, and it can be applied also to more recent contributions to world-systems theory such as Chase-Dunn (1989), and Taylor (1996). Germain (1996a: 204) critiques the appropriation of Braudel by world-systems theory along these lines.

[25] Benjamin Cohen, in a recent review article (1996: 269), defines global finance as "all types of cross-border portfolio-type transactions . . . [including] capital flows associ-

Table 1.1 *The international organization of credit*

Political economy practices	Financial practices
(1) Changing nature of wealth creation in the world-economy	(3) Influence and role of principal financial centers (PFCs)
(2) Inter-state rivalry and dominant ideological predispositions	(4) Capital recycling mechanism

Mapping the international organization of credit and determining the forces which shape it consists in the first instance of identifying the set of practices which comprise the wealth-creating dynamics of the world-economy as they relate to the establishment of pools of internationally mobile capital, and which construct the institutions that organize and channel this wealth in particular ways and for certain types of investments. These practices, which I have identified as political economy practices and financial practices, are summarized in table 1.1.

The first political economy practice ((1) in table 1.1) connects the organization of credit to the world-economy at the level of wealth creation. Understanding the changing nature of wealth creation is critical to the international organization of credit because it affects the location, amount, and social purposes to which wealth is put, as well as the monetary institutions that are best placed to act as points of access to that wealth. When new monetary agents gain access to large sources of capital and begin to recycle that capital abroad, changes in lending and financing practices occur which can have repercussions within the world-economy. Changes in where and who creates wealth in the world-economy affect how that wealth is mobilized and recycled from areas and industries in surplus to those in demand and/or need.

The forces which shape the practices associated with the creation of wealth are most naturally at home in the realm of capitalism. They are most often organized as institutions engaged in the trade and production of goods and services for a mass or world market. For Braudel, this realm is the home of accumulation on a world scale,

ated with foreign direct investment . . . Financial globalization [thus] refers to the broad integration of national markets associated with both innovation and deregulation in the postwar era and is manifested by increasing movements of capital across national frontiers."

where capitalists seek to reproduce their capital by engaging in speculative ventures attended by high levels of risk: the long-distance trade of an earlier era, or the stock market and top-level real estate speculation of the contemporary era (1979/1984: 6??) In contrast to the realm of the market economy, this realm is defined foremost by its lack of transparency. It is here that the organic unity of capital, capitalist, and capitalism is strongest, and where the particular form of wealth creation that dominates a world-economy first takes hold. The realm of capitalism, however, is not completely defined by geography. Its definition is sharpened and focused by the clusters of institutional networks which lie at the heart of wealth-producing commercial activities. In the age of merchant capitalism this cluster of commercial activities was dominated by long-distance traders, while in the age of industrial capitalism it was dominated in the first instance by the giant industrial concerns of Britain and the United States, and secondarily by those of Germany, France, and Japan. As the emergence of the knowledge-intensive economy strengthens in the contemporary period, we may expect the wealth-creation dynamic to become concentrated on high-technology and knowledge-intensive firms. As the key sectors of wealth creation – and the agents which constitute these sectors – change over time, so too does the international organization of credit that is constructed around their activities. We may say that the international organization of credit is fully embedded within the larger wealth-creating dynamics of the world-economy.

The second major political economy practice ((2) in table 1.1) can be characterized as the changing nature of inter-state rivalry and the ideological predispositions of what have been known historically as the great powers. At one level, inter-state rivalry helps to establish the geographic boundaries of a world-economy, demarcating the areas within which established patterns of activity can be expected to continue, and providing a motivational logic to maintain such practices. Inter-state rivalry here helps to set the outer limits on the influence of private monetary authorities within the credit system by providing a boundary which they may cross only with great risk.[26] At

---

[26] These limits are political and clearly visible, although sometimes only after the fact. An instructive example lies in the public response to the international debt crisis of the early 1980s. German banks had lent heavily to Poland and American banks had lent heavily to Mexico, but only American banks received the full support of international efforts to resolve these repayment problems. Poland was in effect part

another level, however, inter-state rivalry helps to set the ideological predispositions of the great powers which in turn inform the latitude public monetary authorities grant to private monetary agents. These predispositions establish the scale of political attempts to mold the institutions through which credit is channeled within the world-economy. Together, inter-state rivalry and the ideological predispositions of the great powers provide the motive forces which shape the level of influence states attempt to wield over the international organization of credit.

The second key set of practices connecting the international organization of credit to the world-economy are more narrowly and technically financial in scope. The first aspect of these practices ((3) in table 1.1) focuses upon the role of principal financial centers within a world-economy. A principal financial center, or PFC, is where the material and social aspects of credit are brought together to form a concentrated point of access connecting the individuals, firms, and governments in need of credit to the resources represented by international credit. A single world PFC is indicative of a highly centralized international organization of credit, while a number of competing or rival PFCs indicates a decentering of wealth creation within a world-economy. The hierarchical relationship among PFCs thus symbolizes the distribution of power between both states and networks of monetary agents within the international organization of credit. Clear lines of dependence and reliance are often, but not always, associated with the direction of capital flows between PFCs.

The density of linkages between PFCs confirms the strength or weakness of these hierarchical relationships. The dominance of selected networks of monetary agents is most importantly a result of operating in the first instance out of a world PFC. Having access to the credit facilities within a PFC allows monetary agents to expand into a world-economy on the basis of the activities of firms based in those cities or dominant national economies, and therefore to become an important element of the centralized organization of a world-economy. Equally important, dense linkages between PFCs ensure an effective movement of funds between centers, so that wealth created in one area and industry may be put to work in others. Another aspect of the density of linkages between PFCs lies in the collection and

of another world-economy, and banks lending to Poland paid the high transaction costs associated with trading outside of their world-economy (Strange, 1987: 569).

transfer of information between PFCs and among networks of monetary agents. Credit, and the value of the claims and obligations it represents, is finely tuned to flows of information between lenders and borrowers and between competitive networks of monetary agents themselves. The constitution of information and the networks through which it flows therefore play an important role in the consolidation and/or erosion of particular PFCs within the international organization of credit.

The capital recycling mechanism ((4) in table 1.1) comprises the second aspect of financial practices within the international organization of credit. It is the means by which capital is recycled from areas of surplus to areas of demand or need. Historically, the capital recycling mechanism has been composed of networks of monetary agents that have been dominated by private, family-controlled firms. Joint-stock banks, which rose to prominence in Continental European countries in the middle of the nineteenth century and slightly later in Britain, have since usurped the central position of family-controlled firms, and since 1945 governments themselves have became actively involved in the capital recycling mechanism. This mechanism is highly susceptible to direct political influence, primarily because private monetary agents operate so clearly within regulatory contexts established by public monetary authorities. It is at the same time a fragile and finely-balanced human artifice, based as much on subjective perceptions of confidence and credibility as on more objective criteria like size and market share. For this reason the constitution of the capital recycling mechanism is a highly technical affair, and cannot be reduced to simple monocausal foundations of a purely political or economic nature. It is with respect to this aspect of the international organization of credit that the call for a genuinely interdisciplinary approach to political economy can be most forcefully made.

The forces which shape the financial practices of the international organization of credit are firmly rooted in the behavior of monetary agents and the institutional networks which develop around their activities. They constitute the means by which credit is channeled throughout the world-economy, and in their public incarnation affect how the activities of private agents are regulated. Historically, however, private monetary agents have been the principal institutions at the center of the global credit system. In this sense both the capital recycling mechanism and the links between PFCs can be understood as growing up and around the preferences and practices of private monetary agents as they are supported and/or constrained by public authorities.

The political economy and financial practices which constitute the international organization of credit are integrally related to one another. The emergence of new centers of wealth creation shifts material resources into networks of monetary agents active in the first instance out of newly emergent financial centers. Rival financial centers thus emerge as points of global competition to established PFCs within the international organization of credit. Great power rivalry contributes to this process by over-taxing the wealth-producing capacities of the strongest states, leading to the kind of imperial over-extension which Paul Kennedy (1987) has associated with the rise and fall of great powers throughout history. Shifts in the availability of material resources alter the existing balance of social power, reinforcing or eroding the ability of a particular network of monetary agents to dominate access to internationally mobile credit. New networks of monetary agents challenge established lending practices, pouring resources into new areas and industries and hastening the decline of older, more traditional industries and areas. Governments involve themselves in the capital recycling mechanism to redress inadequate access to resources for nationally-based firms, or withdraw as part of a strategic plan to limit their exposure to private economic pressures. In these ways, and others, the emergence of competing centers of wealth creation helps to transform the capital recycling mechanism, alter the international organization of credit, and ultimately change the constitution of the world-economy.

This understanding of the international organization of credit is fully consistent with the world-economy approach outlined above. It is broadly structural in nature, in terms of its concern with the overall organization of credit, and international in focus, in terms of its concentration on the organization of capital within the realm of capitalism, understood here in Braudelian terms. Despite this structural and international emphasis, however, it is institutions which lie at the heart of the inquiry, rather than some conception of collectively imputed mass behavior or a metatheoretical understanding of ontologically primitive principles such as rationality or anarchy. It is the institutional nature of power in the modern political economy which demands that the world-economy approach adopt an historically-specific institutional focus, despite its avowed embrace of a structural method of exposition. To understand the nature of change, it is

23

necessary to look to the institutional locus which constitutes the international organization of credit, namely the public and private monetary authorities that dominate credit networks at any given point in time. These authorities not only create and exercise power through their individual actions; they also produce a credit market through their collective interactions. To explore the way in which power is exercised, therefore, the world-economy approach insists that close attention be paid to both institutions and their broader structural (here read market) constraints.

Markets, however, are not understood in their classical definition as mechanisms through which buyers and sellers engage in exchange. Rather, they are structured sets of social practices in which wealth and power are created, appropriated, and then used in particular ways: they are themselves structures of power. The principal social actors within markets are most often private individuals and firms, whose actions both collectively shape the structure of markets and are in turn shaped by this collectively produced behavior. At the same time, the principal social actors standing over markets are states, from whom markets derive the juridical frameworks against which private activities may be judged. The dynamics which markets assume at any given moment in time, therefore, are dependent upon the activities and expectations generated by both public and private institutional authorities. It is precisely the way in which this interactive dynamic arises out of collective practice that helps to impart to a world-economy its overall coherence.

Organizing the argument: monetary order and the international organization of credit

The central argument of this study is that order in the IMS is critically dependent upon a stable international organization of credit, and that this stability is in turn a direct consequence of the way in which public and private monetary authorities are able to channel credit from areas and industries in surplus to areas and industries in demand and/or need, to perform the necessary international clearing transactions in a transparent and effective manner, and to provide adequate long-term credit to the world-economy so as to encourage balanced and sustainable growth. Historically, the effective institutionalization of these practices has been associated with a highly centralized international organization of credit, as centered on

24

Antwerp in the sixteenth century, Amsterdam in the seventeenth and eighteenth centuries, and London in the nineteenth century. When the international organization of credit has become decentralized, the effective institutionalization of these practices has broken down, and disorder has been the result. In the contemporary period, the international organization of credit has come under a host of pressures that have culminated in a profound structural change within the past decade. The result has been a process of decentralization that has called into question the soundness of the international organization of credit, and with it the type of order that the IMS is capable of achieving. This process is identified here as *decentralized globalization.*[27]

The onset of decentralized globalization can be observed in several areas. There are now three PFCs of global importance where New York once stood alone throughout most of the postwar period. International financial intermediation is no longer dominated by one particular type of monetary agent, but parceled out between several types of agents specializing in banking facilities, long-term securities, equities, and innovative financial services. Public authorities no longer command unassailable authority over private monetary agents through their extensive regulatory grip over international capital movements; the power of private monetary agents increasingly shapes the context of state action within the international organization of credit. And finally, the hierarchical concentration of state power in the hands of the American government has been broken in terms of inter-state relations. Here, as elsewhere in international politics, the eclipse of American dominance makes itself felt.

The onset of decentralized globalization contains social, economic, and political implications for the international organization of credit. Socially, private monetary agents now exercise more authority in controlling access to credit than at any time since 1947. It is their criteria which determine who has access to credit, on what terms, and at what cost. Economically, shifts in where wealth is being created within the world-economy, who sits astride that wealth, and who controls access to it, have worked to privilege a new set of private

---

[27] The phrase "decentralized globalization" is in this usage quite distinct from what some sociologists and geographers have called "glocalization" (Agnew and Corbridge, 1995: 185). Whereas glocalization refers to the simultaneous fragmentation of identities within a condition of globalization, decentralized globalization refers to the development of multiple concentrations of public and private authority connected by a highly integrated set of mutually sustaining, cross-cutting financial practices.

economic actors in the world-economy. While transnational corporations (TNCs) of any nationality still maintain preferential access to credit, those TNCs based in Japan are especially privileged by the relatively inexpensive credit available to them and its price in terms of foreign currencies. Here the emergence of the Asia-Pacific region as a dynamic center of wealth creation within the world-economy is having significant consequences for the international organization of credit. Finally, the political implications of a decentralized international organization of credit include a fragmentation in the capacity of any one state to exercise predominant control over credit conditions on a global scale. Despite the contentions of some that the United States still exerts overwhelming structural power within the IMS (Strange, 1990), an increasingly decentralized international organization of credit has robbed the IMS of a single dominant locus of power. As Kindleberger noted in relation to the 1930s, when this occurs it becomes difficult for any type of genuine public interest to be advanced.

Public power is becoming more difficult to exercise in the contemporary financial system, in either instrumental or structural terms, for several reasons.[28] Power is shared more unequally between public and private monetary authorities now than at any time in the postwar period. It is also unevenly shared between state authorities in the sense that policy instruments are no longer uniformly effective. While the United States, for example, exercises immense structural power over global levels of short-term liquidity, structural power over global interest rates is fragmented between the United States, Japan, and Germany. In terms of the IMS more generally, the principal international reserve currency is not the currency of the principal international creditor. Each of the three major world PFCs has very different levels of regulatory supervision, and are integrated into the global financial system somewhat unevenly. In sum, the contemporary international organization of credit is entering uncharted waters in terms both of its decentralized organizational structure and its variegated hierarchy of social and political power, thereby compromising the possibility of achieving a stable international monetary order into the near-term future.

The remainder of the book is organized in two parts. Part 1 offers an

---

[28] I am here following Susan Strange's use of relational versus structural power (1988: 24–9).

historical interpretation of the international organization of credit that begins in Antwerp in the sixteenth century and continues down to the contemporary era. This historical approach is the means whereby theoretical observations can be made with regard to the role of credit in the world-economy. It offers a periodization that is arranged according to how the organization of credit is structured internationally, and it links this to changes in successive world-economies. Although it may seem strange at first to tell the story of monetary history without dwelling upon the mechanism of international currency exchange (i.e., gold standard, gold-exchange standard, dollar standard), the interpretation as a whole has a unity that is suggestive. Most importantly, it indicates that a comprehensive understanding of crucial turning points in monetary history must include changes in the way that credit is organized internationally.

Chapters 2 and 3 explore past IMSs and their organizations of credit. Chapter 2 examines the successive international organizations of credit centered in Antwerp, Amsterdam, and London from the sixteenth through the early twentieth centuries, including the interwar period. The principal focus is upon the role of PFCs and networks of monetary agents within the IMS, and the effects which differing degrees of centralization have on the type of monetary order in question. The contrast between periods of strong centralization within IMSs prior to 1914 and the decentralized IMS of the interwar period is examined through the perspective of monetary networks and PFCs, to construct a stylized version of monetary history that privileges a narrow focus on the international organization of credit. Chapter 3 continues this historical exposition into the Bretton Woods period, concentrating on the foundation of international credit that allowed a stable monetary order to be achieved so spectacularly during this period. It is the international organization of credit that is a key reason for the phenomenal growth of the years 1947–71.

The intent of Part 1 is two-fold. On one hand, it must establish the legitimacy of treating credit as a critical component of the IMS, in order to highlight clearly the important role which the international organization of credit plays in the world-economy. The proper mode of inquiry for this task is historical, in the sense that a story must be told that has not yet received adequate attention. At the same time, because the historical time-frame is imposing, stretching back to the sixteenth century, the historical reconstruction will be schematic at best, emphasizing important themes and drawing attention to certain paramount connections. Part 1 does not pretend to offer a comprehensive revisionist account of monetary history; rather, it has the more modest intent of enriching our understanding of monetary history by focusing on themes that are often obscured or downplayed by scholarly inquiry. On the other hand, by examining the structural characteristics of successive and different international organizations of credit, a clear outline will emerge of what precisely constitutes such a structural organization, and why. Part 1 will therefore amplify this chapter's remarks concerning the origin and utility of the world-economy approach, with the ultimate aim of constructing a viable structural understanding of the international organization of credit.

Part 2 builds upon this interpretation of the international organization of credit to examine changes in the contemporary period, defined here as the years from 1972 to the early 1990s. The availability of information dictates this as a cut-off date, since at the time of writing information for 1993 and 1994 is generally the latest available on a comparative basis. Chapter 4 traces the changes within the international organization of credit during the years since 1972, continuing the form of investigation begun in Part 1 but with more statistical support. In nearly all aspects, it appears that the early 1980s rather than the 1970s stand out as the watershed in contemporary financial history, when the process of decentralized globalization took effective hold on the international organization of credit. Chapter 5 pays close attention to the response of public authorities to these changes, and argues that the contemporary period has witnessed a diffusion of power in monetary affairs not only between states, but more importantly between states and markets. Public authorities, principally central banks and treasuries, have both led and followed the advance of market authority in monetary issues; in almost no cases have they successfully opposed or challenged it. Chapter 6 then stands back and reflects on the future direction of the international organization of credit, and suggests how IPE can incorporate the broad insights offered by the world-economy approach into its development as a distinct social field of study.

Summary

IPE must push ahead in two directions if it is to become a fully self-conscious and reflexive field of inquiry. First, it must reach beyond politics and economics for a genuine interdisciplinary framework within which it can develop. If IPE fails to do this it will remain subject to the imperial pretensions of its intellectual forebears. Second, IPE must articulate for itself an object of inquiry which can provide it with a distinct social field of study, one moreover that neither politics not economics are theoretically inclined to explore adequately. By drawing on the work of a small band of scholars who clearly evince an interdisciplinary approach to political economy, and in particular by embracing the work of Fernand Braudel and other similarly minded scholars, we can fashion an approach to IPE which both provides a distinct object of inquiry and invites genuine interdisciplinary analysis. The study which follows thus explores the international organization of credit as an integral part of the bounded social totality identified as a world-economy in order to help advance the self-conscious identity of IPE as a reflexive discipline in its own right.

In the following chapters, four substantive claims are made regarding the construction and erosion of monetary order within the IMS:

1. The foundations of international monetary order are to be found in the international organization of credit.
2. The international organization of credit is fully embedded within the world-economy, and directly connected to the wealth-creating activities which are at the center of every world-economy
3. The social practices which constitute the international organization of credit include in the first instance the activities of public and private monetary authorities as they engage in international clearance and provide adequate long-term credit to the world-economy.
4. Monetary order is therefore directly dependent upon the effectiveness of these practices as they are fashioned within the broader world-economy.

By closely following how the political economy and financial practices at the heart of the international organization of credit have changed throughout the modern era, this study enriches our understanding of the IMS in the contemporary period. It challenges important aspects of conventional accounts of monetary order during the pre-1914 gold standard era, the interwar years and the Bretton Woods period, and definitively documents the demise of the postwar New

York-centered global credit system in the 1980s. The historical perspective used to advance these arguments points towards an alternative approach for IPE, able to reconcile the competing claims of political science and economics concerning the provision of authoritative knowledge about the construction of monetary order within the IMS. By employing this framework, we can not only place the near-term future of the IMS into the context of the growth and development of the world-economy as a bounded social totality, we can also outline an appealing way to think about IPE as a discipline, with its own particular object of inquiry to understand and its own particular subject matter to explore.

Part 1
The international organization of credit in historical perspective

2   The power of cities and their limits: principal financial centers and international monetary order

Chapter 1 defined a world-economy as the set of relationships and practices that knit together a bounded social totality realized through the creation and diffusion of a certain kind of wealth. It considered the international organization of credit to be those networks of private and public monetary agents that stand at the heart of creating and channeling a world-economy's internationally mobile credit. In the modern period, these networks are rooted in the first instance in a world-economy's dominant city, where monetary agents are able to gain access to the financial resources which accrue to capitalists involved in commercial activities designed to accumulate wealth on a massive scale.[1] Those cities that are home to these dense networks of monetary agents were called in Chapter 1 "principal financial centers," or PFCs, in order to identify them as key access points to international credit. This chapter will develop our understanding of the role of PFCs in the construction of monetary order through a reconsideration of the relationships and practices that historically have served to constitute the international organization of credit. Central to this reconsideration will be the way in which the interaction of banking networks, state activities and the dynamics of wealth creation have shaped and directed the IMS from its inception in the sixteenth century to the end of the interwar era. Such a focus confirms the importance of viewing private monetary agents, international clearance, and the provision of long-term credit as critical dimensions of the IMS, and of the necessity of considering the international

[1] During the Middle Ages credit was mostly associated with individual merchants and/or bankers, rotating from fair to fair with them as they participated in these ancient mechanisms of exchange (Braudel, 1979/1982: 90–2; Ehrenberg, 1928/1963: 309–10; and Pirenne, 1936: 100–2).

organization of credit to be thoroughly embedded within the larger social totality that is the world-economy. Indeed, the main conclusion of this chapter is that the institutional strength and coherence of the international organization of credit cannot be explored apart from the broader patterns of social practice constitutive of a world-economy.

This chapter contains three sections. The first considers in detail how and why Antwerp, Amsterdam, and London emerged as the PFCs of their respective international organizations of credit, and how the erosion of their positions at the center of their respective world-economies brought with it international monetary disorder. The inability of Paris and Berlin to develop as financial centers of the first rank during the nineteenth century will be explored briefly in order to highlight how the international organization of credit funnels power and privilege towards selected centers of gravity. The second section examines the interwar period, and considers the possibilities of constructing monetary order under both the general conditions of international economic rivalry and the specific conditions of inter-city rivalry. Exploring why and how neither London nor New York were able to emerge effectively as the leading PFC of the interwar period adds considerably to our understanding of why the interwar years were marked by severe monetary disorder. The third and final section reflects on the international organization of credit in historical perspective, and offers several specific observations regarding the foundations of international monetary order.

The power of cities: three eras in the international organization of credit

Antwerp and the emergence of the modern IMS

The emergence of the modern IMS can be legitimately dated only from the early sixteenth century. Prior to this time, of course, the international movement of credit (in the form of bills of exchange) and the international activities of bankers (such as the Bardi, Peruzzi and Medici of Florence) were not unknown. English wool, for example, made its way to Rome during the fourteenth and fifteenth centuries, largely financed by Florentine bankers operating out of London and Rome under considerable pressure to recycle Papal funds (de Roover, 1963: 47–8, 195–6). Medieval fairs flourished for long periods of time, providing an infrastructural support for vibrant credit networks that moved with fairs from place to place, on occasion even outlasting the fairs themselves as at Champagne during the late thirteenth century (Braudel, 1979/1982: 91). And as scholars of the World System have demonstrated, sophisticated financial instruments were in existence prior to this time, allowing complex and overlapping circuits of exchange to develop in the thirteenth century linking together the trading nodes of Europe, the Mediterranean, the Middle East, India, and China (Abu-Lughod, 1989). Yet if we look for the steady and consistent growth in a higher volume of funds and credit moving between cities and financial markets as the distinguishing characteristic of an IMS, then it is only in Europe during the sixteenth century that we find such a system becoming constituted around networks of monetary agents located in the first instance in cities.

Money and credit settled in cities for a not insignificant reason. As the Middle Ages waned, both cities – many of whom were independent – and princes waged war; the former to protect their liberty and the latter to extend their rule. While princes were able to obtain funds to the extent that they could cede revenue-producing activities to financiers, cities obtained their funds mostly through the selling of annuities based upon the efficient collection of consistent tax revenues. The result was that by the dawn of the early modern era the credit standing of most princes was very low, while that of most still independent cities was very high. Consequently, activities which required access to credit, and in particular to public credit, grew where such funds were located, bypassing the apparently more secure bastions of princely control (Ehrenberg, 1963: 25–45). This change in the location of credit (and its concomitant institutions) at the close of the Middle Ages can be seen as one part of the general revival of industry and commerce. It complemented the other large-scale change in the source of credit then under way, namely the demise of the Church and the rise of the bourgeoisie as a significant source of credit for commercially-oriented undertakings (Pirenne, 1936: 102–39). As Charles Tilly observes, capital and cities have a long historical association (1992: 17–18, 47–51).

Nevertheless, despite its association with cities, the rise of modern finance cannot be understood apart from the twin processes of state formation and imperial expansion. The financial demands sovereigns faced as they waged war to secure and expand their imperial domains made traditional forms of financing crown expenditures inadequate. At the same time, the expansion of trade and exploration after the stagnant years of the fourteenth and fifteenth centuries placed accumulating reserves of capital with private individuals. The need for money eventually led sovereigns to exploit these rapidly growing sources of private credit, which were located mostly in cities where trading activity encouraged the accumulation of such funds. The shift from self-financed wars and explorations to those which were largely publicly financed was made successfully first by the Castilian crown during the fifteenth century, when it began to offer *juros* and *asientos* to private banking houses based in Germany in exchange for guaranteed tax revenues (Braudel, 1979/1982: 519–25). Thus did the imperatives of war, trade, and exploration combine with international movements of capital and credit to produce the origins not of public finance or debt, which had long been in existence, but of the first truly *international* mechanism by which private wealth flowed into public coffers.

This mechanism, the first modern IMS, emerged as part of the web of international trade and payments centered on Antwerp, where much of the trade of northwestern Europe and the Far East took place. Fernand Braudel argues that Antwerp's central position as the *entrepôt* for trade between the Baltic, the Atlantic, and the Spice Islands was confirmed when the first Portuguese ship, laden with pepper and cinnamon, pulled into its docks in 1501 (1979/1984: 143–4). More importantly, Richard Ehrenberg calls Antwerp one of only two *world bourses* in the sixteenth century, where loan capital and credit were available to crown borrowers on a continual basis in exchange for guaranteed tax revenue or other promises of repayment (1928/1963: 311).[2] The rise of Antwerp, and particularly its bourse, signaled a shift in the structure of public financing that mirrored the expansion of both the resources available to sovereigns (American bullion and revenue from the granting of lucrative trading monopolies) and the imperial demands which they assumed.

Why did Antwerp develop as the first PFC of the early modern period rather than Lisbon, Seville, or Madrid, despite the fact that the sixteenth century witnessed a spectacular movement of silver bullion

---

[2] The other world bourse was Lyons, where the French crown borrowed its funds. Lyons, however, was largely a regional financial center, and did not attract capital from abroad in the same way that Antwerp did. In fact, as the Lyons money market was a direct creation of Louis XI – in order to provide funds for the French crown – it remained largely a creature of French political needs, which were of course not insignificant (Ehrenberg, 1928/1963: 233–5, 281–3).

from the New World to the Iberian peninsula? The answer is that it was in Antwerp rather than in any Portuguese or Spanish city that there occurred the accumulation of capital which is the basis of any extensive credit network. As Antwerp became the trade hub of northern Europe, it attracted merchants and bankers from all over Europe to its markets. The Portuguese elected to sell their spices directly to the European market through Antwerp, probably because their financial resources had been stretched to the limit opening and exploiting the early Indies routes (Braudel, 1979/1984: 149). The South Germans, particularly the large German banking houses such as the Welser, Imhof, and Fugger, were attracted to Antwerp as the source of goods brought into Germany. The silver from their mines flowed in as a consequence. The English had a long history of trade with Flanders, primarily in woollen products. And the Genoese were eventually attracted because of the activities of crown borrowers. In fact, Ehrenberg dates the emergence of Antwerp as a financial center to 1510, when bills of exchange became drawn on Antwerp by the House of Fugger (1928/1963: 257).

It is the peculiar international nature of the Antwerp money market, however, which serves notice that here is the world's first actual PFC. The major suppliers of credit were the large German banking houses, most importantly the Welser and Fugger. (See the appendix, p. 179 for a list of the major banking houses involved in supplying international credit, identified by city and era.) Italian bankers, primarily Genoese but also Venetian and Florentine, were additional sources of credit. The formation of the Antwerp Bourse allowed these bankers access to relatively large pools of capital in order to finance their credit operations. And the Antwerp Bourse provided the first sustained secondary market for public debt, for example the *juros* and *asientos* of Spain, where they were bought and sold by third parties as demand allowed.[3] As a result, when crown authorities required money to fulfil the onerous demands which they had assumed, they turned more and more to the credit provided by German and Genoese bankers, a substantial portion of which was based on the resources available to them through the Antwerp Bourse. The strength of this Bourse was

---

[3] Public loan funds had been in existence for a long time, as evidenced by the *montès* of Venice, Florence, and Genoa. However, shares in these public loan funds, although negotiable and subject to price fluctuations, were not easily transferable, and most importantly, were chiefly bought and sold in the city of issue (Ehrenberg, 1928/1963: 48, 58; Braudel, 1979/1982: 100–1).

37

especially evident during the 1540s and 1550s when, as its own credit position became stretched, the house of Fugger turned to the Antwerp money market for short-term funds to reloan to Charles V (Ehrenberg, 1928/1963: 112–13). When Philip II declared bankruptcy in 1557, the financial positions of the great German banking houses were so compromised that the Bourse was shaken to its very foundation. The "Age of the Fugger" had ended.[4]

The case of Antwerp is instructive, for it suggests how a particular city comes to act as the central linchpin of an international organization of credit. First, a PFC must lie at the heart of a world-economy. That Antwerp lay at the heart of the early sixteenth-century European world-economy is attested to by the fact of its *entrepôt* position between the Atlantic, Baltic, and Far East trade routes. Second, a PFC must draw towards itself the idle capital not only of its own immediate hinterland, but also of foreign areas that see in this city access to profitable employment of those funds through all manner of ventures, including the financing of public debt. In fact, PFCs will always be primary sources of public credit for governments, mainly because of the capital and credit in existence there. Antwerp, for example, drew towards itself the silver of Germany and later of Spain, and a good deal of the capital siphoned out of Italy via Genoa; this provided resources to its bourse for lending to crown authorities. Third, an elaborate set of financial institutions must arise to manage these funds. Moreover, these institutions have demanded a proximity to others which has reinforced the role of cities within all credit systems. The resulting overlap of institutional networks has included commercial banks, investment banks, securities firms, and a bourse, acting as both a secondary market for securities as well as a primary source of investment and speculative capital. The other side of this institutional network is its role as a clearing house, where transactions are balanced against one another in order to minimize the amount of real resources required to keep these transactions occurring. In the

---

[4] Ehrenberg calls the sixteenth century the "Age of the Fugger," primarily because the precarious nature of royal finances allowed internationally active financiers such as the House of Fugger to become extremely influential in politics. The decline of the Fugger was due in part to its over-extension of credit to the Spanish crown, but more importantly to the rise of organized public credit, which removed royal finances from the demands which individual financiers could place upon royalty in exchange for their services. In this way the influence of the collective market, or bourse, was substituted for the influence of the individual financier (1928/1963: 332–3, 375–7). On the emergence of organized public credit in England, for example, see Dickson (1967).

case of Antwerp, Spanish bills drawn on Antwerp bankers routinely paid for Spanish troops as they marched throughout Europe (Braudel, 1979/1984: 150–1). Finally, there must be a certain "remove" between public authorities and the private credit network if a single city is going to be able to act as a financial intermediary for a world-economy. In Antwerp, the civic authorities were so weak, and the Flemish authorities so timid, that very little stood in the way of German and Italian merchants and bankers operating in the city as their interests in the larger world-economy dictated.

During its heyday in the sixteenth century, Antwerp facilitated the movement of goods through Europe by providing the necessary credit to finance their journeys. It drew silver from German mines, through the services of German banks such as the Fugger, to Antwerp, and passed that silver on to the Portuguese who required it for their dealings in the Far East. It extended credit to the Spanish crown through the enormous reserves of its bourse, allowing Spain to finance the exploitation of the New World. The Antwerp Bourse even lent funds to the English crown, and provided one of Queen Elizabeth I's counselors, Sir Thomas Gresham, with the blueprint for the nationalization of the English capital market. When the Bourse could mobilize capital and credit with authority and confidence, the world-economy grew; when it could do so only hesitantly, such as between 1523 and 1535, the world-economy grew in a much less robust form (Braudel, 1979/1984: 150–1). The experience of Antwerp strongly suggests that at the center of an effective international organization of credit stands a PFC, home to powerful networks of monetary agents able to transfer credit on an international scale, undertake international clearance, and provide adequate long-term credit to public and private authorities. Moreover, the monetary order which emerges from such a high degree of centralization has no necessary relationship to a particular state having achieved a position of dominance within the international system. Antwerp, despite being at the heart of the city-led world-economy during the sixteenth century, had no pretensions to political hegemony, and indeed was throughout much of this period under constant threat from the imperial pretensions of the Spanish crown.

Amsterdam and the apogee of a city-led world-economy

After the outbreak of revolutionary activity in Antwerp and the Netherlands generally in the late 1560s, the pivotal role played by

that city in the world-economy's monetary system declined. \
Spanish troops marched north to suppress the rebellion, and silver
from the New World began to flow increasingly towards Genoa,
where the creditors to Philip II maintained their residences. This
movement of silver allowed the Genoese fairs to become for a time
the dominant institutional network through which credit flowed
within Europe. According to Braudel, capital from the Italian main-
land was drawn towards Genoa, and used to advance credit to
Philip II, who was by now engaged in the imperial ventures which
would bankrupt Spain on several occasions over the course of the
late sixteenth and early seventeenth centuries. He repaid this credit
with silver coming in from Peru and Mexico, which went on to
Genoa and from there to other Italian cities, often to be used to
pay for trade with the Levant (Braudel, 1979/1984: 166–70). But as
the Spanish and French bankruptcies took their toll on the
Genoese, and as silver production in America declined, the sources
of credit and the networks through which this credit flowed
underwent a transformation. Most importantly, trade with the Far
East re-emerged in the middle of the seventeenth century as an
especially lucrative activity, and the exploitation of this trade and
its spectacular profits fell to the best organized company of the
day: the Dutch East Indies Company, based in Amsterdam. Thus
the shift from Genoa to Amsterdam was directed in the first
instance by the emergence of a newly constituted world-economy
centered around the trading activities of Dutch merchants and
bankers.

In fact the seventeenth-century world-economy was dominated by
three trading circuits which overlapped in terms of their exchange
and distribution points. The first important trading circuit was the
growing North Atlantic economy, where trade, exploration, and
development with the New World were beginning to move on from
the single-minded exploitation of silver mines by the Spanish. Amsterdam captured this growing trade by virtue of its *entrepôt* position,
especially with the burgeoning plantation economies of the West
Indies. The Baltic and its long-established trade comprised the second
important trading circuit. The traditional raw material products of the
"mother trade," to use Smith's invocation (1991: 101) – timber, grain,
and ship-building materials most importantly – came to be trans-
ported largely aboard Dutch ships to Amsterdam, where they were
warehoused and distributed abroad to Spain, England, and America

for final use.[5] The interaction of the North Atlantic and Baltic trade routes were thus complementary, and their convergence on Amsterdam reflected the ascendancy of its *entrepôt* position. The third important trading circuit became identified with the trade in luxury goods with the Far East, which during the seventeenth century came to be largely monopolized by the Dutch East Indies Company. This trade was grafted onto the other two major trading circuits through the work of Dutch merchants and bankers: American bullion used to pay for Old World exports flowed into Amsterdam and onwards to the Far East, where it was used to purchase spices and luxury goods. These goods were in turn shipped to Amsterdam and from there distributed via convenient river transport to Northern Europe for consumption (Kindleberger, 1978b: 178). During the course of the seventeenth century, then, well established trade routes and the networks of merchants that had dominated them either succumbed to Dutch competition or became allied to them, thus serving to reconstitute a world-economy centered in the first instance on Amsterdam (Smith, 1991: 104–5).

The international organization of credit which grew within this world-economy was also centered in Amsterdam. At its hub was Amsterdam's money market, where crown and merchant alike were able to satisfy their expanding credit requirements. Here was found the dense web of interwoven relations between merchants who traded, bankers who offered credit, and other financiers who could mobilize capital on the Bourse. To this market went merchants in search of the bills of exchange which were their company's lifeblood, and crown heads who could not finance their growing expenditures without recourse to public debt. In fact, Amsterdam easily outdistanced all other European financial centers in the eighteenth century as a source of public credit for foreign states, including Sweden, Austria, Denmark, Russia, France, Poland, Spain, the United States, and of course Great Britain (Riley, 1980). Throughout the eighteenth century much of the money earned by Dutch companies engaged in the *entrepôt* trade returned to the world-economy in the form of loans and bonds for the crowns of Europe.

Amsterdam's position as the PFC of the international organization of credit during the eighteenth century was due in no small part to the

---

[5] Braudel sees in the warehousing capacity of the Dutch the heart of their commercial strategy: it allowed Dutch merchants to shape the supply and demand of their products to a unique degree (1979/1984: 238).

development within this city of what has been called an "information exchange" (Smith, 1984: 987). What distinguished Amsterdam from even its predecessor Antwerp was the density, diversity, and reach of the information-gathering institutions of the day. The most important channel for this information was the extensive network of private merchants, but Amsterdam pioneered the development of other more institutionalized channels of information as well, including the central Exchange Bank, an active commercial press, municipal governments, the Bourse and very significantly the East India Company, which was one of the first institutions to systematically exploit information for its own use. Upon being channeled into Amsterdam, information was collated, aggregated, and analyzed according to the short-term or long-term needs of its end-users. This information network brought down transaction costs in Amsterdam of undertaking foreign business, and helped in the consolidation of an informational hierarchy which at least in the beginning mirrored the organizational structure of the world-economy. That is, Amsterdam stood at the apex of an informational hierarchy which included below it regional information centers such as Hamburg or Cologne, and far away outposts such as those within the Dutch East Indies Company's control (Smith, 1984: 992). The only ambiguous aspect of this information hierarchy is the position of London, which from the early years of the eighteenth century was closely integrated with the Amsterdam capital market.[6] In fact, Amsterdam's status as an information exchange helps to explain why it remained the PFC of the eighteenth century's international organization of credit even after the world-economy within which it came to fruition had irretrievably begun to decline: information requires channels of communication to travel through and a concentration of expertise for its analysis, and once set up such channels and expertise can function long past the eclipse of their founding conditions.[7] We shall encounter this phenomenon again

---

[6] Building upon Smith's work, Neal argues that prices for identical stock traded in both London and Amsterdam traced one another as closely as current communications allowed; they were for all intents and purposes fully integrated (1990: 43). Paris remained outside of this arc of integration until well into the nineteenth century, largely due to the consequences of the South Sea Crisis of 1720 (Schubert, 1988: 305).

[7] Riley (1980: 24–5) notes that as Dutch trade declined relative to others, the volume of commercial paper passing through Amsterdam expanded significantly: "What occurred between 1650 and 1750 was a transition from commerce to commercial and government finance."

during our consideration of the role of London within the nineteenth-century international organization of credit.

At its apogee, then, Amsterdam was the archetypal PFC of what Fernand Braudel identifies as a city-led world-economy. Like Antwerp before it, Amsterdam exercised an enormous sway over the international movement of goods outside of the jealously guarded colonial areas of England, France, and to a more limited extent, Spain. It was an *entrepôt* center of extraordinary dimensions. It drew silver towards itself from the New World and from its trading basins in western France, Flanders, parts of Germany, and the Baltic (Braudel, 1984: 207–10). Amsterdam was also a primary source of funds for the crown heads of Europe during the eighteenth century, with everyone from Catherine II to Louis XVI coming at some point to the Amsterdam money market. And the elaborate network of agents who could mobilize funds for attractive projects was unrivaled in Amsterdam during its heyday. One of these firms, Hope & Co., continued as a leading European banking house well into the nineteenth century (Born, 1977/1983: 52–8). This elaborate network ensured that Amsterdam maintained itself as the information exchange of Europe well into the eighteenth century and long after the volume of commercial transactions in London and Rotterdam surpassed those in Amsterdam (Smith, 1984: 989). Finally, like Antwerp before it, any inclinations which the Dutch political authorities might have had to exert a strong element of control over financial matters was severely circumscribed by the interest which the Dutch financial classes had in maintaining an open market for the movement of capital. This interest not only allowed the Dutch credit network to develop free from the intervention of a politically motivated regulatory agency of any type, it also encouraged foreigners to place their funds in the Amsterdam money market by making potentially damaging actions by the Stadtholders or States-General in these matters almost inconceivable (Braudel, 1979/1984: 193–201).

What Braudel has called the last of the "city-centered world-economies" (1979/1984: 175) slowly dissolved over the course of the late eighteenth century. Caught between increased competition on trade routes formerly dominated by Dutch merchants, new forms of production that began to place more wealth into the hands of producers rather than traders, the retreat of its powerful social classes into the relative safety of *rentier* activities, a small home market and increased protectionism abroad, the dominance of Amsterdam over its world-economy was first called into question and then finally broken by the violent continent-wide repercussions of the French Revolution (Smith, 1991: 107). Between 1793 and 1815 traditional channels of credit were blocked, trade routes – especially between Europe and the Far East, but also within Europe were interrupted, political alliances were rearranged, and new social forces were unleashed: how could any city whose strength rested mainly upon the competitive edge of its merchant capitalists ride out this storm?[8] The newly constituted world-economy that slowly emerged out of the ashes of Napoleonic Europe was centered on a city whose strength rested not only on a network of financial institutions without parallel in Europe, but on a more productive wealth-generating basis as well, namely a national economy. This city, of course, was London.

London and a new world-economy

If state formation and war have provided the overall framework within which we can understand the origins of the modern IMS, this is no less true of its evolution in the nineteenth century. The birth pangs of the nineteenth-century world-economy were registered during the Napoleonic wars, and its death throes during the fighting of the Great War. Nevertheless, just as we were required to inquire more closely into the precise nature of the emerging credit networks of the sixteenth century in order to understand why Antwerp rather than Seville became that period's PFC, so too must we inquire into the changing nature of credit networks centered in London if we are to place the emergence and stability of the nineteenth-century international organization of credit into its overall context. By doing so we will not only be able to confirm the observations made regarding the role of PFCs as indicated by the experiences of Antwerp and Amsterdam, we will also be able to explore an important new develop-

[8] Napoleon's attempt to enforce the Continental System onto a recalcitrant Europe foundered on the problems of replacing sea-borne transport (the most efficient form of the day) with poorly developed roadways, reducing tariff levels within Europe, replacing Asian, African, and American markets, and finally replacing also the flow of gold from the New World which the British blockade cut off. The Dutch, caught in the middle of this, were hard pressed just to maintain their European connections; when the ravages were over it was impossible to reassemble the pieces. On these points see Kindleberger (1978b: 179), Cameron (1966: 6), Crouzet (1964), and Riley (1980: 195–200).

ment that shaped the changing structure of the world-economy – and therefore its international organization of credit – over this period.

This important development was the full-scale emergence of the national market as the principal building block of the nineteenth-century world-economy. In general terms, the emergence of the national market shapes the possibilities open to a PFC within the international organization of credit in three important ways. First, the emergence of a coherent and integrated national market provides a significantly larger primary hinterland to draw on for the purposes of establishing a capital-rich financial center. Credit networks at the heart of a PFC are thus able to reach out beyond the national market from a secure base. At the same time, rival financial centers which do not have such a well integrated primary hinterland to draw upon are relatively disadvantaged. Over the early modern period, although national markets developed only slowly, once they reached a threshold in which the various components of their local economies meshed, they easily outdistanced their main economic rivals, namely city-centered economies. Cities at the center of national economies enjoyed an unrivalled supremacy over cities with no national economy to draw upon. This supremacy may be seen either in the triumph of London over Amsterdam as the eighteenth century wound down (Braudel, 1979/1984: 297) or in the triumph of Britain over France in the early nineteenth century (Schwartz, 1994: 27–30).

Second, by virtue of their size, national economies provide the foundation for denser and more sophisticated sets of linkages throughout the world-economy than do smaller, city-centered economies. This density resides in the control over the production process which firms operating at the heart of a national economy have historically been able to achieve. As they learn to master all aspects of production within the confines of a national economy, these skills and expectations form the basis upon which these firms expand outwards from their initial markets. The dense linkages characteristic of a national economy thus become replicated within the world-economy, intensifying the links between its different realms. In this sense, national economies are better positioned to integrate a world-economy because their central wealth-creating dynamic more strongly imposes itself abroad. During the course of the nineteenth century, for example, industrial capitalism emerged as the dominant form of capitalism within the British economy, supplanting the merchant capitalism of an earlier era. Together, the emergence of industrial

45

capitalism and the consolidation of the British national economy positioned London as the dominant city in the nineteenth-century world-economy.

Finally, the emergence of a national economy provides a greater array of resources to the state, allowing it to exercise a more potent form of political power, either directly or indirectly. Within a national economy, wealth may be appropriated on a larger scale and with more efficacy than is the case under a city-centered economy. While a part of this efficacy is subject to the potential of the wealth-creating dynamic itself and the ability of state authorities to effectively tax its citizens, the sheer capacity of a state to appropriate wealth is increased if it wields power over an integrated and coherent national economy. This increased capacity is also evident in the resources a state may extract from foreigners wanting to trade or do business within the boundaries of a national economy, since state authorities are organized in part to extract payment for such privileges. The strengthened capacity to project political power in turn serves to reinforce the extension of a national economy's hinterland and a deepening of the ties that bind that hinterland more closely to the metropole. In the case of Britain during the nineteenth century, these deepened ties resulted in an Empire linked economically and politically (rather than simply commercially) to the manufacturing and financial power of London. As with the rise of the modern state, the emergence of the national economy concentrated social and economic power within a particular social class, allowing that accumulated "resource" to be used in new and novel ways.

The shift from Amsterdam to London as the PFC of a reconstituted international organization of credit therefore signaled an important shift in the form of world-economy. During the course of the nineteenth century the central integrating factors of the world-economy were transformed from firms and markets anchored in a dominant city to firms and markets anchored in a dominant national economy. Cities were not eclipsed as the central locus of decision-making, rather their roles were altered to reflect the degree to which they dominated their own national economy, including its hinterland. This dominance was projected abroad to the extent that the national economy was joined to and participated within the world-economy as it was constructed throughout the nineteenth century.

Here it is important to note that as powerful as the British economy was during the nineteenth century, its position as the undisputed center of the dominant world-economy did not go unchallenged. The German economy came to dominate much of central and eastern Europe after its unification in 1870, and its phenomenal growth rates soon pushed it into the Near and Far East at the close of the century. The American economy, in absolute terms, surpassed that of Britain some time after the mid-point of the century, and slowly carved out for itself in Central and South America what Walter LaFeber has called a "New Empire," largely at the expense of the British (1963: 242–82). With the relative closure of French, German, and Russian markets after the onset of the Great Depression in 1873, Britain's economic position became more tightly bound to its Empire than ever before, and its capacity to act as the center of a world-economy became more difficult to coordinate. Indeed, many scholars argue that it is precisely during the course of the Great Depression that the nineteenth-century world-economy began to unravel (Cox, 1987: 151; Polanyi, 1944/1957: 19; Barraclough, 1964/1967: 24–5). It is these challenges, they argue, that introduced structural transformation into the British-centered world-economy near the turn of the century.

Yet it is precisely during this time of perceived structural transformation that the high period of London's dominance in international finance is dated, starting anywhere from between 1870 and 1890 and lasting to 1914. Here again the utility of focusing on PFCs and banking networks as critical components of the international organization of credit is confirmed, for the apparent anomaly of dominance in a period of supposed hegemonic decline can be accounted for only with reference to the precise way in which credit was organized during these years. The answer to this anomaly lies in the peculiar structure of the international organization of credit during this period. This structure, which did not come under sustained pressure until the actual onset of the First World War, was influenced primarily by the location of capital, the type of monetary agents utilizing this capital stock and their relationship to public authority, the form which credit and foreign investment took, the nature of international clearing operations allied to the way in which information was collected and processed, and the state of political relations among the major powers of the day. The institutional system of credit, exchange, and capital mobilization that grew up around this order is commonly identified as the classical gold standard, although it is more accurate to call it a London-centered global credit system.

Capital accumulated at a faster rate in London during the nineteenth century than anywhere else in Europe for several reasons. Most important, Britain was the birthplace of the Industrial Revolution, and its phenomenal progress placed relatively large profits into the British banking system that demanded to be invested. The London bankers, many descended from the goldsmiths of an earlier era, proved most adept at finding profitable outlets for the capital first gathered in the country banks and ultimately passed on to London for profitable employment.[9] British overseas trade added substantially to this capital stock,[10] as did eventually the balances kept in London by all manner of foreign firms whose business required a presence in London. So much foreign money was kept in London that by 1873 Walter Bagehot could see in these balances a potential banking catastrophe – the Bank of England did not carry enough reserves to cover these claims in the case of an emergency, such as occurred in 1866 with the failure of Overend, Gurney (1873/1917: 57).

Just as important as the accumulation of an enormous capital stock for the rise of London was the development of a sophisticated banking network which could place the balances deposited in country banks to good use with merchants and traders operating out of London. Many of London's major investment banks had evolved out of firms originally involved in merchant activities: hence their generic titles as merchants and merchant banks in the nineteenth century.[11] Some time during the 1860s, after the triumph of free trade forces, and in order to better service their clients, London's merchant and private banks moved into international financing on a large scale, and began

[9] Although London banks were older than country banks, the importance of country banks after the beginning of the Industrial Revolution is undisputed. Because they were local in nature, they were constantly having to avail themselves either of extra credit to meet the demand for loans or of the opportunities provided by the London money market to earn interest on their over-supply of deposits. The role of London bankers as agents and clearing correspondents of country banks was thus established early in the eighteenth century, to the profit of both partners. See Scammell (1968: 118–23) and Kindleberger (1984/1993: 79–81).

[10] The profits derived from the slave trade were also an important source of capital for many of the early merchant banks, especially those located in Liverpool and Bristol (Williams, 1944/1964: 98–102).

[11] For example the firm of Baring Brothers & Co. grew out of a drapery business first established by Johann Baring in Exeter in the early eighteenth century, and that of Overend, Gurney out of a wool merchant's firm in Norwich. Even Nathan Rothschild began that family's illustrious history in England as a cotton trader in Manchester in 1798 before moving on to banking activities in London (Born, 1977/1983: 21, 53; Scammell, 1968: 127). On the evolution of banking designations, see Roberts (1993).

to develop the correspondents and reputations which would serve them well into the twentieth century (de Cecco, 1974: 84). The outward expansion of private British banks, however, occurred under the watchful eye of the Bank of England, a privately chartered institution that slowly gained regulatory responsibilities over the course of the nineteenth century. William Brown calls the development of empirically sound banking practices in Britain, including the role of the Bank of England, one of two "foundation stones" of the stable nineteenth-century IMS (1940/1970: 778).[12]

It was the very activities of these merchant banks, however, that dominated the working of the gold standard. They undertook three kinds of activities: they financed foreign trade, they brought new bond offerings to the market, and they tried to provide secure investments for the capital which their clients deposited with them. The London merchant banks thus stood at the center of the credit practices which constituted the nineteenth century's international organization of credit. They acted, for example, as the principal conduits through which foreign credits financed the building of infrastructure in Canada, Latin America, and much of Africa, including the development of railroads, ports, and utilities. Their acceptance bills circulated internationally through their vast network of correspondents, and were so secure that London banks often financed trade that did not directly involve the British economy (Bloomfield, 1963: 37). In this sense the dominant credit network of the world-economy was essentially private in nature, i.e., its institutions had no statutory obligation or accountability to public authorities. Where public authority was involved, it was usually as the guarantor of privately funded investments, and even then rarely and only for explicitly "political" reasons (Platt, 1968: 10–17).[13] The

---

[12] De Cecco disputes this claim by arguing that the Bank of England was losing its ability to control the London money market, especially after 1900. The source of this loss of control was the fight between the rising domestically focused joint-stock banks and the internationally oriented "inner circle" of private merchant banks and the Bank of England. The tremendous growth in the assets of the joint-stock banks meant that they would soon control more wealth than the merchant banks, and were determined to gain a say in monetary policy. Their bid to smash the power of the "inner circle" in 1914, he argues, was partially responsible for the breakdown in international clearance through London (1974: 99–102, chapter 7 *passim*). His arguments are supported in part by Ingham, who sees the social divide within the City between merchant banker and joint-stock banker as part of the larger divide between industry and finance in Britain (1984: 164–7).

[13] Of the four major capital-exporting countries during the late nineteenth-century –

intensely private nature of credit in the nineteenth-century international organization of credit is confirmed by examining how governments responded to financial panics: in the 1866 and 1890 panics, for example, it was the Bank of England, in conjunction with private bankers, that led the response, with Treasury officials on the sidelines awaiting the call to suspend the 1844 Peel Act if the situation proved especially difficult (Hawtrey, 1962: 85, 105–10).[14] In the United States, where a rudimentary central banking authority did not even exist until 1913, the job of stemming financial panics fell to bankers like J. P. Morgan and James Stillwell, whose actions during the 1907 panic prevented a widespread collapse in the US financial system (Carosso, 1987: 535–47). The *laissez faire* attitude of government officials towards questions of finance was thus supported in the banking system by the private exercise of monetary authority.[15]

If large amounts of capital were available in London, together with an efficient banking system, then the almost inevitable result of large-scale import and export transactions would be the development of international clearance and a sophisticated system of information exchange centered on London. "International clearance" encompasses both the technical clearing operations that banks perform at the close of each business day and the broader function of providing customers with revolving credit on a day-to-day basis, in the form of either overdrafts or bills of exchange. What makes both types of operation work effectively, of course, is access to information, and here London, like Amsterdam before it, developed into a key information exchange

Britain, France, Germany, and America – only France and Germany exercised any meaningful degree of political control over investment, and even here the investment itself was always of a private nature, that is to say, it was provided by individuals and firms in search of profit (Feis, 1930/1964: 122–42, 169–76). The era of state-sponsored credit did not begin until the Great War.

[14] Scammell points out the differences between the Overend, Gurney and Baring crises as being quite substantial: in the latter the Bank of England worked with private banks to contain the possible failure of Barings, while in the former the Bank of England led the charge to dispose of Overend, Gurney by keeping Bank Rate around 10 percent (1968: 189n.). The point here, however, is that it was the Bank of England rather than the Treasury which made the ultimate choice of who to save and how to do it. It must also be pointed out that the Bank of England was a private institution up until it was nationalized after the Second World War.

[15] This *laissez faire* attitude extended to the relationship between bankers and politicians in Parliament as well. Yousef Cassis's masterful study of City bankers during this time concludes that the influence of finance on politics was subtle and largely informal. In Parliament bankers were a surprisingly quiet lot, while the official banking organs made few deputations to government (1987: chapter 8).

center. This is represented at one level by the important international markets established in London or British port cities like Liverpool for many commodities, such as cotton, gold, and various other metals. Equally important, the London stock exchange, together with the role of the City as the world's premier insurance center, also worked to channel information and transactions towards London and its merchant bankers. The high volume of transactions undertaken in London's various financial markets resulted in large working balances being maintained there by foreign merchants, bankers, and central bankers, which in turn reinforced the scale and depth of international transactions undertaken in London on a regular basis. These provided the raw material of international transactions out of which London's pre-eminent role as an international clearance center and information exchange were built, roles which outgrew the narrow confines of the British economy as the nineteenth century drew to a close. In the end London's role as the PFC of the nineteenth-century international organization of credit cannot be adequately accounted for without taking into consideration its triple dominance in providing finance, clearance, and information to the world-economy.

The state of great power relations during this period comprises the final element of the structure of the nineteenth-century international organization of credit. Despite the claims of some theorists concerning the nature of state power during this time, it is difficult to label British power as truly hegemonic (e.g., Gilpin, 1981: 134–8). Rather, the state of great power relations under the *Pax Britannica* can more accurately be characterized, following Cox (1987) and Polanyi (1944/1957), as a balance of power.[16] The rough equality of armed might assembled on the Continent allowed no one state to carve out for itself an autarkic empire along the lines envisioned by Napoleon at the dawn of the nineteenth century. It also ensured that no alternative to British banking practices could be championed by a great power secure in its access to capital markets: none such existed on the Continent, where all looked to London to set the lead in financial markets. The same can

[16] This difference is largely the result of whether one links the concept of hegemony to the political relations among states, strictly speaking, as do most neo-realist theorists such as Gilpin (1981, 1987). If, instead, the concept is discussed in relation to the structure of world order, where state-to-state relations are but one aspect of such an order, then it is quite legitimate to speak of the balance of power between states as one element in the structure of a hegemonic world order (see Cox, 1987: 123–9; Polanyi, 1944/1957: 259–66; Gill and Law, 1988: 76–80; and the modified neo-realist stance of Keohane, 1984a: 31–46).

be said of America and New York at this time.[17] Where armed might produced a stalemate, and economies, empires, and states' interests remained to be developed, access to the London capital market remained all-important for the financial systems of the great powers. London's role was thus secure up until the international flow of funds was severed by the actual outbreak of war in 1914.

If monetary order in the nineteenth century was constructed around the practices of banks and states within the context of a world-economy increasingly organized through the building blocks of national economies, how did the capital recycling mechanism actually operate? The principal instruments of credit were the modern descendants of the traditional bill of exchange: acceptance bills and finance bills.[18] The use and circulation of these bills gave rise to a large and sophisticated banking network in London with connections ranging over the known trading world. The capital which this credit represented was derived from several sources. Originally it came from country banks, into whose coffers poured the profits of the early Industrial Revolution. These profits made their way to London, where they had access to a wider range of investment opportunities than were available in the provinces. Over time export sales added to the capital stock, as did earnings from activities related to international trade: shipping, insurance services, and commercial commissions. Finally, the capital stock was rounded out by savings from overseas colonial officers, balances from foreign banks and firms doing business in London, and, most importantly, income from previous foreign investments (Imlah, 1958/1969: 40–1). By 1870, the London capital market was unprecedented in its richness and size.

Although bills of exchange constituted the life-blood of commercial exchange, what really distinguished the London capital market from others in Europe such as Paris, Amsterdam, Vienna, and Berlin after 1870 was its ability to fund long-term private and government debt.

---

[17] Throughout this period the United States was a net capital importer, drawing most importantly on the London market. Virtually every Treasury issue, for example, and especially the ones designed to consolidate the enormous Civil War debt, had to include London houses of issue in order to be successfully placed. The Morgan banks cemented their position as America's preeminent financiers by leading the New York portion of these Treasury offerings (Carosso, 1987: 176–200, 311–51).

[18] The distinction between "acceptance bills" and "finance bills" is simply that the former are drawn on bankers in order to finance trade, while the latter are drawn on bankers to finance other investments, often in foreign centers (Bloomfield, 1963: 35–8).

From about 1850 on, London became the place of issue, first for railway investments and then for investments in public securities, that financed the construction of the infrastructure which bound together much of the nineteenth-century world-economy. The merchant banks of London, preeminent among them the Rothschilds, Barings, and J. S. Morgan (later J. P. Morgan), mobilized the capital of an entire generation to flow outwards from London into hitherto undeveloped areas of the world. In cooperation with issuing houses all over Europe and America, these banks, what Polanyi (1944/1957: 9) has labeled as *haute finance*, became the mechanism that saw capital flow from areas of surplus to areas of demand or need, in the process establishing a delicately balanced world credit system centered on London.

To a large degree, credit and investment were provided in a careful, cautious, and prudent manner. Where acceptance bills were concerned, the reputation of firms who offered this form of credit, as well as the needs of firms who used it, ensured that the expansion of credit was not undue or precarious. It was based on the exchange of commodities, and rooted therefore in productive investment and growth in world trade, in what Peter Drucker has called the *real economy*.[19] The Bank of England also had a good deal of control over these credit instruments, as changes in the bank rate had an immediate impact upon the cost of using bills of exchange as a form of credit (Hawtrey, 1962: 44). Investment in securities, on the other hand, whether private or public, was somewhat more prone to speculative excess and/or unproductive employment. That is to say, investors who purchased railway or canal or government bonds could just as easily be investing in productive enterprises as speculative ventures, as the history of the period bears out. The only real indication of the quality of the investment was the reputation of the firm offering the security.

Nevertheless, the rhythm of capital movements remained broadly tied to growth in the availability of funds seeking profitable investment. More often than not this profitability was perceived to lie with overseas investment, where returns were slightly higher than those available in Britain. Several historians have speculated as to why the London money market developed primarily as a market for foreign investment. Their conclusions indicate that, aside from British govern-

[19] Drucker contrasts this with the *symbol economy* of capital movements and credit flows, which he argues is the flywheel of the world-economy today (1986: 781–2).

ment and railway securities, most home investment was raised in the provinces through private negotiation and reinvestment of profits.[20] The separation of industrialists (in the North and Midlands) from bankers (in the City) encouraged this, as did the predisposition of City bankers for liquid assets and large issues. Finally, the need for a secondary market for large issues (to ensure that these financial assets were considered liquid) effectively eliminated all but the largest firms and governments from utilizing the London money market. And despite the industrial development of Britain at the time, the vast majority of its firms were still family-owned and run (Cottrell, 1975: 54; Cairncross, 1953: 90–102). As a result, capital which found its way to London stood a very good chance of being invested abroad.

Not all of the capital which came to London, however, originated in British hands. Although there is some dispute, the evidence seems to suggest that London was a marginal net debtor for short-term claims and of course a net creditor for long-term claims (Bloomfield, 1959: 42, 1963: 71–7; Lindert, 1969: 56; de Cecco, 1974: 119). Individuals, firms, and banks, including central banks, carried short-term balances in London which were in turn invested abroad, on a long-term basis, by London banks seeking good rates of return on these funds. The overall balance of payments deficit that resulted provided a continual and growing source of credit to the world-economy.[21] This is the root of what some have called Britain's role as the nineteenth-century "lender of last resort." It is essential to point out, however, that this role was never performed by a single institution such as the Bank of

---

[20] This serves notice that Braudel's three-fold distinction between material life, the market economy, and capitalism retains its utility even into the nineteenth century. The capital accumulated in London represented the rewards of capitalism, of that sphere of social life which took the world-economy as its preserve. In contrast, much of the accumulated capital of the northern British industrialists represented the rewards of exchange relations more narrowly considered, what Braudel identifies as the "wheels of commerce." This capital was plowed back into individual enterprises rather than risked in potentially lucrative investments abroad. While the City defined the realm of *capitalism* in the nineteenth-century world-economy, many British industrialists remained participants in the *market economy*, which itself remained largely confined within the boundaries of recently consolidated national economies.

[21] Imlah points out that the British economy, throughout the nineteenth century, ran a trade deficit, a current account surplus (due to its surplus in "invisible" earnings like shipping, insurance, etc.), and an overall basic balance in deficit, primarily due to the continual reinvestment overseas of profits earned on previous foreign investments (1958/1969: 70–5).

England, rather it was performed collectively by the London capital market acting as a source of long-term investments.

Liquidity, or assets which can be realized under duress without a significant loss in value, was also provided to the world-economy through the London bullion market. This was where most newly mined gold came onto the world market, and where the link between gold and credit was most tightly bound (Brown, 1940/1970: 776–8). Because the world's major bullion market was located in London, the Bank of England enjoyed a preferential access to gold which obviated the need to hold large gold reserves – it could moderate the movement of gold simply by manipulating its discount rate, which affected the cost of short-term credit, and in turn the movement of gold. If this was inadequate, it had access to gold reserves as a final recourse. This relative abundance of monetary tools meant that British finance never suffered the incredible pendulum-like swings felt by more peripheral economies such as Argentina (Ford, 1960/1985: 149–53). It also meant that the Bank of England could administer its policies with a gold reserve that in retrospect seems absurdly low.

It was not simply increases in liquidity, however, which fueled the tremendous outflow of funds from London. There are few who agree with the contention that the single most important factor in the smooth operation of the pre-1914 gold standard was the happenstance discovery of gold in California, Australia, South Africa, and the Klondike (Rolfe and Burtle, 1973: 12). Rather, more convincing arguments are made by those, such as William Brown, who suggest it was the delicately equilibrated flow of credit that stood at the root of the unparalleled economic expansion of the nineteenth century (1940/ 1970: 777). Credit not only fueled world trade, but funded the construction of infrastructure and industry which produced the goods which then traveled over the world's oceans. As Imlah notes, long-term investment, rather than increases in gold supply, was the major source of purchasing power during the nineteenth century, and was therefore one of the major reasons for the stability of the *Pax Britannica* (Imlah, 1958/1969: 127–8).

London, of course, was not the only source of long-term capital investment in Europe. Paris also developed a large capital market, as did Berlin after 1870. And New York became, near the close of the century, a source of funds for several Latin American and Caribbean governments. None of these centers, however, rivaled London in the depth, sophistication, and political freedom of their money markets

(Cassis, 1991: 54–6). Paris and Berlin became important reserve currency centers, with their central banks exercising a high degree of influence over the movements of their exchanges relative to London (Lindert, 1969: 35).[22] But even here, changes in the Bank of England's discount rate invited immediate response, not only from the French and German central banks, but from Continental investors taking advantage of higher British interest rates by moving their funds to London. This left Paris and Berlin (and to a lesser extent Vienna and Amsterdam) in the position of having to draw on their own monetary "satellites" in order to preserve their liquidity positions, suggesting that it is the more peripheral areas of a monetary order which always bear the brunt of adjustment policies (Lindert, 1969: 78).

But there were other reasons why Paris and Berlin could not compete with London. Berlin was ultimately a "capital-poor" capital market, as the German economy was in the middle of an expansionary boom requiring enormous amounts of investment. What little capital that remained for foreign investment was guided by the dictates of German foreign policy. In the form of credit it financed foreign trade, and in the form of investment it flowed first into Russia and then, after 1890, into the Near East (Feis, 1930/1964: 73–80). Paris had a larger capital market, but deepening political shadows after 1870 ensured that French foreign policy would dictate the direction of French investments. After 1890 this was primarily towards Russia, in a determined effort to bolster first a potential and subsequently a treaty-bound ally (Feis, 1930/1964: 49–59). Many students of the classical gold standard echo Brinley Thomas's argument that even though the combined creditor positions of the Continental powers outweighed that of Britain, the explicit political nature of those investments ensured that the world beyond Continental Europe would turn to London to finance its growing needs (1967: 11–12).

In order, then, to account for why London emerged as the nine-teenth-century's PFC *after* the apogee of British industrial might, and why it continued in its position far after Britain's apparent ability to sustain such a role had been exhausted, we must look to the peculiar structure of the international organization of credit in the nineteenth century. Monetary order was a result of the confluence of practices rooted around a *laissez faire* approach by public authorities to foreign

---

[22] A "reserve currency" is a currency which central banks will hold in their official reserves for use in foreign exchange interventions.

investment (although not banking regulation), the balance of power in Europe, the sophisticated banking network developed in London and able to mobilize enormous amounts of capital, the way in which this capital was mobilized, and the international clearance and information exchange activities that came to be centered on London. The evolution of the gold standard within these practices was primarily a consequence of the smooth recycling of capital and continuous movement of credit through London. The IMS was dominated during this time by the practices of private international bankers, hence it can be characterized as a private, London-centered global credit system.

Our exploration of London as a PFC of the first rank suggests we should add at least one other consideration to our understanding of how a PFC comes into being and modify another of our previous considerations about how that position is maintained. The consideration we should add is that of the national economy, specifically in terms of the resources a PFC is able to draw on as a result of being at the center of an integrated and coherent national economy. In the case of London, its position *vis-à-vis* other potential PFCs such as Amsterdam, Paris, and Berlin was strengthened by virtue of its dominance of the emerging British national economy. The lesson here is that a city must be at the heart of a strong and vibrant national economy before it can seize the opportunity of becoming a PFC.[23] Yet, as the experience of London also demonstrates, the requirement of being at the center of the *entrepôt* trade of a world-economy is not a continuous one. While such a position seems necessary to launch a city on its way to becoming a PFC, if its network of financial institutions becomes strongly enough established, the financing of trade and long-term investment can become partially disembedded from these trading networks, although it will not become disembedded from the actual practice of trade. To a certain extent, the artifice of finance can take on an institutional life of its own, together with its own logic and dynamic.[24] At the same time, the autonomy of

---

[23] As we shall discuss in part 2, the necessity of being at the center of a vibrant national economy may be relaxed if that national economy is in turn part of a larger regional economy.

[24] This artifice gains strength to the extent that banking networks are able to insinuate themselves into prevailing structures of power, such as dominant social classes and state agencies. By most indications City bankers had been extremely successful at integrating themselves into the prevailing British power structures prior to 1914, forming an élite that, as one scholar notes, was "if not new at least renewed" (Cassis, 1985: 212; cf. also Ingham, 1984: 128–51).

finance and the power of cities have their limits which are clearly visible in the experience of the interwar period.

The limits of cities: inter-city and international rivalry in the interwar years

The interwar years stand as another period of transition in the international organization of credit, similar in outline to the transition from Antwerp to Amsterdam that was occasioned by the Revolt of the Netherlands in the late 1560s, and the transition from Amsterdam to London that was consummated by the two decades of European war beginning in 1793. It was a transition, in other words, that was embedded within a larger set of transformations ongoing in the world-economy. Of particular significance for the reconstruction of international monetary order were the emergence of new centers of wealth creation, changes in how public authorities became involved in the capital recycling mechanism, the almost complete emasculation of the pre-1914 global network of private monetary agents, and shifts in the state of great power relations. These changes had knock on effects in terms of international clearance, the collecting and processing of information, and in the freedom and direction of credit flows internationally. The experience of the interwar years thus confirms the limits of cities as organizational linchpins within the international organization of credit: in the end they can neither construct nor sustain monetary order against the grain of severe political and economic dislocation.

The failure to establish monetary order in the 1920s

Much of the instability of the interwar period had its roots in the economic and financial immiseration of Europe during the Great War. The war itself destroyed much of the productive base of north-east France, the heartland of French industry. The ten *départements* that saw most of the combat lay in ruins by 1918. German productive capacity was exhausted, due both to its tremendous war effort and to the lack of investment in plant and technology imposed by war finance. What little Russian industry that existed prior to 1914, while not actually destroyed by the war, was rendered virtually inoperable by the civil war that began shortly after the signing of Brest–Litovsk in 1918. And British industry, suffering as it was from underinvestment since the

58

turn of the century, exhausted itself in much the same manner as its German counterpart. It was not until 1925 or thereabouts that 1913 levels of output were again reached (Maddison, 1976: 502–3).

In financial terms, the war nearly destroyed both the currencies and the capital markets of all belligerents save for the United States. By the end of the war, for example, Germany's currency retained less than 10 percent of its prewar value (Clarke, 1967: 19), while the Paris capital market received a crippling blow once the Bolshevik Government declared its intention not to honor any of the overthrown tsar's debt. For virtually every belligerent, the consequences of the war effort undermined the capacity of capital markets to provide adequate postwar investment.[25] Even for the United States, which emerged from the war as the world's largest international creditor, the effects of war finance were not entirely benign: inflation, a suddenly expanded national debt, and the new experience of being owed huge sums by wartime allies worried policy-makers more comfortable with balanced budgets and a minimal governmental role in the national and international economy.[26]

While the economic and financial dislocations of the war set important constraints on the way in which international monetary order could be reconstructed, three sets of financial practices also contributed to the disorder of the interwar period. The first problematic financial practice was the aggressive way in which public monetary authorities responded to the threat of inflation in 1919–20. This response took the form of high interest rates which produced a severe deflationary spiral within the main industrialized economies and tight credit conditions lasting until the early 1930s.[27] The second problem-

---

[25] The effects of war finance on the capital markets of the belligerents varied in line with their prewar depth and liquidity. Here, the preeminence of London is again confirmed, as the London market was able to substantially ease the difficulties faced by Britain in financing the war as compared with its main German enemy (Balderston, 1989: 237–41).

[26] After 1915, the United States in effect became the "lender of last resort" for both the British and French governments, who in turn financed Russia's flagging war effort. This was the first time that the American capital market was opened up to Europe, and the heritage of inter-allied war debts proved to be a postwar difficulty of immense proportions. See Thomas (1947: 205–8), and Kindleberger (1984/1993: 292–7) on the provision of credits to the allies, and Gilbert (1970) more generally on the effects of war finance in the United States itself.

[27] An important aspect of this practice was the set of intellectual beliefs regarding the gold standard that heavily influenced how policy-makers approached international monetary issues. It was only by relaxing or abandoning the belief in the legitimacy of

atic financial practice was the abdication of leadership in international monetary matters by governments, and its transference to central banks and to private international banks such as J. P. Morgan. This practice was part of the overall retrenchment on the part of public authorities from exercising active leadership in monetary and financial matters after 1919, and had its most important consequence in the refusal of American authorities to address the issue of war debts and reparations as a unified set of issues. The third problematic financial practice was the inability of private banks to adequately recycle capital from areas of surplus to areas of need. This problem was aggravated by what Brown identified as an unbalanced world-economy with no dominant international center of credit. The shaky interwar capital recycling mechanism allowed only a fragile capacity to deal with systemic crisis, because there was no single set of actors, public or private, individual or collective, with access to the appropriate amount of resources necessary to support currency values or engage in adequate long-term lending. The way in which these three sets of financial practices interacted compromised the reconstruction of international monetary order until well into the 1930s. We will examine each of these in turn.

After the war, all of the major governments were faced with a tremendously expanded credit base, a result of financing the war with borrowed money rather than taxation. A brief price explosion occurred in 1919 and 1920, and this was used by the two most important central banks of the interwar period as the opportunity to return to financial orthodoxy via a deflationary policy.[28] Under the leadership of Benjamin Strong, the Federal Reserve Bank of New York steadfastly maintained high rates for nearly a year, thereafter lowering and raising them according to crude indicators of economic performance which were developed in the early 1920s (Wicker, 1966: 93–4).[29] Across the Atlantic, the Bank of England continued the high discount rates it first implemented in 1919 throughout the 1920s, in a determined bid to regain the prewar purchasing power of the pound, and

what Eichengreen terms the "golden fetters" that the condition was set for an end to the Great Depression (1992: 390–5).

[28] In the United States this policy began to take effect in early 1920 (Wicker, 1966: 45), while in Britain it began in late 1919 (Clay, 1957: 120–33 *passim*).

[29] The Federal Reserve System did not succeed in becoming a centralized structure until after the death of Strong in 1928. Until then, the New York bank exercised remarkable influence over the entire system, and especially over the international aspects of American monetary policy. See Chandler (1958) and Wicker (1966).

its concomitant role as an international currency. The major result of this policy was a slowing of capital exports out of London and an overall restriction in the availability of credit to British industry. Reconstruction in Britain had therefore to be financed within a context of severe deflation and investment uncertainty, particularly as it related to the as-yet-unsettled question of reparations and inter-allied war debts.

The second problematic financial practice was the reluctance on the part of major monetary powers to assume responsibility for monetary questions beyond support of currency parities.[30] It was most importantly a denial of the radically altered power that belligerent governments had assumed over the supply of money during the war, a supply which had expanded significantly as the war was fought. The strongest indicator of this expanded public control lay in the unprecedented rise in the use of the short-term treasury bill as the chief means of financing government activity during the war.[31] These securities were offered "on tap" during the war years, that is, they were offered as often as the government needed money to finance its operations. Central banks resorted to two other measures to allow for sharply increased deficit financing: they stepped up the circulation of notes and pumped increased liquidity into banking systems to enable private individuals and banks to purchase war bonds. In this way governments kept actual taxation within politically acceptable limits while allowing private individuals and companies to fund the increased government debt. It was these individuals and firms in turn who purchased the various treasury bills and war bonds offered throughout the conflict (Kindleberger, 1984/1993: 285-9).

One major consequence of war finance should have been the assumption of specific responsibilities after the war for the allocation

---

[30] For example, the United States refused to become involved in negotiating an overall solution to the closely linked wartime issues of reparations and inter-allied war debts. Kindleberger (1973/1986: 17-26) and Block (1977: 19-20) deal thoroughly with these issues.

[31] Moggridge comments that prior to the war, the treasury bill was the "small change" of the London money market, accounting for less than 1 percent of outstanding short-term securities (1972: 35). The use of the treasury bill to finance a growing portion of government expenditure resulted in the selling and buying of these securities on the open market, and the beginning of "open market operations" on the part of central banks. The Bank of England initially began such operations in 1915 and moved to make them a permanent part of their money market operations in 1922, while the "Open Market Investment Committee" of the US Federal Reserve Banks was formed in 1923 (Balderston, 1989: 239; Moggridge, 1972: 26; Wicker, 1966: 73).

of financial resources within and even between national economies. Yet neither of the two most powerful states in the postwar period chose to do so.[32] Both the United States and Britain had deep-seated concerns about the consequences of war finance, yet after initial hesitations related to giving up the benefits of unlimited treasury bill auctions, both devolved monetary policy to their respective central banks.[33] This abdication of responsibility notwithstanding, the new tools of control held by governments set the stage for the deflationary contraction in money supply, production, prices, and wages that marked 1920 and 1921. The United States in particular refused to even consider international governmental cooperation on monetary matters on anything other than American terms until 1923, when the chaos of the French army's occupation of the Ruhr made clear the link between reconstruction and reparations, paving the way for the negotiations that culminated in the Dawes Plan (Costigliola, 1977: 915–19; McNeil, 1986: 36–48).

The third set of problematic financial practices was the inability of the formerly dominant network of London-centered financial institutions to reconstitute itself on a fully workable basis. Most clearly visible was the inadequacy of available flows of internationally mobile credit to fund the reconstruction costs of the immediate postwar era. Table 2.1 details the new foreign securities issued on the London and New York markets from 1921 to 1924. These were the only significant sources of international credit in the early years of the decade, as other major European capital markets remained closed to foreign placements until after 1924. Only $2.47 billion in securities were placed on the London money market, while $2.373 billion were placed on the New York money market.[34] To put these figures into perspective, the 1921 London Schedule of Payments for German Reparations

---

[32] In France and Germany, governments did take explicit responsibility for the allocation of financial resources within national economies. Both governments ran large budget deficits as a consequence of directly financing reconstruction costs, and the German government went so far as to try and coordinate international borrowing by German firms and municipal authorities when such borrowing became possible under the Dawes Plan (Kooker, 1976: 97; Eichengreen, 1990: 86–8; Schuker, 1988: 20–3; McNeil, 1986: 48–68).

[33] In the early 1920s, the Bank of England was still an independent, private banking institution, while the Federal Reserve banking system in the United States had been established by law only in 1913. The ability of political authorities to control either of these institutions was extremely limited.

[34] All references are to the US dollar.

Table 2.1 *Issues of new foreign securities, New York and London, 1921–4, US$ (million)*

Year	New York	London	
		Foreign	Total
1921	567	116	525
1922	666	298	662
1923	317	204	643
1924	823	299	640
Totals	2,373	917	2,470

Sources: Brown (1940/1970: 328) for London figures and Lary (1943: 219, table III) for New York figures. The pound has been converted at $4.75. Total British lending includes Colonial and Dominion borrowing.

called for a total payment of some $33 billion over fifty years (Schuker, 1988: 16); the French estimated reconstruction costs to approach 15 percent of their total national income in 1921 alone (Kindleberger, 1984/1993: 335); and America was owed about $11.9 billion in loans and advances to its wartime allies (Kindleberger, 1973/1986: 40). With a pool of just under $5 billion of internationally mobile capital available to help finance reconstruction in Europe, it is clear that a world-wide credit shortage existed between 1921 and 1924.

Inadequate foreign lending during the early part of the decade was aggravated by the partial emergence of New York as a PFC within the international organization of credit. The war provided the first real stimulus to New York's potential as an international financial center, by allowing American banks to step into the breach created by the suspension of clearing through London in July 1914. They began to finance American foreign trade in dollar-denominated bills, and to compete with British banks for the financing of international trade, especially in Latin America (Brown, 1940/1970: 144–5). The floating of large bond issues for the belligerents also contributed to the development of New York as an international capital market, as did the redistribution during the war of working balances (of central and private international banks) from London to New York, largely a result of heavy allied wartime purchases (Brown, 1940/1970: 152–3).

New York's ability to act as a world PFC, however, was only partially developed during this time. Major markets for raw materials remained in London and Liverpool, where long-established exchanges determined their price. International clearance, interrupted by the war, resumed afterwards in London, where it remained until 1931. At the same time, New York emerged as a competing magnet for international funds, first as a haven from uncertainty, and perhaps later as a source of speculation.[35] Finally, New York was still the major source of capital for a developing continent, and as such had fewer funds to lend abroad (Brown, 1940/1970: 784–5). Far from being unwilling to assume its role as the world's PFC, as Kindleberger and others have advanced, it is more accurate to conclude that New York was not yet able to step into the gap created by a weakened London.

The global credit network which was re-established during the first part of the decade finally began to resume capital recycling on a substantial basis after 1925, with the inauguration of the Dawes Plan. The most thorough analysis of the period estimates that between 1924 and 1929, some $6.4 billion flowed out of New York towards foreign destinations, while the comparable figure for London was some $3.3 billion (Kindleberger, 1973/1986: 56). Yet this credit network channeled resources in a very unbalanced manner throughout this period. A close examination of capital issues for government accounts from 1924 to 1928 in four creditor countries reveals the direction of long-term capital flows, at least to the extent that they can be identified.[36] Out of a total of $1877 million floated, fully $1138 million went to European or Dominion authorities. Only $587 million flowed into the accounts of governments in underdeveloped or semi-developed countries. This imbalance is even more pronounced if only securities placed on the New York market are considered. Out of a total of $1142 million placed, $732 million went to European or Dominion borrowers. The single largest borrower was Germany, which attracted nearly 20 percent of all foreign government financing placed in New York. What capital there was available during this period largely

[35] There is some dispute as to how much foreign capital entered New York to speculate in the stock market bubble of 1928–9. What is certain is that after June 1928 foreign lending out of New York collapsed, and many foreign securities were sold or liquidated in order to transfer money into speculative loans to the stock market. The result was that New York clearly became a drain on the international monetary system in 1928 and 1929 (Kindleberger, 1973/1986: 70–6).

[36] The information is scanty and not always comparable. Nevertheless, it is an indicator of the direction of long-term portfolio investments. The four creditors are America, Britain, the Netherlands, and Switzerland. All figures are from UN (1949: 17–34).

found its way to European countries,[37] placing other areas at a funding disadvantage.[38]

The international organization of credit that came into being over the course of the 1920s thus had particularly weak foundations. While the newly emerging world-economy's center of wealth creation had shifted from one side of the Atlantic to the other, the hub of its dominant financial network had not yet followed. In fact, the historically close connections between London and New York suffered throughout the 1920s as New York-based firms competed fiercely with London-based firms.[39] As a consequence credit flowed, with few exceptions,[40] through rival financial networks towards their own areas of privilege: British colonies and the Dominions in the case of London-based bankers, and Germany and Latin America in the case of New York-based bankers. Working balances and clearing operations, with their concomitant information exchanges, became fragmented between these two rival PFCs, and the critical mass of internationally mobile credit failed to accumulate in any one city so as to allow monetary authorities (public or private) ready access to adequate liquidity in the event of a crisis. The stability based upon ready access to internationally mobile credit that lay at the heart of the nineteenth-century monetary order was thus denied to the international organization of credit in the 1920s. It was instead fragmented and decentralized, prey to a complete collapse should any part of its fragile capital recycling mechanism come under undue pressure.

This collapse arrived with the 1931 financial crisis in Germany and

---

[37] The picture of FDI out of the United States is more balanced, since a very large proportion of it went into Latin America and Canada. British FDI was similarly more balanced in its dispersion, although here too Dominion investments were a large component of overall investments (UN, 1949: 31–2).

[38] This was especially the case with respect to the agricultural sector of the world-economy, which was in depression from 1926 onwards (Kindleberger, 1973/1986: 70–94).

[39] This competition is evident in the interwar experience of Kleinwort, Sons & Co., one of the City's leading merchant banks. One of its major prewar activities was the acceptance business, with American acceptances the single largest component valued at about 30 percent of its overall total. During the 1920s, this proportion fell to about 3 percent, as New York houses successfully competed for the trade credit that London firms had historically provided (Diaper, 1986: 64).

[40] Within the Dominions, Canada had historic ties to the New York capital market dating back to the funding of the CPR. More ominously for British bankers, South Africa and Australia both considered closer ties to New York during the 1920s as a means of overcoming the scarcity of international credit in London (Costigliola, 1977: 923–4).

Britain. As credit conditions tightened in the United States and Britain in 1928, London-based banks found it increasingly difficult to draw on the mobile international loan fund as they had prior to 1914 (and in a much more limited manner during the 1920s). Previously, in times of recession or depression, London's status as an international clearance center allowed it to attract funds from abroad and lend these onwards; although they used their "own" funds, so to speak, City banks also had access to working balances and mobile capital placed in the London money market because of its high rate of return, liquidity, and security. This is what Williams means when he asserts that London was both the major financial center and major clearing house of the pre-1914 IMS (1963: 514–17).[41] Over the course of 1928–1931, London had been left as the only source of loan funds to much of the depressed agricultural regions of the world, and when the credit crisis of Austria and Germany hit, starting a run on the pound (caused in large part by European central banks repatriating their sterling holdings), London and the Bank of England simply ran out of resources to stem the flow (Williams, 1963: 518–25). In this way the credit shortage of the reconstruction period, initiated by the Bank of England's high discount rate policy in 1919, returned full circle as an immediate currency and liquidity crisis in 1931.

1931, then, marks the end of the private, London-centered global credit system. It had been under extreme pressure throughout the 1920s, and it fell apart in 1931. It did not collapse, however, only because Britain no longer stood at the center of the nineteenth-century world-economy. Equally important, the structure of the pre-1914 monetary order that had allowed London to maintain its position at the center of the global credit system finally collapsed as well. This is evident most obviously in the institutional network of monetary agents that had maintained access to the capital and credit of others, channeling those resources to areas of demand or need at whatever

---

[41] It must be emphasized, however, that London's position in the pre-1914 system was not simply a function of high interest rates. It also included confidence in the stability of sterling and in the general liquidity of the money market produced by the necessity of keeping money on call in London as working balances. The sophistication, depth, and breadth of the London money market, and the determination of the British government to respect the priorities of the City, produced what Brown (1940/ 1970: 154) has called the "deposit compelling" power of London prior to 1914. After the war, London was forced to adopt a "deposit attracting" stance, as it had to rely more and more on Bank Rate alone to attract capital to London. This stance became inadequate in the face of the run on the pound in 1931.

price the market would bear. The collapse of clearance first in 1914, and then again in 1931, irrevocably damaged this intricate network. Public authorities were slow to respond to the root causes of the collapse: providing adequate credit facilities and ensuring that capital can move from areas of surplus to areas of demand or need. When they did begin to respond, such as with easy money discount policies after 1932, they did so incompletely and with much hesitation, providing inadequate liquidity to the major national economies for a recovery to occur. The Keynesian response had still to be formulated.

Continuing monetary disorder, 1931–1947

The financial history of 1931–47 is marked by several attempts to reform the IMS by stabilizing exchange rates and providing credit facilities to nations undergoing international adjustment. These include the 1933 London Monetary and Economic Conference,[42] the 1936 Tripartite Agreement between Britain, France, and the United States,[43] and the 1944 Bretton Woods meetings. None of these attempts, however, addressed the impairment of international clearance or the moribund nature of private capital markets, especially in the United States.[44] These issues were addressed only on a national

[42] The London Monetary and Economic Conference of 1933 was dealt a death blow on the eve of its opening by President Roosevelt's announcement that the first priority of America would be to maintain stable domestic price levels. This "America-first" policy effectively killed any hope of cooperative expansionary fiscal activity, since US gold reserves were a crucial component of overall world liquidity. For a discussion of the 1933 conference, see Clarke (1973).

[43] The Tripartite Agreement provided mutual support for the currencies (in reality only the pound and franc) and the promise that dollars presented to the Federal Reserve by the Bank of England and Banque de France would be converted into gold at $35/ ounce. Although it is unrealistic to claim that the Tripartite Agreement foreshadowed the post-1945 global dollar standard (as does Cleveland, 1976: 51), it is not inaccurate to claim that it re-established a rudimentary form of monetary cooperation that attempted to address one of the main elements of uncertainty in the interwar monetary system: volatile exchange rates (Clarke, 1977: 57–8). For an argument that the Tripartite Agreement brought only the shadow of international monetary co-operation bereft of substance, see Drummond (1979, 1981: chapters 9–10).

[44] On the moribund state of private capital markets, especially in the United States, see Kindleberger (1973/1986: 282–3). Kindleberger points out that it was under conditions of private capital scarcity that public financing for exports found a beginning. Public support for international adjustment, however, still had no place in the lexicon of American governmental responsibility. For a discussion of the pressures which faced Dominion borrowers in the London capital market after 1931, see Drummond (1981: chapter 5).

basis, and were successful to the extent that national resources permitted. That is, they could be successful only when undertaken by states presiding over a largely self-sufficient economy or economic bloc, such as in the United States, France, or Germany later in the decade. Even here, it is often pointed out that recovery was successful only when predicated upon heavy military spending, as in Nazi Germany from 1936, Britain from 1938, and the United States from 1940.

Much more so than either the 1933 Monetary and Economic Conference or the 1936 Tripartite Agreement, the discussions held at Bretton Woods in 1944 began to address the issue of how to provide for adequate credit facilities (and liquidity) within the IMS.[45] This problem was situated within the context of the immediate postwar transition period. It was realized that large sums of money would be needed both to rebuild Europe's devastated areas and to ensure that repaying the large balances produced by wartime purchases (in both sterling and dollars) would not destabilize postwar monetary aims. One proposal was to endow an International Bank with some $10 billion for this purpose, but opposition within Congress eventually made this option impossible (Gardner, 1969: 84–5). The remaining options, namely Harry White's Stabilization Fund and Keynes's International Clearing Union, were not actually designed to provide the amounts of credit needed for reconstruction purposes; they were rather intended to allow economies to adjust to imbalances in their payments' positions under "normal" circumstances of trade. It fell by default to bilateral negotiations between creditor and debtor states, i.e., between the United States, Canada, and Britain, to negotiate postwar reconstruction loans. The British loan of 1946, part and parcel of the Bretton Woods negotiations in the eyes of British and American policy-makers alike, was a prime example.

The problem of providing adequate credit for the immediate postwar period was especially important for two reasons above and beyond the obvious necessity of rebuilding a shattered economic infrastructure. The task of reconstruction would be more complicated

---

[45] The literature on the discussions themselves focuses primarily on the plans put forward by Harry Dexter White and John Maynard Keynes; the pressure exerted by the Americans on the British and French for some form of multilateral framework; and the very different postwar problems envisioned by American and British policy-makers. See Gardner (1969), van Dormael (1978), Block (1977), Helleiner (1994), and Harrod (1951) on various aspects of the negotiations.

than simply providing investment capital because the actual capital goods which were needed were available in large enough quantities only from the American economy. Hence reconstruction would involve importing hundreds of millions of dollars' worth of equipment from the United States, all of which would have to be paid for in US dollars. This problem was replicated all over western Europe. The second problem was peculiar to Britain, and this was the immense overhang of sterling balances which had accumulated in London as a direct result of British costs incurred while prosecuting the war. These balances were held by Dominion and Colonial authorities and firms, who would need them in the postwar period for investment and procurement purposes. During the war these balances were blocked, and the thought of unfreezing them upon the cessation of hostilities presented British policy-makers with some unpleasant prospects (Gardner, 1969: 218–21). In short, the problem of providing adequate credit in the postwar period was very much a problem of capital recycling and international clearance.

The question of providing sufficient liquidity to allow for an orderly expansion of economic growth and trade also occupied the minds of postwar monetary planners. Both Keynes's and White's plans gave this question serious consideration, proposing to alleviate liquidity shortfalls through institutional means. The principal difference between the two plans lay in the scale of liquidity provided and in the conditions of its dispensation. Keynes's International Clearing Union originally called for some $26 billion in credit to be made available to national economies in the form of an overdraft, which would be politically neutral as to the terms of its availability and applied symmetrically to both deficit and surplus countries. White's Stabilization Fund was more modest in its funding, some $5 billion, and was directed solely at alleviating some of the distress which national economies in deficit on balance of payments might incur as a result of undertaking corrective measures (Gardner, 1969: 74–9). While both plans thus situated the question of liquidity within the context of balance of payments imbalances, they differed in important respects on how receptive a national economy should be to international pressures towards equilibrium.

In the main, however, the Bretton Woods discussions centered around the highly charged questions of what to do about adjustment procedures and how to establish and maintain stable exchange rates. The various ideas put forward very much reflected the interwar experiences and interpretations of the two principal creditor nations. The Americans, having the fortunate experience of maintaining a trade and current account surplus during these years, wanted to ensure that deficit economies adjusted appropriately, albeit not under extremely deflationary conditions. The British, having experienced trade and current account deficits as well as deflation throughout the entire interwar period, worried that deficit economies would be made to bear the entire adjustment burden. They accordingly wanted to ensure that economies in a position of surplus be made to recycle that surplus or face some kind of penalty. The eventual result reflected the desperate straits of Britain and the relatively secure position of America: the IMF and IBRD, together with the British Loan, confirmed the American view of the basis of monetary stability in the postwar world, as well as the belief that deficit economies should bear the brunt of adjustment costs.[46]

As for the issues of capital recycling and the provision of credit, those were momentarily left to the private sector. This was not expected to be a problem, though, as capital flows in general were not expected to be large in the postwar world (Helleiner, 1993). Credit would be provided in the traditional manner, through private banking institutions, while liquidity would be increased in the immediate postwar era by bilaterally negotiated inter-governmental credits. Extreme uncertainty surrounding reconstruction in Europe, however, literally closed down the prewar networks of capital mobilization in the years immediately following 1945. Capital markets remained tightly regulated in Europe, and governments other than that of the United States found it impossible both to fund the investment needs of a wartorn industrial complex and to commit themselves to an open multilateral trade and payments system under the impending specter of massive imbalances. When it became clear that western European governments were more likely to sacrifice the emergent multilateral trade and payments system to the exigencies of reconstruction, and that this decision was possible even in the face of the rapidly crystallizing contours of the Cold War, a new departure forced itself upon

---

[46] The Americans did, however, recognize and incorporate some of the British demands, such as the inclusion of a "scarce-currency" clause in the Bretton Woods Agreements, to be used if a creditor country ran persistent current account surpluses with its trading partners (thus denying these countries the opportunity of earning foreign currency to pay off their international loans by running offsetting trade surpluses).

the postwar economic planners of Washington and other erstwhile former allies. This departure was the Marshall Plan and its associated framework for international trade and payments, which while similar to the system envisioned at Bretton Woods, nevertheless marked a radical departure as far as the international organization of credit was concerned.

The most critical aspect of this departure was that the American money market had to be tapped through the medium of Washington rather than the traditional Wall Street banking community. It was the Truman Administration which took the lead in providing credit to Europe, through the Marshall Plan, in turn paying for this with bills and bonds purchased by American banks and institutional investors. The mechanism of recycling thus took a decisive turn towards a quasi-public form, with governmental assistance assuming a responsibility unthinkable only a decade before. This marks a structural transformation in the organization of credit of the first order, in that governments, after a generation of resistance, finally began to accept that the idea of public intervention was no longer confined only to the sphere of monetary relations, but that finance too was a legitimate object of intervention. The relatively self-sufficient American economy accepted as the price of multilateralism both publicly funded international investments and a continuing role in the operation of the international payments system.

It was of course only the most feared of political outcomes that provided the necessary condition for such a *volte face* in American thinking. This is evident in two ways. On the one hand, much American diplomacy during the war consisted in ensuring that American business opportunities abroad were as favorable as possible consistent with the emerging national security aims of the government. Whether attempting to open up the Sterling Preference Area or ensuring that international trade was as open and fair as possible, American diplomats had a clear idea of the kind of postwar order they desired and of what kinds of policies that entailed on the part of its allies (Paterson, 1973: 1–29). On the other hand, a non-communist and balanced Europe was an important part of that world order; thus American diplomats were reluctant to see any state dominate the Continent as Germany had attempted to do in the 1930s. With the emergence of the Cold War in 1946–7, the worst fears of American policy-makers threatened to materialize: a Soviet-dominated Europe launched on the course of economic autarky. The Marshall Plan suddenly became the key to realizing the American vision of the postwar world (Hirsch and Doyle, 1977: 31).

The foundations of monetary order

Considering the international organization of credit through successive eras dominated by Antwerp, Amsterdam, and London, as well as the counter-example of the interwar period, confirms the importance of networks of credit institutions, international clearance, and long-term credit to a more sophisticated analysis of the construction and erosion of international monetary order. Standard accounts of monetary order – emphasizing the aims and interests of states and the generation of wealth and power as a consequence of shifts in national economic efficiency – only partially incorporate the insights offered by this consideration. We can now outline with a greater degree of precision the structural foundations of monetary order by reflecting on the historical constitution of the international organization of credit and its successive transformations during the early modern period.

These reflections begin with the strong relationship between the structure of the world-economy and the international organization of credit. Historically, since the dawn of the early modern period, a leading trade-oriented *entrepôt* city has stood at the center of the international organization of credit. This dominant position in trade does not necessarily correlate exactly to where wealth is produced; in the sixteenth century it was produced in the silver mines of the New World, in the eighteenth century it was produced in the Far East, while in the nineteenth century it was produced in the British Midlands. The *entrepôt* city, however, is where this wealth is *realized*, or in other words where the payments of cash and/or credit occur such that goods and services obtain a value. This helps to explain why it was neither Seville nor Birmingham which became the linchpin of a particular international organization of credit, but rather Antwerp and London. The historical evidence is clear that an international organization of credit forms around the wealth-creating patterns of a world-economy, which in the past have been tightly linked to trade (especially in luxury goods). This is the historical truth behind the bankers' saying that "capital follows trade."

Yet the experience of both Amsterdam and London also suggest that while it may be a necessary condition for the construction of international monetary order that an international organization of credit be built upon the foundations of a strong world-economy, the evolution of monetary order can under certain conditions outlast those foundations, just as the medieval credit mechanisms of the Champagne Fairs outlasted their trading origins in the thirteenth century. Here we must look to the fragile artifice of banking networks to understand how they can both draw credit from outside of their "natural" constituencies and channel it abroad to fund all manner of economic and political activities. This recycling capacity lies at the heart of international monetary order, and reflects the solidity of the trading and wealth-producing relationships of the world-economy as well as the political relations within and between major states. As solid as these relations may be, however, they can of their own accord neither effectively conduct the transfer of payments between different types of money that comprise international clearing operations, nor adequately collate and analyze the information flows that are the source of much value within the financial system. Herein lies the potential for credit networks to be partially autonomous from trade patterns and economic relations between national economies, in the sense that once established these credit networks can exist by feeding on trade patterns and wealth produced elsewhere by virtue of their peculiar position within the world-economy. Simply put, they are the most significant institutions providing access to the internationally mobile credit required by other actors.

The role and position of credit networks thus provides the key to understanding both the power of cities and their limits. Under conditions of a concentration in the wealth-producing dynamics of a world-economy and a balance of power amongst the leading states, together with a consensus in the appropriate treatment of finance by government, PFCs and their networks of credit institutions can serve to establish the hierarchies within and among other credit networks that allow effective practices of international clearance and the provision of long-term credit to develop. Such an international organization of credit will have a clear center of financial gravity which will last as long as the dominant network of credit institutions is able to maintain these effective practices. Historical experience also shows that these dominant networks are usually only broken up through warfare; outside of the twentieth century, the occasion of each collapse in an international organization of credit has been war rather than economic change. The twentieth century provides an anomaly that can be explained only with reference to the legacy of war finance and the decentralized reconstitution of international monetary order after 1919. Decentralization within the international organization of credit thus marks the limits of the power of cities, when their dominant networks of credit institutions find it impossible to engage in clearance and long-term lending on a global scale. At this point the exigencies of the world-economy take over, as a new international organization of credit must be constructed, based upon a changed set of structural foundations. The post-1947 period offers such a situation, and is the subject of chapter 3.

3   Between change and continuity: reconstructing "Bretton Woods"

1947 stands as a watershed in terms of the structural transformation of the international organization of credit. Between the wars, the private London-centered global credit system that had so effectively supported the nineteenth-century world-economy proved impossible to reconstruct in its entirety: its capital recycling mechanism remained only imperfectly operative during the 1920s; international clearance centered on London broke down completely in 1931; and throughout the 1930s the very possibility of creating a network through which international credit could pass was stillborn. Immediately after 1945 the task of resurrecting effective international banking networks proved equally difficult, precisely because the international dimension of credit – as a material resource as well as a set of social practices – had itself to be reconstituted. This required finding new sources of internationally mobile capital and re-establishing the means of transferring it abroad. In other words, a new international capital recycling mechanism had to be constructed. This was made possible only through the active intervention of public authorities, who took it upon themselves to reverse a decade and a half of inadequate private capital recycling. The story of the Bretton Woods era, therefore, revolves around the ways and means in which public authorities worked to re-establish a global credit system consistent with the domestic aims and ambitions of those states with the strongest and most important postwar economies.

Once established in the years after 1947, however, the structure of the international organization of credit proved extraordinarily resilient. In fact these foundations proved so sturdy that documenting the definitive end of the "Bretton Woods" era in 1971 is a slightly disingenuous exercise, for many of its foundations remained solidly intact throughout the 1970s and indeed ended only in the 1980s. This chapter explores the strength of these foundations by carefully considering the way in which the practices which served to define them displayed both change and continuity over the course of the twenty-four years between 1947 and 1971. It begins by placing the construction of the international organization of credit into the context of the establishment of the *Pax Americana* during what Eric Goldman (1956) so aptly identified as "the crucial decade." The anatomy of monetary order during Bretton Woods is then considered, followed by reflections on the significance of 1971 in the light of the international organization of credit. Although the move to floating exchange rates is indeed a significant aspect of the Nixon Administration's August 1971 declaration, more importance is laid here on the implications of this move for the abandonment of public control over the credit system more broadly considered. In particular, the technical end of Bretton Woods made possible the emergence of a private multi-centered global credit system that became realized only during the 1980s. The overall intention of this chapter, therefore, is neither to offer a revisionist account nor a complete history of monetary affairs during this period; these are enormous tasks in their own right and well covered elsewhere (Strange, 1976; Volcker and Gyohten, 1992; Helleiner, 1994). Rather, the intent is to explore in a systematic manner those dimensions of international monetary order that are so inadequately reviewed by contemporary IPE scholarship.

Bretton Woods and the international organization of credit

Outlining the Pax Americana

The broad outlines of the dominant postwar world-economy can be initially identified with the consolidation of an Atlantic-centered political economy. It was dominated by the global expansion first of American and later of European and Japanese corporations, and predicated upon the production and distribution of goods and services throughout the industrialized world. Ancillary to this were the linkages developed with other less industrialized economies as a source of both raw materials and cost-competitive labor for certain types of production. American capital, originally in the form of Marshall Plan aid, but later on as foreign direct investment (FDI) and military aid, poured into Europe, north-east Asia and Japan, fueling the postwar reconstruction that rapidly regained for these areas their former levels of production and relatively high living standards. Since access to the wealthy American consumer and capital market was the key to success in the early postwar world-economy, the term that has come to identify it, *Pax Americana*, is entirely accurate. The world-economy thus consolidated was both centered on the wealth-producing American market and international in scope, as American transnational corporations (TNCs) expanded their activities to span the known trading world.

The geographic boundaries of this world-economy were only occasionally ambiguous. Included within it were all of North America and western Europe, Japan, Australasia, South Africa, the oil-producing countries of the Middle East plus the newly created state of Israel, and the nominally independent quasi-US protectorates in Asia: the Philippines, Taiwan, South Korea, and South Vietnam. Outside of the dominant postwar world-economy stood the Soviet Union and its conquered wartime satellites, soon to be joined by China, North Vietnam, and North Korea. They in effect constituted a second world-economy, predicated upon an autarkic and command-driven mode of development. More ambivalent were many of the economics of Africa and Latin America, whose colonial links provided historic connections to the dominant world-economy but whose future development had yet to confirm their full participation. This ambivalence also applied to many of the emerging economies in Asia such as India, Burma, Indonesia, and Thailand, whose colonial links allowed for inclusion into the Atlantic-centered world-economy but whose developmental strategies, like much of the colonial world, remained to be decided. Nevertheless, it is possible to identify the boundaries of the dominant world-economy as largely following the military orbit of the United States.

Over the following decades, the world-economy that evolved within these boundaries expanded in two ways. First, it made inroads into the more marginalized and peripheral areas of the world-economy, and those that in 1945 stood on its edge. This is most obvious in the case of Asia, where Singapore, Thailand, Hong Kong, Indonesia, and others oriented their development towards the United States even if they did not necessarily adopt American-led development strategies. In Africa and Latin America, too, economies that had partially withdrawn from a fragmenting world-economy in the interwar period had by the late 1950s fully embraced its successor.

Second, the central dynamic of wealth creation within the world-economy – the production of goods and services for an increasingly global world market – reached out to subsume in a systematic way greater swathes of activity throughout the world-economy. The intensification of production, stimulated in part by the expansion of corporate capital across borders, contributed to the decentralization of wealth production and the globalization of productive capacity that marked the later years of the Bretton Woods period. Here the very success of the *Pax Americana* in promoting the generation of wealth amongst its non-US-based upper echelons encouraged the transnationalization of productive firms, and through this the spread of the dominant world-economy. As the Bretton Woods era drew to a close, it became characterized more by its transnational and global foundations than by those rooted in the US economy. The world-economy underlying the *Pax Americana* had become transformed into a more decentralized and globalized social totality.

The anatomy of monetary order: the New York-centered global credit system

Within the confines of the early postwar world-economy, an international monetary order was established that was far removed from its nominal precursor, the pre-1914 gold standard. If the pre-1914 gold standard is more accurately understood as a London-centered global credit system, then the Bretton Woods fixed-exchange rate standard can be more accurately understood as a New York-centered global credit system. Its monetary order can be identified by outlining its principal sources of credit, the form which that credit took, the dominant channels of international clearance and information exchange, the capital recycling mechanism, and the state of great power rivalry. To begin with, the most important source of long-term capital within the industrialized world was the US economy. Figure 3.1 illustrates the magnitude of long-term American capital exports throughout the Bretton Woods period in comparison with the capital imports and exports of Britain, Germany, France, and Japan. American capital exports to Europe were a key part of the web of trade, investment, and security relations that served to establish the core of the Atlantic-centered world-economy. What must not be overlooked, however, was the actual *source* of American capital exports: in these early years the long-term capital that moved from the United States to

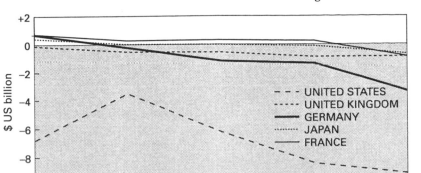

Figure 3.1 Net long-term capital movements, United States, United Kingdom, Germany, Japan, and France, 1947–71, five-year averages

Source: IMF, *Balance of Payments Yearbook*

Europe was predominantly public in origin. The turn to public capital was the means whereby international credit was reconstituted after the war, and it symbolized in a dramatic way the US commitment to a reconstructed Europe. Between 1947 and 1950, over $18 billion worth of long-term American government credits, and $10.5 billion worth of private long-term investments, flowed abroad. In the immediate postwar years, then, the international organization of credit that came to be established reflected its origins in the public character of US long-term capital exports. Table 3.1 details the public and private proportions of these capital movements.

In the early 1950s, after the Marshall Plan concluded, the public proportion of these capital movements out of the United States declined, and the slack was picked up by American multinational corporations moving into Europe in order to take advantage of profitable investment opportunities. Long-term capital movements out of the United States from about 1956 onward thus came to be dominated by FDI, which rose from a net outflow of $1111 million in 1947 to a net outflow of $7717 million in 1971. Equity and security issues combined to form the vast majority of the rest of private long-term capital flows, followed by bank lending, but they are completely overshadowed by the magnitude of FDI. The emergence of FDI as the major form of international long-term capital movement marks a

Table 3.1 *Public and private breakdown of selected American net long-term capital movements, 1947–71, $US million*

Year	Public	Private	Total
1947	−5,491	−5,015	−10,506
1948	−4,569	−2,096	−6,665
1949	−5,412	−1,542	−6,954
1950	−2,619	−1,875	−4,494
1951	−3,787	−1,822	−5,609
1952	−2,054	−2,150	−4,204
1953	−2,150	−1,458	−3,608
1954	−1,527	−1,675	−3,184
1955	−1,295	−1,071	−2,366
1956	−1,885	−2,407	−4,292
1957	−2,786	−4,004	−6,790
1958	−2,820	−3,729	−6,549
1959	−2,259	−3,030	−5,289
1960	−3,014	−3,508	−6,522
1961	−3,066	−3,322	−6,388
1962	−2,747	−3,964	−6,711
1963	−3,474	−4,555	−8,029
1964	−3,475	−5,338	−8,813
1965	−3,636	−6,428	−10,064
1966	−3,837	−5,092	−8,929
1967	−4,834	−5,320	−10,154
1968	−4,465	−1,681	−6,146
1969	−4,119	−3,622	−7,741
1970	−4,370	−5,180	−9,550
1971	−5,102	−7,241	−12,343

Source: IMF, *Balance of Payments Yearbook*

major change in the way in which the world-economy was provided with credit.[1]

It is worthwhile considering the implications of this change for the international organization of credit. Three considerations stand out. First, the particular form credit takes has a direct impact on the ability of monetary authorities to control overall levels of international capital movements, and therefore also international liquidity. Some forms of capital exports are more easily amenable to regulatory scrutiny than others. The extent to which FDI can be done "in-house," for example (perhaps financed out of retained earnings), has a direct

---

[1] It will be recalled from chapter 2 that under the London-centered global credit system, the world-economy was provided with international credit primarily through the issuance of securities, bills of exchange, and acceptance credits.

impact on the capacity of regulators to control this form of capital export, as regulators must rely on the integrity of firms' reports if they are to scrutinize the investment plans of a great many individual companies. The diffuse sources of FDI thus render close regulatory scrutiny problematic. The early experience of the Johnson Administration in the implementation of its Voluntary Credit Restraint Program proves this point: a large bureaucracy was required to make this form of capital control effective. This can be contrasted with the relative effectiveness of the Interest Equalization Tax, the brainchild of the Kennedy Administration and designed to make the placing of foreign securities on the US market more expensive for US investors to purchase. Because securities (and equities) tend to be concentrated in terms of where they are "brought to market," and because they are channeled through a centralized regulatory procedure, this form of capital export can be monitored much more effectively. Even here, however, the problems inherent in drafting legislation that is acceptable to those who provide and use international credit (domestic and foreign) should not be underestimated (Volcker and Gyohten, 1992: 33–5). Nevertheless, this regulatory asymmetry worked to disadvantage portfolio investment as a form of capital export out of the United States during the Bretton Woods period (Hawley, 1987: 45–86). The growth of FDI as the major form in which credit was provided to the expanding world-economy during this time in effect represented the loosening of political and regulatory control over a crucial element of the international organization of credit.

Second, the way in which credit is provided to a world-economy helps to determine the influence which its PFC wields. Here we must note the ambivalent relationship that American FDI has had to the central role played by New York as the postwar world-economy's PFC. While capital and credit were in fact more available in New York than elsewhere during the early postwar period, the highly decentralized nature of banking in the United States allowed FDI to be raised by financial intermediaries throughout all of America's major regional centers. Although regional banks often kept working balances in New York, their regional intermediation tended to disperse the centralizing force of New York. Thus, unlike the power of London during the nineteenth century, based on concentrating both financial balances and information on international credit conditions in the square mile of the City, New York could neither fully establish nor completely maintain these essential foundations of financial power for long in the postwar period. There were simply too many options available to American corporations intent on raising funds for FDI in an economy organized along strong regional lines.[2] The prominence of FDI thus both weakened the hold of New York as an organizational linchpin of the postwar global credit system and indirectly complicated the ability of monetary authorities to regulate the international movement of funds.

Third, the form which capital exports take contributes to the specific ways in which a world-economy is consolidated within its boundaries. Unlike securities issues, FDI is predominantly associated with investment in productive enterprises, often modeled on similar enterprises in the home market. The output of these enterprises may be exported back to the home economy, sold in the immediate market, or exported to another destination altogether, but in any case economic expertise, social norms, and cultural habits are transmitted by the investing firm. This ties the recipient economies into the larger social totality out of which the investment has come, thereby broadening the base of social relations upon which it rests. In other words, the strength of FDI as the predominant form of international credit more tightly integrates the space within the boundaries of a world-economy, in this case the space bounded by American security interests.

Recognizing the predominance of FDI as one cornerstone of the international organization of credit under Bretton Woods helps to account for three later developments. First, large-scale FDI worked to undermine the capacity of authorities, especially in the United States, to regulate international flows of capital efficiently. The eventual abandonment of capital controls in the 1970s was therefore not such a *volte face* as commonly perceived, since from the earliest years of the Bretton Woods period the most important form of capital movement had been subject to only limited controls in the world's largest creditor economy. Second, the predominance of FDI hindered the establish-

---

[2] The regional organization of the American economy has long fostered regional financial centers. In fact, early competition among regional banking centers like Boston and New Orleans, and in particular Philadelphia (home to the second Bank of the United States), ensured that the eventual concentration of finance in New York during the nineteenth century would mirror German development with its multiple financial centers (e.g., Berlin, Frankfurt, Hamburg) instead of British and French development (Hammond, 1957, chapter 1; Kindleberger, 1974). Indeed, this reality is institutionalized in the Federal Reserve System, with regional representation on the Federal Reserve Board in Washington.

ment of New York as the world's PFC, opening up a niche which London-based firms exploited in the 1960s as they worked to re-establish the role of the City in international finance. New York's position as a PFC thus evolved in response to a more sustained competitive challenge than London had faced from Paris and Berlin at the turn of the century. This serves notice that even though city-centered economies have been eclipsed by national economies, the peculiar strengths of certain cities at the center of international financial networks may well continue to exert a powerful influence on the development of the IMS. Finally, the integrative strength of FDI allowed the world-economy identified with Bretton Woods to survive the collapse of its exchange rate system, precisely because FDI tied together in a highly systematic way the productive and consumptive space of the world market. Far more than portfolio investment, FDI unites production and consumption within a world-economy by continually expanding the domain of the world market. In part because FDI had expanded and deepened its productive core, the Bretton Woods international organization of credit remained largely intact even after shedding some of its monetary attributes in 1971.

International monetary order in the early postwar period, however, rested on wider foundations than simply the provision of long-term credit by the US government and FDI by US multinationals. A second constituent foundation was the way in which international trade and payments were reconstituted in the postwar period. In order to be successful, it was clear that European reconstruction would have to embrace a multilateral form for the purposes of managing cross-border trade and payments. After the war, however, economic planners remained stubbornly in favor of balance of payments surpluses in all of their trading relationships, principally in order to conserve and/or accumulate desperately needed foreign exchange. This line of thinking threatened to lead to permanently lower intra-European trade levels, as multilateral clearing was eschewed in preference to a series of strictly controlled bilateral relationships. Yet bilateralism could neither overcome the tangled credit shortage facing western European nations nor help to ameliorate the political turmoil which they all confronted. These were in effect multilateral issues in search of multilateral responses. Recognizing this fact, the first round of Marshall Plan allocations made in 1948 included an announcement that funds would be made available for the construction of some type of intra-western European clearing system.

The European Payments Union (EPU), the name given to this clearing system, moved to eliminate strict bilateral accounting payments between its members by providing a limited amount of credit to be used for the purchase of goods and services from other European countries.[3] Settlement occurred at the end of each month, with only the net amount owed being paid to member nations through the accounts of the payments union. While several reasons account for the subsequent success of the EPU, there is little doubt that a substantial portion rested on the public support provided by the United States, namely an initial $350 million contribution to its revolving credit facility and a US agreement to fund $150 million worth of potential sterling balances. The EPU uniquely allowed the governments of western Europe to mesh their domestic reconstruction plans with their need to earn foreign currency, particularly dollars, through international trade (Milward, 1984: 320–35; Eichengreen, 1993: 81–97). In this sense it was part of the attempt to institutionalize the postwar domestic settlements across western Europe, whereby the fruits of productivity increases, reached in part through the suppression of wage demands by trade unions, were reinvested in industry rather than withdrawn as profits by industrialists. But equally importantly, the EPU contributed to the institutionalization of a new system of international clearance centered on the recently formed Organization for European Economic Cooperation (OEEC) and the once moribund Bank for International Settlements (BIS). In other words international clearance became reconstructed outside of a London-based network of financial institutions and within the context of strong support from public authorities. This support extended, in the case of the United States, to government-provided insurance for trade with areas of limited currency convertibility, i.e., Marshall Plan recipients plus other associated US allies (Eichengreen, 1993: 115–16). We can see here how far the EPU contributed to the quasi-public nature of the Bretton Woods international organization of credit, providing an excellent example of what Ruggie (1982) has called the "embedded liberalism" of the postwar economic order.

Throughout the crucial decade of the 1950s, therefore, international

---

[3] The negotiations for this mechanism were slow and tortuous, and bore fruit only after it became obvious that the system envisioned by the Bretton Woods planners would not materialize. The EPU, in this sense, like the GATT, was a second-best alternative to the truly multilateral framework originally pushed by American policy-makers (Milward, 1984: 333).

clearance was fully supported by public authority not only in the mechanism of clearing (the EPU itself) but also in its funding. It was only with the arrival of full currency convertibility for many European nations that private international clearance re-established itself through London on a global scale (surpassing the servicing of the sterling area already undertaken), paving the way for the withdrawal of direct public support for the organization of clearing operations. This suited the British, who had been vociferous opponents of the EPU all along, and who agreed to its implementation only after the US State Department applied extreme pressure (Block, 1977: 101). It was the pull of Britain's still important international position, however, which ensured that London would retain a substantial role in international payments once the EPU ended in 1958.

Britain's international position was based on two factors. First, it remained a net capital exporter throughout the entire Bretton Woods period. This provided City credit institutions with the material resources around which to reconstruct their global banking networks, focusing in the first instance on the Commonwealth and former Empire countries. Second, Britain's economy remained a principal importer of foreign goods from all over the world, but especially America and Britain's traditional suppliers such as Canada, Australia, South Africa, and Argentina. Many of these goods were invoiced in sterling, providing City institutions with powerful incentives to restart their international clearing operations. Under sustained pressure from City interests, the British government reopened London as an international financial market in 1951, primarily as a means of protecting and promoting these commercial activities.[4] Such a move immediately raised the possibility of repeating the interwar experience with international clearance, when the IMS was fragmented between London and New York. In the postwar period, however, the absolute dominance of New York as a source of long-term capital to the world-economy prevented history from repeating itself.

---

[4] This decision was not made without some trepidation, based on Britain's disastrous experiences with sterling convertibility in 1947 and devaluation in 1949. Permission to participate in international financial clearance in sterling was withdrawn in 1957, after a run on the pound had seriously depleted the Bank of England's gold reserves. London banks responded by resuming clearing operations in US dollars, thereby forming the beginnings of a market in dollars outside of the United States. This market developed into the Eurocurrency market (Strange, 1976: 180; 1986/1989: 37–8).

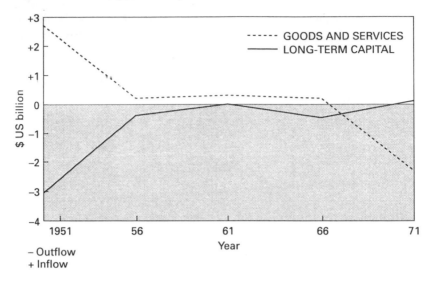

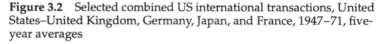

Figure 3.2 Selected combined US international transactions, United States–United Kingdom, Germany, Japan, and France, 1947–71, five-year averages

Source: IMF, *Balance of Payments Yearbook*

Throughout the Bretton Woods period the United States consistently exported more long-term capital than the other four major creditors combined. And although these nations had divergent bilateral relationships with the United States, their combined overall payments balance indicates that the United States was a net provider of dollars on both current and long-term capital accounts. This is especially the case from the late 1950s onwards, as figure 3.2 portrays. When combined with the dominant position, both absolutely and relatively, of the American economy in the flow of international transactions, it is easy to understand both why the postwar world-economy had America at its center and why New York, despite its own ambivalent relation to the US economy, occupied such a key position.

First of all, New York was a major *entrepôt* destination for American imports and exports connected with the Atlantic economy. New York had the single greatest concentration of US corporations active abroad, and served as the staging ground for those corporations not based in New York but nonetheless active abroad. It was where the new world met the old. Like London in the nineteenth century, New York in the 1950s and 1960s acted as the commercial heart of an expanding world-economy. Its proximity to Washington, furthermore, ensured official contacts and influence on policy at all levels of government. It was no accident, for example, that the Council on Foreign Relations was established in New York in the early years of the twentieth century; it is an excellent location for an organization dedicated to forging links between business, government, and academia in the United States.[5]

The force of these links is indicative of the emergence of New York as the principal information exchange center of the postwar international organization of credit. Chapter 2 noted that two channels dominate the flow of information within any IMS: private channels built around the flow of information within and between financial institutions and their associated networks, and public or quasi-public channels built around the collection and analysis of information by industry-specific agencies, financial exchanges, think tanks, the media, and public and private international institutions. The rise of US banks to a position of preeminence within the global banking industry after 1945 ensured that their channels of information would be the strongest and most widespread during this period. Their global networks combined with burgeoning research departments to support the global approach adopted by leading American banks such as Citibank as they expanded out of the United States in the 1950s. Other channels, however, were equally important in the postwar period. Preeminent among them during the Bretton Woods period were the New York Stock Exchange, the best capitalized and most liquid exchange in the world, and the New York-based media, including the big three television companies (ABC, CBS, NBC) and two of the most prestigious English-language newspapers in the world (the *New York Times* and the *Wall Street Journal*). Together with the private channels of banks and their associated networks, these institutions ensured that New York stood at the crossroads of critical information flows within the world-economy.

This central position is reinforced if we consider the plethora of think tanks and private and public international institutions which rose to international prominence during these years along the New

[5] The Council on Foreign Relations was founded in 1921 by a group of influential Americans including Herbert Hoover, General Tasker Bliss, Christian Herter, and Charles Seymour (Gill, 1990: 126; Higgott and Stone, 1994: 17–19).

York–Washington axis. The concentration of expertise in the IMF and World Bank is an obvious foundation upon which to build an information exchange. So too are the roles played by the Brookings Institution and the Institute for International Economics as centers of information and sources of expertise for public authorities, as well as the close relations between leading faculty of the prestigious Ivy League universities of the eastern seaboard and these institutes. Private international institutions have also enhanced the concentration of information flows and analytical expertise along the New York–Washington axis. One of the most prestigious such institutions was the Trilateral Commission, conceived by elite New York- and Washington-based American citizens during the final years of Bretton Woods and coordinated initially out of its New York office. Finally, the preeminence of industry-specific agencies such as Standard and Poors and Moodys, both based in New York, confirm this city's position at the epicenter of information flows during the Bretton Woods period. Like London and Amsterdam before it, New York's position as the unparalleled information exchange center of the postwar world-economy helps to explain both its dominant role within that period and the continuation of that role after the apparent decline of the American economy within the world-economy.[6]

In addition to its role as the principal information exchange of the Bretton Woods period, New York boasted both an enormous pool of capital and the sophisticated secondary markets which dominate the capital recycling mechanism of any IMS. New York's capital market provided effective intermediation between international savers and borrowers, led in the first instance by US banks. Discounting facilities were available in its secondary market, where bonds, bills, and securities of all types could be discounted when needed. Together, these provided a source of loan funds for international investment which corporations and governments utilized throughout the Bretton Woods period. Richard Cooper has demonstrated the overwhelming preponderance of New York as an international capital market in the early 1960s, and this view is strengthened if the primary focus is on long-term capital movements. To use his words, "agglomeration begets agglomeration" (1968: 115, 127–39). The position of New York

---

[6] For discussions of the ways in which private institutions can be seen to be part of the governance structure of the emerging world order, see Gill (1990), Sinclair (1994), and Higgott and Stone (1994). For a discussion of the role of information within the context of understanding financial power, see Strange (1990).

and its financial institutions at the center of the Bretton Woods capital recycling mechanism was not seriously challenged before the 1970s, despite the re-establishment of London as a significant international financial center and the subsequent rise of the Eurocurrency markets.

London was of course the only possible rival financial center to New York during this period, with its banking traditions, practices, and connections stretching back well over a hundred years. The role London carved out for itself in the postwar period, however, came to rest primarily on its *entrepôt* capacity, earned initially as an intermediary between capital-rich America and capital-poor postwar Europe, and subsequently consolidated as the undisputed home of the early Eurocurrency markets. Throughout the 1960s London worked to establish itself as the premier Eurocurrency banking market by virtue of the number of "Euro-banks" operating in the City and the dramatic growth in the volume of Eurocurrency transactions undertaken there. By 1971, London had more than four times the number of active "Euro-banks" than its closest rival, New York, while over 40 percent of all business transacted in the Eurocurrency markets took place in London (Lomax and Gutmann, 1981: 12–13). Nevertheless, beyond its role in the Eurocurrency markets, London was usually a net taker of long-term capital for investment and social infrastructure purposes outside of Commonwealth and former colonial areas. Therefore, in terms of being a rival "world bourse" (to recall Ehrenberg's phrase), where all manner of borrowers come in search of long-term investment funds, London bore only a pale comparison to New York. It provided substantial long-term investment only for Commonwealth and former colonial countries, and its international role was confined to operations in the emerging Eurocurrency markets.

Although the Eurocurrency markets might be considered as another possible challenge to the supremacy of New York, several factors suggest that the impact of these markets on the Bretton Woods international organization of credit was not particularly significant prior to the 1970s.[7] First and most importantly, the majority of funds

---

[7] The term "Eurocurrency market" is somewhat misleading, insofar as the phenomenon which it was coined to describe, namely the growth of a market in funds denominated in currencies residing outside of their legal national boundaries, has now spread far beyond the confines of London. These markets are now global, and are often referred to as offshore capital markets, in order to indicate the ambivalent state of their regulatory supervision. I will use the term "Eurocurrency markets," however, primarily because this was how they were described during the Bretton Woods period.

in the Eurocurrency markets are short-term in nature. For example, in 1976, 86 percent of all UK bank assets in the Eurocurrency market (i.e., loans) matured in less than one year. At the same time, 93 percent of their liabilities (i.e., deposits) were guaranteed for less than one year (Dufey and Giddy, 1978: 28). While many of these assets and liabilities are merely rolled over upon their maturity dates, the short-term nature of these claims suggests that they are used more for operational needs than for long-term investment. Since the origins of the Euro-currency market lay in finding a safe and profitable haven for mobile short-term funds, it should not be surprising that the overall structure of the market reflects this.

In addition to being primarily short-term in nature, the Eurocur-rency market is dominated by the interbank claims of both public and private institutions. It is largely a bankers' market, and was especially so prior to 1971. Estimates of the size of the interbank portion of the Eurocurrency market range from 40 percent to over 50 percent, excluding the participation of central banks (Dufey and Giddy, 1978: 223). One reason for this is the large size of typical transactions, often in the $5–10 million range (Clarke, 1984: 4). Only the largest and most creditworthy institutions seek and place funds through this market. In the 1960s, as well, central banks were major players in the Eurocur-rency markets, principally as a source of revenue for their large dollar-denominated holdings. As late as 1981 one scholar noted that official institutions were the principal sources of growth in the market, in effect fueling its growth in the 1970s (Cohen, 1981: 64–5).

Prior to 1971, then, the effect of the Eurocurrency markets upon the source and direction of long-term capital movements was ambigu-ous.[8] While there can be little question that they provide an efficient source of international financial intermediation,[9] the major effects of this market prior to the 1970s must be seen to reside in the large volumes of short-term funds which could be moved into and out of particular currencies, and the volatility which this entailed for the management of fixed exchange rates and balance of payments imbal-

---

[8] In the 1970s, however, these markets became increasingly important sources of bank credit first to blue chip corporations and then to governments and corporations from the industrializing world (Crough, 1979: 179–208).

[9] For two analyses which point this out from a banking–economic perspective, see Dufey and Giddy (1978: chapters 3 and 6) and Lomax and Gutmann (1981: chapter 1). Swoboda concurs in this assessment (1980: 28–9). Strange, generally a critic of the impact of Eurocurrency markets on the international monetary system, concedes that they have helped to establish a truly international banking system (1976: 184).

ances. Of course, there is no neat dividing line between short- and long-term capital movements. Private sector short-term balances are usually associated with operating balances which, while analytically distinct from capital investments, are part of a firm's overall budgeting targets. Operating budgets thus support long-term investing strategies, and often subsidize start-up costs until returns begin to come on stream. Furthermore, short-term flows of private capital, undertaken to profit from interest differentials or as hedges against currency fluctuations, help to promote the very thing they seek protection from: speculative pressures on currency parities. For these reasons we cannot ignore the impact of short-term capital movements on the IMS prior to 1971.

Nevertheless, it is also clear that the underlying sources of capital and credit did not undergo significant alteration throughout the Bretton Woods period. The New York capital market remained the preeminent world PFC throughout, whether measured in terms of securities offerings, government financing, equity placements, or concentration of large money-center banks. The only sustained competition New York faced was from the new form of capital recycling which gained ground after 1945, namely FDI. Because these investments were financed in part out of profits and in part out of financial intermediation of the kind often found in New York, its organizational centrality was compromised after 1963. It was still, however, the single most important world PFC.

As serious rivals to New York, then, both London and the Eurocurrency markets lacked a diversified, capital-rich domestic market to act as an important source of loan funds. New York, by virtue of its *entrepôt* location and historical connections to both the American government and the collection of transnational corporations based in the industrial heartland of America, had a capital-rich hinterland to draw on. Whereas New York money-center banks had a steady stream of deposits filtering through their networks, London banks and "Euro-banks" were constantly having to bid competitively for the privilege of using other people's money. While this made them efficient and aggressive, it also promoted razor-thin spreads between assets and liabilities and, consequently, thin profit margins. This in turn encouraged short- and medium-term lending as a way of limiting exposure to uncertainty, as well as speculative activity in highly volatile markets such as foreign exchange dealing. In other words the Eurocurrency markets, and significant sections of the London money market, were structurally prone to short-term lending, leaving New York to act as the largest single source of long-term funds throughout the Bretton Woods period.

Where the rise of Eurocurrency markets did mark a significant departure from the postwar monetary order was in the role they began to assume in the shift from a quasi-public to a more fully private monetary order. That the evolution of monetary order was towards a more private form of organization can be seen in two inter-related trends: on one hand, the slow withdrawal of the United States from providing long-term credits and grants to expand and deepen the boundaries of the world-economy after the early 1960s; and on the other hand, the slow shift away from the IMF and towards the Eurocurrency markets as the prime vehicle through which balance of payments deficits were financed. We noted earlier that the public component of American net long-term capital movements fell from approximately 65 percent of the total in the 1947–51 period to approximately 45 percent of the total in the 1962–6 period, before rising again to about 50 percent during 1967–71. If military expenditures are factored into these totals, it becomes apparent that a much smaller percentage of American official capital movements abroad were for productive investment after the end of the Marshall Plan. As table 3.2 indicates, military expenditures formed a significant portion of American government transfers abroad throughout the Bretton Woods years, serving primarily to cement the outer boundaries of the postwar world-economy.

The Eurocurrency markets developed within these protected boundaries as part of the web through which private capital moved out of the United States, whether destined for public or private institutions.[10] Even though it was primarily a market for short-term funds, public institutions began to tap into Eurocurrency markets for funds in the late 1960s; it was considered a less onerous provider of funds by most public institutions, who had to satisfy increasingly

---

[10] The reasons for the growth of these markets are usually linked to some combination of US financial regulations, which inhibited the unfettered movement of funds out of the United States; the persistence of an American balance of payments deficit, which placed large volumes of US dollars abroad; the desire of some banks, largely state-owned trading banks from eastern Europe and the Soviet Union, to use dollars free from US control; and the desire of the British government and London bankers to retain London's historic role as an international financial center. All of these reasons focus on the capacity of private actors to secure funds for investment, operating, and speculative purposes, or in other words for classic capital recycling purposes.

Table 3.2 *Selected American net international government transactions, 1947–71, $US million*

Year	Military	Other	Total
1947	−447	−5,491	−5,938
1948	−800	−4,569	−5,369
1949	−588	−5,412	−6,000
1950	−566	−2,619	−3,185
1951	−1,256	−3,787	−5,043
1952	−1,925	−2,054	−3,979
1953	−2,343	−2,150	−4,493
1954	−2,424	−1,527	−3,951
1955	−2,804	−1,295	−4,099
1956	−2,910	−1,885	−4,795
1957	−2,793	−2,786	5,579
1958	−3,116	−2,820	−5,936
1959	−2,807	−2,259	−5,066
1960	−2,713	−3,014	−5,727
1961	−2,552	−3,066	−5,618
1962	−2,422	−2,747	−5,169
1963	−2,304	−3,474	−5,778
1964	−2,129	−3,475	−5,604
1965	−2,115	−3,636	−5,751
1966	−2,935	−3,837	−6,772
1967	−3,138	−4,834	−7,972
1968	−3,140	−4,465	−7,605
1969	−3,344	−4,119	−7,363
1970	3,377	−4,370	−7,747
1971	−2,907	−5,102	−8,009

Note: In Table 3.2 the data represent all loans, credits, and transfers that fall under the designation of "long-term capital movements and military expenditures." The latter expenditures are normally reported under the "goods and services" category. Outright military grants are often not reported at all for security reasons. The actual figures for military expenditures are therefore higher than what is available through the public record.
Source: IMF, *Balance of Payments Yearbook.*

harsh adjustment practices as a condition of obtaining bridging loans through the IMF. Although the private financing of balance of payments deficits for developing nations did not begin in earnest until after the first OPEC oil price rise of 1973–4, the groundwork was laid during the closing years of Bretton Woods, as banks in the Eurocurrency markets sought out borrowers in increasingly aggressive ways.

The final foundation of international monetary order during the Bretton Woods period was the state of great power rivalry. This rivalry played an instrumental role in establishing the boundaries of the postwar world-economy, and therefore in the consolidation and evolution of monetary order. US aid and credits both consolidated an Atlantic-centered world-economy and brought new areas into the pull of the most important instrument of this powerful social totality, the world market. American-financed investments, together with the efforts of the IMF and World Bank, brought entirely new economic sectors into production for the world market, centered in the first instance upon access to the wealthy American economy. These included areas in Latin America and Africa, as well as certain parts of former colonial areas in Asia, such as Vietnam, Korea, and Taiwan. All told, the world-economy throughout the postwar period expanded both internally and externally; it was a far larger entity in 1971 than in 1945.

The Marshall Plan comprised the original impetus to this process. It had the aim of assisting in the reconstruction of western Europe and tying it irrevocably to the Atlantic economy as part of the anti-communist and democratic bulwark against perceived Russian expansionism (Paterson, 1973: 231–4). The creation of NATO cemented the military component of this bulwark, ensuring that the core of the Atlantic economy was visible in outline form by the middle of the first postwar decade. The extension of American aid to Turkey and Greece through the Truman Doctrine, and the rapid deployment of American troops in South Korea upon the outbreak of hostilities in Korea in 1950, confirmed the outer geographic perimeters of the postwar world-economy. These changed little over the course of the next three decades, and indeed would be expanded only in the 1980s and 1990s with the opening up of China to international trade and investment and the collapse of the Soviet Union and the Eastern bloc. But it was the exigencies of American global political aspirations which defined the world-economy's boundaries throughout much of this period, expanding as American security interests broadened and stagnating during times of relative quiescence.

Where American military interests flowed, American aid and trade followed. This required the presence of American banks and banking capital, and meant that involvement in the world market would not be far behind. Within the rough geographical boundaries of the postwar world-economy, new sectors were continuously brought into production for the world market, whether automobile manufacturing in Canada or Brazil, cash cropping in Africa or Asia, or the exploitation of mineral rights in Central America or Australia. Each of these extensions of the world market intensified contact between that particular sector of production and its dominant market, fueling the need for access to the investments which would facilitate the exploitation of resources under competitive pressures. The extension of the monetary system proceeded accordingly, routed through the hierarchy of capital markets established during the early years of Bretton Woods. The end result was the emergence of a global monetary system rivalling the pre-1914 one, except that it was both deeper in terms of its capital stock and more extensive in terms of its network of monetary agents. It covered the world-economy far more completely than did the pre-1914 gold standard.

Great power rivalry therefore played a role in Bretton Woods from start to finish. It established the outer perimeters of the world-economy, and played a crucial role in consolidating the Atlantic core of this economy. The global nature of US political ambitions that lay at the root of this rivalry gave American corporations a clear advantage when it came to exploiting the new opportunities opened up by American aid and military assistance. Within these friendly confines American financial institutions had a privileged position in the capital recycling mechanism, with their access to the New York money market and preferred position in Washington. It is not surprising, then, that American banks dominated the IMS throughout this entire period. Although not as active in the Eurocurrency markets as London banks, American banks were larger, had excellent global connections, and most importantly, were the prime source of capital for large American corporations. Taken together, the structure of monetary order during Bretton Woods reflected this predominance, since neither American banks nor New York were seriously threatened with rivals throughout this period.

Reconsidering 1971: the abandonment of public control

The common perception of the Nixon shocks sees them as sounding the death knell for the Bretton Woods system. Fixed exchange rates, the centerpiece of the system, were jettisoned in favor of a more flexible adjustment mechanism, while the idea of international adjustment itself was turned on its head, with countries in surplus on current and capital account with the United States now expected to face adjustment pressures rather than the deficit-prone US economy.

95

If, however, we consider the foundations of international monetary order as outlined above, the answer is not so clear. In the first place, the United States became an even larger supplier of net long-term funds to the world-economy after 1971 than before, so that during the 1970s it maintained its position as the largest international creditor. As a result, New York maintained its position as the world's key PFC. Much like London in the twilight of the nineteenth-century world-economy, its capacity to offer financial services to a world market remained unimpaired. The sudden emergence of a trade deficit began also increasingly to drain more private short-term funds and trade credits out of the American economy. After 1971, America was transferring wealth to the world-economy on both its current and capital accounts, thus becoming an even larger net supplier of funds.

In terms of international clearance, New York maintained its position after 1971 at the center of international clearing networks, although this foundation of monetary order came under increasing pressure due to the rise in international transactions volumes undertaken through London. Both New York and London continued to be major *entrepôt* destinations for their respective economies, which were two of the three most internationally active economies in the world. Germany was the second largest trading nation after the United States, while Japan and France were fourth and fifth in line. With the rise of Japan to the topmost ranks in the late 1970s Tokyo would begin to assume a more important role in international clearance, especially for Asia, but it played only a minor role in the so-called "collapse" of Bretton Woods. As for Frankfurt acting as a clearing house for the bulk of German international trade, many German banks were already active in London and Luxembourg, a result of Eurocurrency trading and German exchange controls imposed in the late 1960s. The channels of international clearance thus remained largely unchanged throughout the later years of the Bretton Woods period, and did not play a significant role in the events leading up to the Nixon shocks.

The "collapse" of Bretton Woods, therefore, only marginally affected the international organization of credit. Capital continued to be recycled as before, with the same financial centers providing the majority of the world-economy's internationally mobile funds. International clearance continued much as before, being largely located in London or New York, with important regional centers like Paris, Vienna, Toronto, Chicago, Johannesburg, Tokyo, and Hong Kong establishing subordinate positions. Notwithstanding the increased volatility of exchange rates after 1971, the impressive continuity exhibited by the international organization of credit throughout the 1970s helps to explains why 1971 did not turn into a repeat of 1931: unlike the 1931 financial crisis, the Nixon shocks tampered with only one dimension of monetary order rather than its entire foundation.

The abandonment of gold in 1971, however, did point towards the eventual embrace of a more fully privatized capital recycling mechanism. Not only did the United States abdicate responsibility for the management of the world's key exchange rate between gold and the US dollar, it also began to withdraw its financial support from the provision of long-term grants and credits and medium-term liquidity that had allowed nations to surmount temporary balance of payments difficulties. After 1971, banks emerged as the primary source of balance of payments financing, as well as a prime source of funds for public and private infrastructure investments. Many of these banks were American, and many were active in the burgeoning Eurocurrency markets, especially after the 1973 OPEC oil price rises. Their new high-profile role within the capital recycling mechanism brought the quasi-public nature of the international monetary order under increasing pressure throughout the 1970s.

Why, then, did the United States go off gold? We can begin to answer this question by recalling what Robert Triffin long ago pointed out, namely that one of the major changes in the operation of the IMS in the postwar years had to do with the way in which central banks carried out their responsibilities. He argued that central banks have assumed an explicitly political function by accepting responsibility for the balance of payments position of national economies (1960: 32–4). They are no longer simply responsible for the value of the national currency, but also for the manner in which economies adjust to the changes induced by the cumulative results of international economic transactions. Their major tools, however, continue to be a combination of policies focused around the value of the national currency: interest rate movements, foreign exchange dealings, and other types of open market operations. High levels of reserves are crucial to the success of these operations, but these have failed to grow in step with the growth of capital movements. The end result is a holding pattern in which officials seek to contain the effect of short-term movements of capital with inadequate resources.

This problem was especially acute in American monetary policy during the later years of the Bretton Woods period, which saw a steady deterioration in its gold reserve position. In addition to this, however, the global ambitions of the American government opened the American economy to mounting pressures from changing patterns of wealth creation in the world-economy. The wide-ranging pattern of military bases and military assistance, when coupled with insistent American demands for other economies to be open to American capital, created a situation in which wealth flowed from the American economy abroad in increasingly large amounts. Eventually, this began to affect the movement of short-term funds into and out of the United States itself. Speculative economic pressure and political pressure from resurgent European and Japanese allies began to mount against American government policy, presenting a series of very unpalatable choices for American policy-makers and political leaders. The end result, justified in the name of balance of payments pressures, severed the public responsibilities of the United States to manage its currency in line with previously established rules and agreements. One must agree therefore with Fred Block that the Nixon shocks represented the final unilateral attempt by the United States under the Bretton Woods system to ensure its freedom of action in pursuit of its own narrowly defined interests.[11]

But even this unilateral US action failed to gut the structure of monetary order under Bretton Woods, although it did reinforce the pace of other transformations which were to come into full effect in the early 1980s. The principal significance of the Nixon action lay rather in its explicit abandonment of public control over exchange rates and long-term capital movements. Even though the quasi-public nature of capital movements had been eroding for some time, the Nixon shocks released a dramatic surge in private capital movements towards economies in balance of payments difficulties that was short-term in nature. The significance of 1971 for the international organization of credit thus resides in the new opportunities it provided to private financial institutions due to the withdrawal of active public participation in the capital recycling mechanism. Caught between change and continuity, the Bretton Woods international organization of credit persisted into the 1980s before succumbing finally to the

[11] This conclusion is echoed by Volcker and Gyohten (1992). That American actions have been a success is attested by the record of international monetary coordination since 1971, which clearly establishes that the United States has been able to conduct its monetary policy with little recourse to the demands or interests of its major trading partners. This is discussed in chapter 5.

reorganization of credit networks around the transnational financial circuit of New York, London and, more ambiguously, Tokyo.

Summary

The international organization of credit during the Bretton Woods period exhibited both change and continuity. Its principal foundations included:

1. The consolidation of an Atlantic-centered world-economy built upon trade and investment practices aimed at an increasingly global world market.
2. A capital recycling mechanism finely balanced between public and private participation in the movement of credit from areas of surplus to areas of demand or need.
3. A clear hierarchy between the two major PFCs, and a slowly globalizing network of monetary agents anchored in the first instance in New York.
4. A strongly entrenched great power rivalry which firmly established the boundaries to the world-economy, and behind which flowed the resources of American transnational enterprises.

By 1971 change had begun to encroach upon these foundations in a number of respects. The very success of the *Pax Americana* in promoting the creation of wealth outside of the United States had produced competing centers of wealth creation within the world-economy. While these centers did not seriously rival the American economy, they were the harbingers of increased competition in the 1980s. Although the state of great power rivalry had begun to relax by 1971, most importantly with détente, it still showed no signs of changing in a dramatic and enduring way. The Cold War would end only at the close of the 1980s, but not before flaring up once more. New York was clearly the most important PFC within the global credit system, but London both retained an important position with regard to the Commonwealth and its former colonies and had established its primacy in the fast-growing Eurocurrency markets. This erosion of the centralization of the Bretton Woods international organization of credit was reinforced by the globalization of networks of monetary agents during this period. First American and then European banks began to establish a global presence in the 1960s, giving these firms options in how to run their operations unavailable to their precursors. The most important change, however, was the emergence of an increasingly private capital recycling mechanism. Although the impact of this change would not be felt for another decade, its beginnings could be seen in the emerging infrastructure of the Euro-currency markets and in the withdrawal of public authorities from providing long-term international capital investment. Herein lies the crucial importance of the Nixon shocks of 1971: they signaled a newly emergent balance within the IMS between public and private monetary authorities. The transformation from a quasi-public, New York-centered global credit system to a private, multi-centered global credit system anchored in a select few international capital markets was now to begin in earnest.

Part 2
The contemporary international organization of credit

4 The era of decentralized globalization

Although the events of 1971 shook the postwar foundations of international monetary order, they did not collapse in the same way that the cessation of international clearance through London in 1931 prompted the complete breakdown of monetary order in the interwar period. Certain elements of the postwar monetary order did of course change, such as the determination of exchange rates, the value of the US dollar, the role of gold as a reserve asset, and the expectation that deficit economies would, in the normal course of events, adjust their international accounts. But the overall international organization of credit, as chapter 3 argued, remained remarkably stable in the face of changing political and economic circumstances. As the 1970s wore on, however, a number of important changes gathered pace which did occasion a major structural transformation of monetary order in the mid-1980s. These changes are most clearly represented by the emergence of Tokyo as a PFC that began to rival New York and London, and by the globalization of the world's major monetary agents. Twenty-five years from the formal end of Bretton Woods we are at the point where a relatively small number of highly capitalized firms operating out of a select number of PFCs wield an enormous amount of influence over the access which firms and governments have to international credit. The phrase which best evokes this two-fold movement, and which serves to define the contemporary period, is *decentralized globalization*.

To identify the international organization of credit as being marked by decentralized globalization is to recognize that its central institutional nexus of credit networks has no definitive *hub*. The absence of a clear and geographically representative center, however, does not mean absolute fragmentation in the international organization of credit. We must recognize that the way in which monetary networks have globalized over the past twenty years has worked to offset many of the fragmenting tendencies that decentralization might have been expected to produce. We should therefore consider decentralization and globalization to be complementary dimensions of the contemporary international organization of credit. While the globalization of monetary agents has allowed decentralization to occur, decentralization has in turn itself strengthened the dynamics which are directing monetary agents to continue globalizing their activities in line with the growing integration and international responsiveness of markets. The notion of "decentralized globalization" thus indicates precisely how the structure of monetary order is marked by diverse sources of credit knit together through global networks of monetary agents active across a range of financial practices.

The motor force of decentralized globalization has been the progressive privatization of the global credit system as it has evolved over the post-1972 period. Whether it is deciding who has access to credit or who assumes the role of balance of payments financier, private banking authorities today play a more central role in the organization of credit than they did throughout the Bretton Woods period. When coupled with the emergence of multiple PFCs, this structural transformation ensures that public control over levels of credit and liquidity will in the future come from international coordination rather than the exercise of power by a single state, since as we will see in chapter 5 the ability of individual states to influence the international organization of credit remains extremely asymmetrical. Additionally, with much of the capacity to grant access to credit now lodged in the hands of private authorities, traditional means of monetary policy such as the determination of interest rates, the setting of reserve requirements, and the selective use of open market operations, have lost some of their efficacy. The challenge of preserving stability in a private, multi-centered monetary order is increasingly becoming the challenge of ensuring that credit moves *throughout* the system in particular ways rather than simply *into* the system, and this is a challenge with which public monetary authorities are only beginning to grapple.[1]

---

[1] Alan Greenspan, the Chairman of the US Federal Reserve Board, recognized this problem in the early 1990s when he claimed that his repeated lowering of interest rates were not having the intended effect of making credit more available to the American economy. Accordingly, he moved to combine lowered interest rates with a 2

One of the principal consequences of the privatization of the global credit system has been an explosion in the availability of private liquidity which governments are hard pressed to control. Part of this expansion of liquidity and credit can be simply explained through changes in exchange rates: with the sustained depreciation of the US dollar against other major currencies, the measurement of capital stocks will increase simply by virtue of being valued in US funds, irrespective of actual increases in funds available.[2] Part of this expansion can also be accounted for by inflation, which was especially high in the mid- and late 1970s. But the largest part of this liquidity expansion, as will be argued below, is the result of a combination of more efficient financial intermediation and the creation of new financial instruments which have expanded the ability of those in need of capital to gain access to it. In other words, it was not only that the pool of capital available for investment expanded; the instruments whereby credit could be realized in the form of resources for potential borrowers also changed dramatically. Private banking authorities, primarily global banking concerns but also securities firms, have been at the heart of this change.

These authorities have been the primary beneficiaries of the era of "decentralized globalization." As a collective entity they have larger proportions of internationally mobile funds under their control than at any time in the past. They are also more securely positioned as critical components of the IMS than at any time since the early interwar period, given their newly consolidated roles in balance of payments financing and foreign exchange operations. And through the medium of the Eurocurrency markets they are now less dependent on central banks for liquidity than in any previous era. This structural transformation in the intensity of private monetary authorities'

percent drop in the reserve requirements for federally chartered American banks in early 1992, the first such move in over ten years (*Globe & Mail*, February 18, 1992). This move, however, had little impact on the willingness of banks to begin extending significant amounts of new credit to customers (*The Economist*, 3 April 1993: 71). See also Feinman (1993: 580–1).

[2] This problem of measurement is more intractable than may at first appear. Any attempt to measure capital stocks must use a common currency for valuation, but the wide fluctuations in the value of the most widely traded currencies distort efforts at measuring *actual* versus *nominal* increases in levels of credit and liquidity. Neither the use of a basket of currencies nor the PPP (purchasing power parity) model can alleviate this problem, as they must in turn rest on a standard comparison of value. Although the problem of measurement tempers the analysis which follows, it does not impair it.

involvement in the international monetary order is further supported by the vertical and horizontal concentration that has occurred in the financial services industry since the mid-1980s. The integration of financial markets has not only prompted the global reach of monetary giants such as Deutsche Bank, Citicorp, and Dai-Ichi Kangyo Bank, and of securities firms such as Nomura and Goldman Sachs, but also of the many connections that tie the two types of monetary agents together, such as between Swiss Bank Corporation and S.G. Warburg or Deutsche Bank and Morgan Grenfell. The ability of these monetary agents to exploit regulatory differences and assume significant market shares of new debt issues marks a new departure in the historical balance of power between public and private authority within the IMS, and therefore of the ability of states to shape the international organization of credit.

Within the world-economy, the structural power of finance, in both institutional and market terms, has increased markedly over the course of the last twenty years. The transformation in the nature of financial intermediation on a global scale, along with the re-emergence of portfolio and bank lending as the major components of long-term capital movements, has placed the position of global finance today at a crossroads, pulled in two directions: towards an arm's-length relation to production by virtue of the portfolio nature of long-term investment and the imperatives of the Anglo-Saxon transaction-oriented financial system, and towards further integration of finance with industry by virtue of the operational principles of Japanese and Continental European banks, who are now the largest internationally active banks and who come out of home markets structured against transaction-based finance. In either case, however, it appears that the structural power of finance can only be strengthened by the direction of change taken in the international organization of credit since 1972.

This chapter will explore these changes by first briefly outlining the altered dynamics of the world-economy in the post-1972 period. In particular, fundamental changes in its Atlantic-centered core and in the state of great power rivalry have opened up future trajectories to more than one possible avenue of development. Within this fluid condition the practices which constitute the international organization of credit will then be explored, focusing upon the links that have been established between large banking concerns and major capital markets via their integration with traditional investment houses and securities firms. The emerging international regulatory web linking public authorities with responsibility for key national financial markets is also a crucial dimension of this transformation, and will receive proper attention in chapter 5. Here, the stress is upon the role of private monetary authorities in terms of how credit is created and transmitted throughout the financial system. Finally, the chapter will end by reflecting upon the irony that capital and credit, although now more readily available to firms and governments than at any time since 1947, is at the same time better able to impose stricter terms of financial discipline upon those in need of such access.

The structure of the contemporary world-economy

There can be no neat line drawn between the present and immediate past. In the case of the Bretton Woods period, as chapter 4 argued, it was marked as much by continuity as by change throughout its existence. Any attempt to outline the broad structural parameters of the world-economy as it has evolved over the past twenty-five years must therefore be somewhat circumspect in its judgment of parameters which are by their very nature fluid. Nevertheless, from the point of view of the international organization of credit, three structural changes stand out as necessary conditions for the era of decentralized globalization to come into being. The first structural change is the lapse of the Atlantic-centered economy as the identifiable core of the world-economy. As late as 1968 we could talk about the emerging problems of interdependence solely with respect to the Atlantic economy (Cooper, 1968). Today the bonds of interdependence stretch far beyond the Atlantic. The emergence of Japan, China, and the economies of south-east Asia as a growth pole of significant importance attest to the decentering of wealth creation within the world-economy, as does the continued deepening of the European Union. Regionalization, to the extent that it can be said to exist, confirms the new diversity of production, trade, and investment links within the world-economy (Henderson, 1994). They are no longer dominated either by US-centered bilateral relationships as in the immediate aftermath of the Second World War, or by US corporations as they were during the 1960s. Today, regional concentrations of wealth creation within the world-economy both overlay and complicate its global structure. The world-economy may have a transnational core (Gill and Law, 1988: 146–56, chapter 11), but it is not a core defined with reference to past geographically contained cores.

The second important structural change is a transformation in the nature of wealth creation itself which, while not yet consolidated, appears to be shaping the changing patterns of wealth production in the industrialized world. Much of the twentieth century has been predicated upon the development of large-scale mass production processes that associate the creation of wealth with the creation of physical goods: trains and railways, cars and roads, houses and factories, electrical grids and capital goods. As the twenty-first century approaches, the creation of wealth has become increasingly associated with either the production of non-physical goods that are more accurately identified as knowledge or information products, or with physical products that are not amenable to mass production: computer software packages, bio-technology, financial products, education and training, and sophisticated communication technology. These are risky but immensely lucrative activities, and they have become the preserve of highly trained and extraordinarily entrepreneurial individuals and/or unusually structured corporations. In this sense the emergence of competing forms of wealth creation predicated upon different kinds of economic and commercial activities presages a social struggle between collective actors with alternative stakes in the economic and political organization of society. These struggles have implications for the organization of the world-economy, because as the knowledge-intensive economy consolidates itself and provides its beneficiaries with increasing social power, it is their ideas, norms, mores, and forms of social relations which will emerge as the standard against which others are judged. And while these standards may bear some affinity to corporate élites that have dominated the Bretton Woods period by virtue of their importance to the generation of wealth within the Atlantic-centered world-economy, they will also contain important points of difference.

The third important structural change is the end of the Cold War and the resulting ambiguity in the exercise of political power in the new international environment. The end of the Cold War irrevocably shattered many barriers to the expansion of the world-economy that existed since 1947. The postwar world-economy thus stands on the threshold of an era of significant expansion in its boundaries as the territories and economies of the former Soviet bloc are integrated into the imperatives and dynamics of the world market. The new openness of political boundaries in Europe to the expansion of the world-economy comes on the heels of a similar experience in Asia, where first China and then India reopened their doors to western investment in the 1980s. While there are today economic and cultural costs associated with expansion throughout the world-economy, there are very few insurmountable barriers to such expansion anywhere. The kinds of barriers that Fernand Braudel used to distinguish one world-economy from another – "a zone which it is only worth crossing, economically speaking, in *exceptional circumstances*" (1979/1984: 26, emphasis in original) – have more or less disappeared with the end of the Cold War.

At the same time, and as a consequence of the end of the Cold War, the way in which political power is exercised internationally has changed. The demise of an erstwhile opponent against which the United States could offer itself and its principles, and around which it could attempt to rally support, has opened up considerable space for pluralism in western political circles. This is true at the level of inter-state relations as well as domestic politics, and has made alternative political trajectories now a very real possibility, subject of course to the prevailing strictures of contemporary social relationships. Yet precisely because these prevailing social strictures can no longer rely on the constitution of the Soviet Union as the indefatigable enemy to be used to help convince others to fall into line, the power of both the United States and its previously dominant sets of social relations has eroded. While still absolutely powerful in terms of material capabilities, the sources of American ideological and ideational power have been weakened. It is in this sense that the end of the Cold War has made the exercise of political power more ambiguous in the world-economy: where social and political allies within "the west" once felt more or less compelled to provide a united front on many economic issues because of overlapping security considerations, freedom of maneuver now exists. The future of the world-economy has become more open to contestation and far less a prisoner of its immediate past.

These three broad transformations in the world-economy carry very specific implications with respect to the international organization of credit. First, the lapse of a single clearly identifiable core to the world-economy has allowed finance itself to become decentralized. As wealth creation within the world-economy has fragmented in terms of its centers of concentration, banking networks anchored in rival centers of wealth creation have begun to compete on a global basis. Yet, the global nature of this competition should not obscure the recognition that there are very few truly "global" banks. Most banks, while having sometimes large and often growing international opera-tions, remain very much creatures of their home markets.[3] Second, the emerging force of the knowledge-intensive economy privileges finance in a very special way: finance, and global finance in particular, is both a voracious user of and an institutional pillar for the develop-ment of complex information systems. Finance will thus profit from the gathering strength of the knowledge-intensive economy even as it occupies a privileged position in the shaping of its future. Finally, the end of the Cold War and the reshaping of political power has served to complicate the regulatory parameters of finance, especially where the exercise of public authority rests on the success of international negotiation. Regulating global finance has never been an easy task, and the loss of a single center from which public authority can be efficiently exercised now makes it an especially tricky task. As in the past, changes in the structure of the world-economy have direct implications for the way in which the international organization of credit, and therefore international monetary order, are constituted.

Reversal of fortune: reconstituting international credit

Since the early 1970s, the principal foundations of international credit as they were established in the Bretton Woods period have been fundamentally transformed. The first point of transformation has been a complete turnaround in the sources of internationally mobile capital. Here the Japanese economy has emerged as the single largest source of international credit in the global financial system, while the US economy has at the same time become the single largest consumer of international credit. The second point of transformation has been the decisive rise of private monetary authorities to a position of leadership concerning how credit is allocated within the global capital recycling mechanism. Together these transformations in the sources of

[3] The trade magazine *The Banker* has done some trail-blazing work on the subject of assessing the degree of globalization of banks. In their 1995 survey, which reflects figures for 1993, 39 of the world's 100 largest banks had at least 25 percent of their assets outside of their home country, up from 38 in 1992, while 18 had more than 40 percent. Twelve of these highly globalized banks were European, three were Amer-ican, and there was one bank each from Australia, Canada, and China. For the third year in a row a UK institution topped the list as the bank with the highest degree of globalization (*The Banker*, February 1995: 68–71).

credit and in the form of its authority herald the reconstitution of the international organization of credit in the contemporary period.

Changing sources of credit

Taking the former reversal first, figure 4.1 traces the net long-term capital movements of the five main creditor economies over the entire post-1947 period.[4] The US economy was the largest single source of international credit until the 1977–81 period, after which it reversed its historic postwar role from that of a net provider to a net recipient of international credit. Between 1984 and 1992 the US economy was a net provider of long-term capital in only one year, and its average net position on long-term capital transactions moved into deficit on the scale of $24 billion annually during 1982–6 and about $32 billion between 1987–91. 1992 and 1993 have seen a halt to this string of deficits on long-term account, with the United States unexpectedly registering large net outflows of just over $46 billion in each year, but it is unclear whether this will be maintained. Some of the reasons for the reversal of the 1980s are narrowly economic, reflecting the under-valued costs of investing in the United States from the perspective of non-US internationally active corporations. Broader reasons begin with the growing protectionist sentiment of the American Congress, which made it prudent for foreign firms to protect their American market share by investing in US industry. The American propensity to consume rather than save, both individually as households and collectively in terms of the budget deficit, cannot be underestimated. In particular, the US budget deficit, which expanded significantly during the early 1980s, is now financed by foreigners to an unprece-dented degree. While the reasons for this reversal may be difficult to separate analytically, the shift in the American economy from that of a net creditor to a debtor is a major transformation in the foundations of the international organization of credit.

Significant new sources of international credit took some time to develop after the so-called "collapse" of Bretton Woods. Of the four remaining major creditor economies of the postwar period, for example, France was actually exporting nearly the same volume of long-term funds in the 1981–6 period as in the 1967–71 period, with

---

[4] Once again, these figures are based on five-year averages and denominated in US dollars.

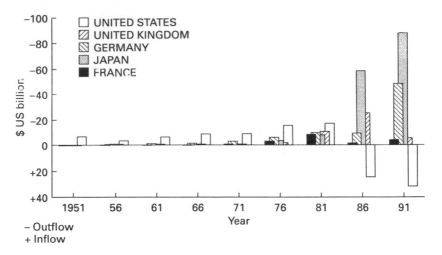

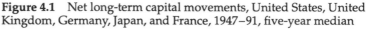

Figure 4.1 Net long-term capital movements, United States, United Kingdom, Germany, Japan, and France, 1947–91, five-year median

Source: IMF, *Balance of Payments Yearbook*

this climbing to just under $4 billion per year during 1987–91.[5] France can no longer be counted as a major provider of international credit to the world-economy, although in exceptional years it may export significant amounts of long-term capital, such as in 1993 when nearly $10 billion flowed out. Germany, despite accumulating massive trade surpluses from the mid-1970s onwards, did not begin to invest large amounts of capital beyond its borders until very recently. It was only after 1987 that average annual capital exports moved above the $9 billion plateau. Between 1987 and 1991, however, German capital exports averaged about $48 billion, vaulting Germany into the position of the second largest long-term capital exporter within the world-economy. Occasionally, as in 1990 and 1991, it has been the largest. More recently, Germany has been transformed into a net recipient of international credit to cover the costs of unification, with a massive $78 billion net inflow of funds occurring in 1993. If, as is expected, Germany's status as a major consumer of long-term international credit proves temporary, German capital will in the late 1990s occupy

[5] Since the figures I am using refer to net long-term capital movements I will specify only those capital movements which are not long term. It must also be noted that these figures are not adjusted for inflation, which means in the case of France that it was actually exporting less capital in the 1982–6 period than in the 1967–71 period.

a key position in the newly constituted international organization of credit. Similarly, British capital exports should also occupy an important place in this new situation. Since 1972 Britain's average annual capital exports have increased more than ten-fold, rising from under $1 billion per year in the mid-1970s to nearly $25 billion per year in the mid-1980s. The greatest increases took place after the election of Margaret Thatcher in 1979, when the outflow of long-term capital steadily increased from just under $11 billion in 1979 to $35 billion in 1986. Such increases are all the more incredible if it is remembered that these figures do not include money lent out or taken in on the Eurocurrency market, since those funds represent neither a drain nor an increase on British capital stocks.[6] British capital exports have become more volatile since 1986, averaging about $5 billion per year but occasionally registering substantial outflows. In 1989 and 1992, for example, British long-term capital exports were over $30 billion, while in 1993 this figure rose to $77 billion. Equally important, British capital exports are distinguished by their diversity; unlike Japan, whose capital exports are concentrated in the United States and east Asia, British international credit is diversified on a global basis. It is upon this diversity of destinations as well as upon its volume that the British economy's position in the newly constituted international organization of credit is being secured.

Nevertheless, Britain's long-term capital exports are dwarfed by the sheer scale of recent Japanese long-term capital exports to the world-economy. Here the reversal of fortune in terms of the sources of international credit is crystal clear. During the Bretton Woods period, Japan moved from a net debtor position in terms of long-term capital movements to a net creditor position prior to 1971, on the order of some $700 million annually. Still, in the 1967–71 period, it was the least important of the major long-term creditor economies. Between 1972 and 1986, however, the Japanese economy, buoyed by record trade surpluses with its trading partners and a continued high personal savings rate, increased its average annual long-term capital exports from nearly $4 billion in the 1972–7 period to over $57 billion in the 1982–6 period. In 1986, 1987, and 1988, the Japanese economy invested respectively $134, $138, and $121 billion abroad, three or four times the amount of the next largest capital-exporting economy. This

[6] It is worthwhile to recall that Eurocurrencies are currencies borrowed and lent outside of the issuing country's borders. Hence Euromarket activity within London does not record itself on the capital account of the British balance of payments.

Table 4.1 *Saudi Arabian long-term capital transactions, 1972–93, $US million (rounded)*

Year	1972	1973	1974	1975	1976	1977
Total	· 364	−1,590	−6,042	−12,821	−15,467	−12,910
Year	1978	1979	1980	1981	1982	1983
Total	−4,965	−10,017	−37,376	−37,574	−12,720	3,237
Year	1984	1985	1986	1987	1988	1989
Total	9,373	456	−3,386	−3,260	−9,333	−13,182
Year	1990	1991	1992	1993		
Total	−17,113	−19,605	−18,628	−8,288		
5-year averages	1972–76	1977–81	1982–86	1987–91	1992–93	
Total	−7,257	−20,568	−608	−12,499	−13,456	

Notes: − = Outflow   + = Inflow.
Source: IMF, *Balance of Payments Yearbook*.

unprecedented outflow averaged nearly $87 billion between 1987 and 1991, and continued into the 1990s. In 1993, for example, the Japanese economy again invested over $87 billion of long-term capital abroad. Almost without exception, Japan has from 1984 on been the single largest source of international credit to the world-economy.

There is one other creditor economy which might be considered an important source of international credit, and thus a key element of the foundation of international monetary order: Saudi Arabia. Its meteoric rise to prominence in credit markets was fueled by the OPEC oil price increases of 1973–4. Oil revenue, the principal source of Saudi export earnings, rose from $2 billion in 1970 to over $110 billion in 1981 before dropping to $18 billion in 1986. Long-term capital movements followed a similar trajectory. In 1972, for example, Saudi Arabia exported $364 million of long-term capital. That figure climbed to over $15 billion in 1976, and after a short respite to over $37 billion in 1980 and again in 1981. Table 4.1 details Saudi Arabia's long-term capital movements.

The impact of Saudi capital movements on the international organization of credit, however, cannot be equated with that of other key international creditors, for three reasons. First, the sums involved, while significant (and especially so in 1980 and 1981 and again from 1989 to 1992), are not of the same magnitude or composition as the other principal creditor economies. By 1982 oil revenues were declining, and Saudi Arabia was actually a net importer of long-term

capital from 1983 to 1985. When it again became a significant international creditor in the late 1980s, the single largest component of its
long-term capital transactions were private unrequited transfers,
mostly workers' remittances. This component of Saudi Arabia's
capital account mushroomed from between $2 and $4 billion per year
in the late 1970s and early 1980s (a small proportion of its international transactions) to between $15 and $20 billion by the late 1980s
and early 1990s. A significant part of Saudi Arabia's capital exports,
therefore, while important for recipient families and economies, have
not become institutionalized within the international organization of
credit. Second, the investments made by Saudi firms and investment
trusts are largely denominated in US dollars and were originally
placed in non-Saudi banks for investment purposes. They were
especially important for the Euromarket activities of American and
British banks during the 1970s, and accounted for nearly 25 percent of
all OPEC foreign investments between 1974 and 1983 (Mattione, 1985:
14). These funds, however, were and still are denominated in another
currency and are often managed by non-Saudi banks. Finally, there is
no principal financial center in Saudi Arabia to complement the large
amount of funds accumulated by Saudi oil production. Without a PFC
Saudi capital exports have become absorbed into the international
organization of credit without transforming its foundations. All of
these factors point to the conclusion that the influence of Saudi capital
on the international organization of credit was transitory in nature.[7]

The reversal of fortune within the international organization of
credit raises several questions regarding monetary order. As chapters
2 and 3 outlined, PFCs require the accumulation of capital for lending
abroad if they are to either acquire or maintain their vibrancy.
Although such an accumulation may occur in a number of ways –
from being an *entrepôt* center, or at the center of a complex network of
wealth-producing enterprises, or as a destination of bullion – in the
past century this has been accomplished first and foremost by being at
the center of a strong international network of trade in goods and
services.[8] With the emergence of Japan as the world's leading "trading

---

[7] Helleiner (1989: 345–6) also points to the military dependence of Saudi Arabia on its
major debtor as another factor in this equation, while Mattione (1985: 185–9)
emphasizes the pressures for safe and liquid investments which have limited the
ability of Saudi Arabia (and other OPEC producers) to influence the international
financial system in a major way.

[8] It is also clear that the rate of savings is an important factor in the accumulation of

state" (Rosecrance, 1986), together with the dominance of Tokyo and its environs over the Japanese economy, we must ask whether Tokyo and the banking networks anchored within it have the capacity to act as a new world PFC, and with what kinds of implications. It is in Tokyo that decisions are made concerning the disposal of this surplus, and in Tokyo that decisions are made concerning who might have access to the credit represented by it. Tokyo now seems to have in place many of the elements necessary for its emergence as a key world PFC.

In terms of how credit is constituted, however, this reversal of fortune is also ambiguous, because the American economy is still the largest single economy in the world, and it produces enormous sums of capital for international investment even as it maintains a voracious appetite for foreign capital. The sheer volume of capital moving into and out of the American economy will therefore exert a powerful impact on the organization of credit. When this is added to the still significant role of New York, as both a source of internationally mobile funds and of financial intermediation on a global scale, it becomes clear that the global financial system will not in the near future become centralized around a single principal financial center. Rather, it seems entirely probable that the international organization of credit will assume a triadic form. New York's position as one part of the triad will be based upon its global heritage and how it stands astride the colossal American economy. London's position will be secured by its dual *entrepôt* role at the center of the Euromarkets and a capital-exporting British economy. And finally, Tokyo's position will be maintained by its dominance of the world's premier export-oriented wealth-producing economy. Adrian Hamilton (1986: 111) has gone so far as to characterize this as a "three-legged stool," and while

capital, especially in providing funds to invest in industry and technology. With reference to Japan, it historically has had a high rate of savings, with individual savings providing over 50 percent of funds to the banking system for lending. Bank loans, in turn, have been the predominant source of investment funds in postwar Japan (Shinkai, 1988: 253). Many economists in fact draw causal linkages between high savings rates, trade surpluses, and capital exports, on the assumption that a "high savings economy" requires both trade surpluses to replace forgone domestic sales and capital exports to provide an income-earning outlet for the unused portion of national savings. In essence, a high savings rate dampens domestic economic activity, thereby necessitating an export-led growth strategy. In the case of Japan, therefore, much discussion revolves around how to absorb excess savings with tax incentives and government deficits designed to promote domestic consumption. See, for example, Ridley (1987: 172–4).

the fortunes of each "leg" may wax and wane on the margins, his metaphor is likely to be accurate into the near-term future.

Such a decentralized international organization of credit raises questions concerning its overall stability. While such questions can be answered definitively only with the aid of hindsight, it is useful to consider some of the broad economic characteristics of the contemporary period with reference to past monetary orders. Under the *Pax Britannica*, the role of London and the British economy in the world-economy assumed certain characteristics. Britain ran a merchandise trade deficit during most of the nineteenth century and throughout the first three decades of the twentieth century, but made up for this by running a large surplus on its invisible accounts. In addition, short-term trade credits were provided by brokers, and long-term capital by merchant banking houses. Capital earned by or within Britain was thus recycled abroad, and paid for with exports back to Britain. There was a certain symmetry to the London-centered global credit system that helps to explain the overall stability which we have come to see in this period, despite some important caveats.[9]

In the *Pax Americana*, this symmetry was not re-established. The American economy ran a trade surplus rather than a deficit throughout the entire Bretton Woods period, further augmented by a surplus on its invisible accounts. It was also a large-scale capital exporter to all parts of the globe, although certain regions were clearly preferred. Capital earned by American multinationals was recycled abroad through foreign investments, while lowered trading barriers encouraged trade with the United States in order to pay for these investments. Since the American economy ran both trade and invisible surpluses, however, in accounting terms it acted as a net drain on the growing wealth of the world-economy, in so far as balance of payments figures represent accurate transfers of wealth between national economies. In other words, although the United States ran a deficit in its overall or basic balance of payments throughout the Bretton Woods period, the wealth represented by that deficit was bound to return (subject to either commercial failure or loss of assets through nationalization). The only portions of the American balance of payments deficit which were irretrievably "lost," so to speak, were

[9] The two most important caveats are that the period was punctuated by a long and deep depression (1873–96) and that the *Pax Britannica* imposed highs costs on the periphery of the world-economy, where boom and bust growth was prevalent (cf. Ford, 1960/1985).

the aid grants and military expenditures abroad, and these as we saw were a declining portion of the total American balance of payments picture. From this point of view, the stability of the postwar international organization of credit rested almost entirely upon America's export of long-term capital, which provided foreign economies with the means to purchase the products of US producers. Any compromise in this propensity to export capital would therefore undermine one of the principal foundations of international monetary order.

This structural imbalance is accentuated if we examine the position of the Japanese economy within the contemporary global credit system. Like America before it, Japan is generating merchandise trade surpluses, but on a scale far surpassing what America ever produced. These are somewhat attenuated by a small deficit on its invisible accounts. Similar also to postwar America, it is supplying long-term capital to the world-economy at a phenomenal rate. These capital exports, of course, represent claims on future wealth which will either be returned to Japan or reinvested abroad once again. Finally, unlike America or Britain before it, the Japanese economy is not particularly open to imports from its major North American and European trading partners, although it is incorporating larger chunks of south and east Asia into its growing economic orbit. The result is that Japan is acting like an immense black hole, into which is flowing the wealth earned by other areas of the world-economy, primarily North America and Europe. Although this appropriated wealth is currently being recycled back abroad through capital exports, the underlying structural imbalance should not be obscured. In fact, it can be argued that this imbalance is being sustained only through the effective operation of the capital recycling mechanism, or in other words through the activities and practices of the monetary agents which collectively comprise the global financial system.

The rise of private monetary authorities

The decentralization of the organization of credit since 1972 has been accompanied by the privatization of the capital recycling mechanism and by the globalization of the major actors involved. Chapter 3 argued that Bretton Woods should be seen as a quasi-public international organization of credit. This was especially evident in the proportion of public to private long-term capital exports. If we turn to examine the post-1972 period, however, a substantial change in this

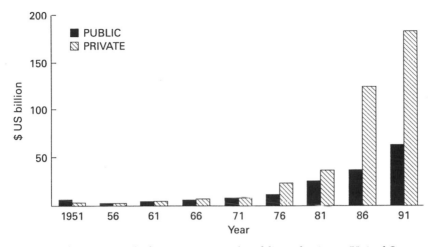

Figure 4.2 Net long-term capital, public and private, United States, United Kingdom, Germany, Japan, and France, 1947–91, five-year median

Source: IMF, *Balance of Payments Yearbook*

balance becomes apparent. As figure 4.2 indicates, this balance began to break down almost immediately after the technical demise of Bretton Woods in 1971. Whereas the proportion of public to private long-term capital exports remained relatively balanced and stable during the last fifteen years of Bretton Woods, it quickly assumed a two : one ratio in the 1972–6 period, with approximately $23 billion worth of international private investments to about $11 billion worth of public long-term capital investments being made annually. This rose to $36 billion worth of private capital to $25 billion worth of public capital in the 1977–81 period, and $124 billion worth of private capital to $36 billion worth of public capital in the 1982–6 period. In the latest full five-year period for which figures are currently available, this proportion leveled off at $182 billion to $62 billion, or a ratio of nearly three : one of private over public sources.[10] Private monetary authorities have found themselves in control of more long-term

[10] 1992 and 1993 saw a return to the ratios of the mid-1980s, when private capital flows dwarfed public ones. Over these two years, private capital flows comprised 83 percent of all long-term international capital transactions within the economies examined here, and public transactions a mere 17 percent.

Table 4.2 *Combined assets of American, British, German, Japanese, and French banks in* The Banker's *top 50 Banks, 1972–95, $US billion (rounded)*

Year	Assets	Year	Assets
1972	620	1984	3,071
1973	883	1985	3,552
1974	926	1986	4,869
1975	1,013	1987	5,975
1976	1,343	1988	6,957
1977	1,366	1989	7,498
1978	1,870	1990	7,788
1979	2,126	1991	8,330
1980	2,361	1992	9,337
1981	2,458	1993	10,345
1982	2,580	1994	12,172
1983	2,825	1995	14,584

Source: The Banker (London, various issues).

capital movements since 1971 because they have been the source of an increasing share of these movements.[11]

The rising ratio of private to public sources of international credit has been complemented by a rise in the proportions of resources held directly by each of these different monetary authorities, deposit assets in the case of banks and official reserves in the case of central banks. We can use the trade magazine *The Banker* to compile the assets of the largest fifty banks headquartered in the five major postwar creditor economies, and compare this with the total official reserves of the corresponding five major monetary powers, as portrayed by the IMF's *International Financial Statistics*. The results are displayed in tables 4.2–4.4.[12] Combined bank assets rose from $620 billion in 1972 to $14,584 billion in 1995, while official reserves rose from $70 billion in 1972 to some $437 billion in 1995. These numbers indicate that the ratio of official reserves to bank assets declined from just over 11 percent in 1972 to 3 percent in 1995. On the basis of five-year averages, which are a better indicator of longer-term trends, the ratio has been

[11] This conclusion reinforces and updates the work of Cohen (1981) and Aglietta (1985), who were among the first to point to the increased prominence of private actors in, respectively, balance of payments financing and credit creation.

[12] The number of fifty was chosen as an indicator of this ratio rather than as categorical evidence of it. Fewer than the top fifty banks seems not to provide a large enough proportion of banking assets to official reserves, while more than fifty does not appear to alter the figures to any great degree.

Table 4.3 *Total official reserves of United States, United Kingdom, Germany, Japan, and France, 1972–95, $US billion (rounded)*

Year	Reserves	Year	Reserves
1972	70	1984	144
1973	74	1985	149
1974	76	1986	194
1975	81	1987	267
1976	83	1988	284
1977	110	1989	290
1978	133	1990	309
1979	137	1991	299
1980	167	1992	310
1981	150	1993	321
1982	139	1994	358
1983	142	1995	437

Source: International Financial Statistics (various issues).

Table 4.4 *Ratio of combined bank assets of American, British, German, Japanese, and French banks to total official reserves of United States, United Kingdom, Germany, Japan, and France, 1972–95, five-year averages, $US billion (rounded)*

Years	Average bank assets	Average official reserves	% ratio of reserves to assets
1972–6	957	76	8
1977–81	2,037	139	7
1982–6	3,380	153	5
1987–91	7,310	290	4
1992–5	11,610	357	3

Source: The Banker and *International Financial Statistics* (various issues).

more than halved from about 8 percent in the 1972–6 period to just over 3 percent in the 1992–5 period. Not only has the underlying basis of liquidity creation within the global financial system been largely transferred to private monetary authorities, the actual resources available to public authorities have not kept pace with those available to private authorities. States today simply have fewer resources to use in their attempts to influence the behavior of market participants compared with what those participants themselves possess; what authority states do wield must come from other sources.

In addition to the recycling of capital becoming largely an affair of private monetary agents, these agents themselves have undergone an incredible metamorphosis since the mid-1970s. For example, in 1972 the world's largest bank holding company, BankAmerica Corp., had assets of some $33 billion. By 1994 the world's largest bank holding company, Sanwa Bank, had assets totalling nearly $582 billion, an eighteen-fold increase in size that outstripped even the fourteen-fold increase in overall assets of the world's largest fifty banks. Concomitant with the tremendous growth in the size of financial markets, therefore, has come a tremendous growth in the size and diversity of the major international banks. The biggest banks have become true leviathans, taking advantage of the opportunities presented by a global capital market anchored in several principal financial centers. Indeed, this globalization and concentration within the transnational banking industry explains a good deal of the integration of the global capital market itself: large banking concerns, with branches in all major financial centers and activities in all aspects of global finance, are now able to obtain and grant access to funds on a world-wide basis, thereby undercutting state attempts to regulate the movement of money across borders.

One in fact may argue that the global concentration of the transnational banking industry is one of the key reasons why the organization of credit has not itself become impaired in the face of mounting regional economic and political pressures since the 1970s. Continually growing levels of concentration, however, are not a forgone conclusion. As measured by the proportion of banking assets held by the largest ten of the top fifty banks, this ratio approached 40 percent in 1972, meaning that 40 percent of the assets held by the top fifty banks were concentrated in the hands of the world's ten largest banks. This ratio declined to about 30 percent in 1976, and was still at 30 percent in 1981. It has only recently begun to increase again, reaching about 35 percent in 1994. The reasons for the slow development of concentration are manifold, including a proliferation of new banking concerns arising out of the first attempts at deregulation; a proliferation of new international financial centers competing with established financial centers, and supporting new banking concerns in the process; and phenomenal growth in banking systems in south-east Asia, Latin America, and the oil-rich Gulf states. The shocks which the debt crisis administered to the largest American and European banks also contributed by lowering their asset base (i.e., their loans) when considered against the relatively healthier portfolios of smaller, regional banks, or large banks that did not actively seek out sovereign loans to developing countries. Nevertheless, it is precisely these large banks which are most involved in recycling capital and credit globally, and they have grown steadily, and at times spectacularly, since 1972.[13]

Implications of the credit revolution: exploring the capital recycling mechanism

During the 1970s and 1980s, the form through which international credit was provided to the world-economy changed. The impact of this change, when coupled with the changes in the sources of international credit, raises the question of who now creates international credit and who controls access to it within the world-economy. If we accept that the capacity of states to control or influence the international organization of credit is circumscribed by how credit is recycled in the first place, then exploring the nature of these changes clarifies who provides what kind of credit to whom, and how. We have already outlined the reversal of fortune amongst sources of international credit, with the American economy becoming in the 1980s a net recipient of international credit flows and the Japanese and German economies subsequently becoming the largest providers of international credit to the world-economy. It is not clear, however, what implications this change has for the capital recycling mechanism, and what if any new powers accrue to Japan and Germany as a result of their new-found creditor status (Helleiner, 1992; Murphy, 1989). We may bring some clarity to this debate by reflecting upon changes in the form of financial intermediation within the capital recycling mechanism and upon their effect on the financial institutions which lie at the core of this mechanism.

We may briefly recall that the predominant form of American private capital exports during the Bretton Woods period was foreign direct investment (FDI). This was in part a response to the interwar experience with bond-payers' defaults, in part a response to the

---

[13] It is interesting to note in this regard that as of 1989 *The Banker* changed its reporting format on the top 500 banks from an emphasis on size to an emphasis on capital adequacy and profitability. This shift in focus marked the realization that sheer size is not an unambiguous indicator of health and vitality, and that some of the largest international banks – and especially the biggest Japanese banks – were both undercapitalized and operating on fragile profit margins.

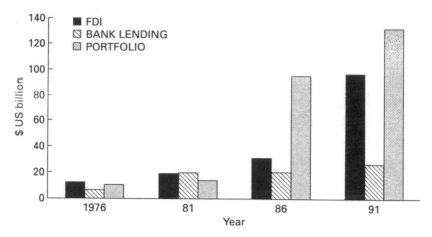

Figure 4.3 Net long-term capital movements, by type (FDI, bank lending, and portfolio), United States, United Kingdom, Germany, Japan, and France, 1972–91, five-year median

Source: IMF, *Balance of Payments Yearbook*

erection of a common tariff around the European Community, and in part a response to the particular demands of American commercial expansion, driven as they were by the mass-production and consumption dynamics of corporate America. The 1963 Interest Equalization Tax, by making investments in foreign bonds more expensive, also contributed to the use of FDI as the principal vehicle by which capital was recycled in the postwar era. Indeed, on a yearly basis, it was not until 1980 that FDI was dislodged as the single largest component of long-term capital movements on a global scale.[14]

As figure 4.3 makes clear, however, the 1980s were a dramatic decade of change in terms of the form taken by international credit. FDI as a component of these flows declined from a high of 43 percent during the 1972–6 period to a low of 21 percent in the 1982–6 period, before rebounding to about 38 percent of all long-term credit flows in

---

[14] It was not until 1984 that portfolio investment significantly outdistanced FDI as the largest single component of long-term capital movements into and out of the United States. This development can be primarily accounted for by the large-scale financing of American budget deficits by foreigners, especially Japanese. It should be noted that by the early 1990s FDI had re-emerged as the single largest component of US long-term international transactions.

the 1986–91 period. And although FDI again declined in 1992 and 1993 to about 23 percent of all long-term capital movements, it seems likely that it will recover to comprise about one-third of long-term capital movements into the forseeable future. Over the same period, portfolio investment increased from 36 percent in 1972–6 to 65 percent in 1982–6, before falling back slightly to about 50 percent of all long-term credit flows into and out of the major postwar creditor economies. In 1992 and 1993 this proportion rocketed upwards to nearly 72 percent, but it appears that on a longer-term basis about 60–65 percent of international credit will be constituted by portfolio investment. Finally, long-term bank lending gyrated wildly from 23 percent of all long-term credit flows in 1972–6 to 37 percent in 1977–81, but now accounts for only between 5 percent and 10 percent of such flows. Broadly speaking, then, these changes indicate that the form which long-term credit takes has moved away from direct control of productive enterprises and back towards arm's-length financial relations, where credit for large enterprises is accessed primarily from capital markets directly via security offerings.

Although this change in the form in which capital and credit are recycled has yet to run its full course, it is clearly one of the most significant developments in the capital recycling mechanism since the emergence of government-sanctioned but privately organized currency stabilization loans in the early interwar period (Meyer, 1970). It is possible to discern a number of implications for the global financial system that arise out of these changes. We can begin by reflecting on how new forms of intermediation are making the channels of credit and networks of monetary agents linking savers and borrowers far more complex and far less amenable to public control than has historically been the case. These channels and networks include layers of institutions such as corporations undertaking FDI, governments advancing aid, international institutions such as the IMF and World Bank providing certain kinds of loans, banks providing various types of funding, securities firms and investment houses undertaking to sell securities and bonds for clients, and information-processing institutions such as Standard and Poors, often all operating in several capital markets at once. This can be contrasted with financial intermediation under the pre-1914 London-centered credit system where merchant banks were the primary institutions involved in capital recycling on an international basis, and with the Bretton Woods period when money-center banks, corporations, and governments were the principal sources of capital recycling. The global financial system itself has thus become far more complicated than its historical antecedents.

One implication of changes in the form of intermediation therefore concerns the capacity of public monetary authorities to control increases in the availability of credit to private enterprises and to adequately supervise the financial operators themselves. Traditional monetary tools and regulatory practices developed by states no longer seem sufficient. This implication is examined in more detail in chapter 5. Four other implications, however, remain to be explored within the context of the changing role of private monetary authorities in the global financial system. These are the use of money as a commodity, the involvement of finance in the productive process, the tiering of financial actors, and what might be called, following Gill and Law (1989), the changing structural power of finance within the world-economy. Each implication will be considered in turn.

The recognition that money has become a commodity, or as Richard O'Brien (1992: 7) terms it, an "information product," has arisen out of the development of very deep secondary markets, in terms of both discounting and futures products, which has been a constituent part of the re-emergence of long-term financing via the issuance of various types of securities. The promises to pay which these financial instruments represent are thus increasingly being traded as commodities according to supply and demand. The impact of this practice on the company or government whose instruments are traded is direct and immediate, and makes further access to financing dependent upon the extent of the commodification of past debt. This of course means that the issuers of debt not only have to worry about how their general operations and long-term strategies are evolving, but also how financial actors are reacting to these practices through secondary markets on a daily basis. It adds an extra layer of complexity and uncertainty to the activities of these enterprises, draining resources and energy away from more directly relevant concerns.[15] In the long run, as Susan Strange has pointed out (1986/1989: 106), the respect for money as a legitimate and credible pillar of economic activity might well be undermined.

One can also expect the manner in which financial actors are

[15] Increased turnover of securities on secondary markets also poses problems for governments, since these securities represent claims on particular currencies. Increased buying and selling translates into increased pressure on exchange rates, whose volatility may have no direct link with government activity or policy.

involved in the production process to be influenced by changes in the form of financial intermediation. There are two contradictory tendencies to this implication. On one hand, if more capital recycling takes the form of portfolio investments, the global production process will remain at least in the hands of those who know that production best: the corporations directly involved, with financial discipline tied to their need to service accumulated debt payments. In this case the influence of finance will arise mainly out of the demands of debt servicing and the ability to grant access to new credit, which of course is not insignificant. Still, historical experience suggests that efficiency and productivity are closely tied to freeing individuals and firms as far as possible from the collective myopia of bankers; keeping them out of the day-to-day operation of manufacturing will in all likelihood promote such efficiency.[16]

On the other hand, the differences in the traditions and practices of Japanese, French, German, British, and American banks and investment houses must be recognized. British and American financial services firms, for example, are more purely purveyors of finance and information than their European and Japanese counterparts. It is precisely these kinds of banks, however, which have recently supplanted American and British banks at the apex of the global financial hierarchy. They have a history of involvement in the firms which they finance, and should they continue to dominate the financial system as they have done in the mid- to late 1980s, we can expect to see increased interconnections between finance and industry on a global scale. This would compromise the trend away from direct financial influence on the productive process by virtue of the sustained involvement of the largest banks in the long-term business strategies of their clients. The role of Japanese house banks in their *keiretsu* organizations and the history of German banks is instructive here, for it points the way to an emerging global structure of enmeshed industry–finance capital whose levels of concentration would indeed be unprecedented. This history has itself become compromised, however, for as financial markets liberalize and become more transparent, the historic role of European and Japanese banks will come

---

[16] A caveat to this is the use of debt to further corporate buyouts, a practice which resulted in the introduction of junk bonds in the 1980s. Such mergers and acquisitions involve bankers and investment houses directly in the running of productive enterprises, and experience suggests again that this lowers the efficiency and productivity of these firms, at least in the short term.

under pressure to become more transaction-oriented, in effect to become more "Anglicized." As the market structures within which European and Japanese banks operate change, the configuration of incentives and priorities which currently shape their strategies will change as well. This can already be seen in the way in which these banks are expanding into markets dominated by investment banking, where they are buying established firms and then allowing them to continue in their traditional lines of business.[17] The battle between what Michel Albert (1993) dubs the Anglo-Saxon and Rhenish models is not at all clearly defined, first and foremost because the agents associated with these two models are no longer self-contained ideal types.[18]

The change in who provides credit through which form of inter-mediation is also contributing to the tiering of the financial system in important new ways. Especially since deregulation swept through financial markets in the late 1980s, there has been a separation between global and more regional players in nearly all types of financial services. In the United States this has resulted in a spate of bank mergers in the 1990s that has largely concentrated the global players in New York and San Francisco, with several of the largest merging to protect their global share against foreign competitors.[19]

[17] Although Japanese banks have been conspicuous by their absence in the commercial–investment bank mergers of the 1990s, recent mergers suggest that European banks are adopting Anglo-Saxon financial market practices as the key means of protecting their global presence. The takeovers of Morgan Grenfell by Deutsche Bank, Warburg by Swiss Bank Corporation, Kleinwort Benson by Dresdner Bank, and Baring by ING have all been presented as the only genuine method for these European banks to become "global" players in markets dominated by "Anglo-Saxon" norms.

[18] Not only are the agents of the so-called Rhenish model adopting Anglo-Saxon characteristics. Many regulators and senior officials active in global financial markets see a move back from a purely transaction-oriented financial system occurring in the 1990s, which incorporates a more relational approach to finance and which will strengthen the relationship-bound element of the financial system. This sense of the perceptions held by bankers and central bankers has been gathered as part of another research project I am engaged on, through confidential interviews with senior officials at the Bank of England (London), Bundesbank (Frankfurt), Federal Reserve Board (Washington), Federal Reserve Bank of New York, Citibank (Washington), Hongkong & Shanghai Bank (London), Crédit Suisse (Zurich), and Deutsche Bank (Frankfurt).

[19] Among the most important mergers were those in 1991 between Security Pacific and BankAmerica, and Chemical Bank and Manufacturers Hanover. 1995 witnessed a spate of regional mergers in the United States, culminating in the announcement in August that Chemical Bank and Chase Manhattan were to join. This process was not confined to the United States: in Japan 6th-ranked Mitsubishi Bank and 10th-ranked

These global players have all established a presence in the global financial system's three PFCs: New York, London, and Tokyo. Equally important, the concentration of financial firms has proceeded not only vertically, with the biggest becoming bigger in terms of their direct competitors, but horizontally as well, with banks purchasing shares in or outright ownership of securities firms. There are few independent securities firms still operating, because the global presence demanded of the biggest players requires capitalization ratios beyond all but the very strongest. In London, for example, the biggest investment banks outside of the US bulge-bracket firms (see the appendix, p. 179) are now owned by banks, many of them non-British.[20] Similar results have been seen in the United States.[21] The financial services industry is now concentrated both vertically and horizontally to an extent unknown in the past.

The tiering of the financial services industry, especially in its banking sector, is helping to segment the way in which finance is linked to economic activity. The largest and most basic level is where banks primarily lend money to individuals and small businesses and provide them with services connected mainly with retail banking. These banks, often specialized institutions such as building societies in Britain, thrifts in the United States, and the *Sparkassen* banks in Germany, make their money by providing mortgages and loans to individuals, overdrafts and increasingly financial advice and services of a fairly basic sort to small businesses and similar types of clients. They act as genuine intermediaries between savers and borrowers within a contained area, most often eschewing recourse to global capital markets altogether and letting their deposit base fund their loan portfolio. These banks are tied directly to the local economy, whether national or sub-national, and are stable in their orientation and not overly speculative by nature, although manias such as that

Bank of Tokyo merged early in 1995, while later in the year in Britain Lloyd's Bank and TSB Bank merged.

[20] Since deregulation in the stock market in 1986, many of the best known firms have sold out to larger full-service financial institutions, among them Morgan Grenfell (to Deutsche Bank), Kleinwort Benson (to Dresdner Bank), Samuel Montagu (to Midland Bank, which was subsequently bought by the Hongkong & Shanghai Bank, or HSB), James Capel (to HSB), Warburg (to Swiss Bank Corporation), and Baring (to ING), although the last was under threat of liquidation.

[21] In the United States, the largest securities firms are a part of financial services empires such as American Express, Sears Roebuck, and Prudential Insurance (Hamilton, 1986: 13–14).

which culminated in the so-called "S & L" fiasco in the United States do occasionally occur. We should view them as part of what Fernand Braudel understands as the domain of "material life," that sphere of activity where expectations and custom change only slowly. Indeed, with respect to retail banking, it is astonishing that despite the promised advances of automated teller machines and computer-based home banking, the local branch – with its offer of face-to-face human contact – continues to dominate the trade. For individuals and small businesses, for whom money is a medium rather than a commodity, banking remains a basic part of the fabric of their everyday lives, largely untouched by the pressures of international competition. Goldman Sachs is not about to begin peddling twenty-five-year mortgages in Lincoln, Nebraska.

The banking activity associated with what Braudel called the "market economy" is concerned with providing financial services to medium and large firms engaged in fairly standard commercial activities. It is defined by the practices of commercial banking, and banks involved in this tier of the financial system provide the trade and investment funds required by small, medium and even some large firms for their activities. These firms have markets that often range beyond their immediate local economies, but usually stop short of full participation within the world market. A good example of this tier of the financial system is the growing number of banks in Europe who have expanded their services across Europe as their clients have traded further afield. They are part of a growing regional network of financial institutions servicing the European economy, and which is composed predominantly of banks domiciled in EU countries (Germain, 1996c). The Frankfurt-based Commerzbank and the Brussels-based Generale de Banque exemplify this tier of banks, having established European networks precisely to provide their corporate customers with the financing they require, but set within a competitive context that is open to international pressure. Their larger corporate customers, after all, have the option of turning to global financial institutions in a way that corner dry-cleaners do not. This tier thus mediates between the financial practices associated with the domain of material life and those associated with what Braudel identifies as the domain of "capitalism," the true home of those who direct their activities to the massive accumulation of capital within the context of the world market. Nevertheless, these banks maintain a regional and corporate focus, ensuring that they are tied directly to the market economy (i.e., that part of the economy that is constituted by stable and transparent investing, producing, and trading relationships). This focus encourages them to concentrate on responding to shifts in the demand and supply for their products, rather than on trying to engage in more purely speculative activities. Ultimately, it is this last point which differentiates the banking tier tied to the domain of the market economy from that tied to "capitalism" proper.

This last tier of the financial system is directly tied to world markets, and most importantly to the activities of transnational firms that span the world-economy. One element of this activity directs itself to the trading and investing needs of companies running global operations. Transnational firms thus engage globally oriented financial institutions to design and operationalize various kinds of foreign exchange and hedging practices to minimize the specific risks of doing business world-wide. The domain of capitalism, as Braudel sees it, contains its own special logic and demands. At the same time, there is a growing element within this financial tier which is engaged more directly in speculative activities, and which has embraced the commodification of money as a means of accumulating capital on a world scale. This tier embraces speculation and risk as its *raison d'être*, and attempts to exploit such opportunities through the aggressive use of its own capital. The archetypal institutions of this tier are hedge funds and investment or merchant banks, especially where their activities embrace arbitraging risk and exploiting speculative dynamics, such as top-level real estate, foreign exchange arbitrage, and stock market speculation. This is the "symbol" economy outlined by Peter Drucker (1986), and although omnipresent in the financial activity undertaken in New York, London, and Hong Kong, for example, it is not necessarily connected to the production of goods and services for the trading economy. This speculative element differentiates the top tier from both the commercially-oriented tier and the retail banking tier, and serves to define the way in which finance constitutes part of the domain of capitalism within the present world-economy.

It is within the top tier of finance that the horizontal and vertical concentration of globally-oriented financial institutions contains direct implications for the future power of global finance in the world-economy. Following Susan Strange (1988: 25), we may consider the power of finance in both relational and structural terms. At the relational level, the major banks and investment houses will wield power to the extent that recipients require access to credit for reasons which they deem to be important. Here the power of individual banks makes for interesting reading concerning their ability to influence the actions of firms, industries, and even governments.[22] From the overall standpoint of the international organization of credit, however, the structural power which lending practices both represent and help to create is more critical to outline, for it is these pressures that public and private actors must respond to if they wish to gain access to needed operating and investment capital.

Here it is clear that the structural power of finance can only be strengthened by the continued vertical and horizontal concentration of the global financial system. If access to internationally mobile capital continues to become concentrated in fewer hands, the lending criteria of those particular banks will emerge as the dominant criteria by which requests for credit are judged. Similarly, if these criteria are established to be those which work best for the biggest banking concerns, they will slowly but inevitably filter down in various forms through the tiers of the financial system. The exigencies of global finance will thus impose themselves upon the regional and national financial systems which serve the needs of actors not completely enmeshed within the world-economy. Access to international credit will come ultimately to depend upon the fulfillment of these criteria, to the detriment of any number of public and private needs which fall under the category of social or basic needs.

What might such criteria look like? They would in the first instance be oriented towards a combination of profit- and market-share maximization, with a clear preference for larger investments in order to put to work the large pool of savings that banks and pension funds are accumulating. Larger investments both carry profit premiums and reduce information-processing overheads; globally-oriented financial institutions are thus predisposed to considering larger projects with their limited but highly specialized staffs. This of course prejudices those economic activities with only a local focus and those activities which offer a lower rate of return on investments. These would include small business, except for those professional services ancillary to large corporate activity, small-scale farming, and entrepreneurial activity associated with new and untried technologies in the hands of

[22] Research into the House of Morgan is the most outstanding example, although work done on the influence of bankers on statecraft is also useful. In this regard see Carosso (1987), Frieden (1987), Cohen (1986), and Meyer (1970).

individuals, or small firms. It also prejudices firms tied to national economies who are attempting to expand internationally. It is typically investors and strategic partners rather than banks which underwrite such expansions. In this sense these criteria stunt the growth of local and national economies not producing for a world market, while at the same time supporting the globalization of world market-oriented firms. In this way the structural power of finance reinforces the integration of the world-economy, rewarding those who accept its demands and penalizing those who resist.

There will therefore be clear winners and losers as the emerging international organization of credit becomes consolidated. Clear winners will be world market-oriented firms active in both industrialized and industrializing economies, who can escape local credit conditions by accessing global credit networks outside of their domicile. The fate of large Mexican companies after the peso devaluation of 1994 illustrates this point. Mexico's Cemex, the world's fourth largest cement firm, was able to gain access to global credit markets within months of the devaluation, while its Mexican competitors and indeed most Mexican businesses were forced to rely on the domestic banking industry to fund their operations, at interest rates often approaching 50 percent (*Financial Times*, 14 February 1995: 24; 25 May 1995: 5). World market-oriented firms are thus able to gain access to global credit networks by virtue of their position and status within the world-economy, while their local and even nationally-oriented competitors are not. It is clear, therefore, that one set of winners will comprise transnational firms irrespective of geographic domicile.

Aside from transnational firms, smaller firms situated within the orbit of the three world PFCs will also be winners in the emerging international organization of credit. Although this is clearest for firms located in the fast-growing economies of Asia, who are slowly gaining preferential access to Japanese banks by virtue of Japanese investments in their economies, it is also true of smaller firms in Mexico, Brazil, and Argentina who are benefiting from the influx of foreign and American banks and the competition they provide for the corporate market. These two areas are belatedly catching up to one of the main financing advantages held by smaller European firms, who have at their disposal Europe-wide financial networks aimed specifically at servicing the growing financial needs associated with a European economy. As regionally coherent economies in North America and Asia strengthen in line with the European economy, those firms with preferential access to financial networks based in New York, Tokyo, Singapore, and Hong Kong will increasingly be able to tap into internationally mobile credit. Just as the British Dominions were favored by London-based financial institutions at the close of the nineteenth century, and Latin American and the Caribbean governments by New York-based financial institutions in the early decades of the twentieth century, so too will certain Asian firms benefit from Tokyo–Hong Kong–Singapore-based financial institutions in the early twenty-first century.

Relative losers in the race for access to international credit, however, will not be without recourse to financial institutions. They will certainly retain access to local institutions and even in some cases to regional financial networks, especially where their product or service has an appeal beyond their immediate local economy (although not necessarily to the world market). As long as the ambitions of smaller-scale producers, farmers, and certain kinds of craftsmen remain focused on providing a livelihood for themselves and their families, they will be able to retain their niche in what Braudel identified as the domains of material life and the market economy. But scope for growth in these kinds of activities will be limited, and in effect determined by competitive pressures beyond their control. These participants in the slower-paced domains of the world-economy will both pay a premium for credit that will be above that of blue chip corporations and be more tightly bound by the lending criteria of their financial institution; yet they will not be cut off from credit altogether. Rather, their choice with regard to obtaining credit will be restricted to the institutions which participate in their domains. While these institutions are in turn themselves partly circumscribed by the global networks of monetary agents active in the realm of capitalism, they are also partly free from the competitive dynamic at the heart of global finance precisely because their natural constituency is not a niche that is particularly attractive to global capitalism.

The exception to the general implications of tiering in the global financial system will be the continued ease with which governments in the industrialized world will be able to raise funds on international bond markets.[23] Despite rising deficits, governments are able to place large security offerings relatively easily, due mostly to the need which

---

[23] The Canadian province of Ontario, for example, has had no difficulty funding its historically unprecedented budgetary deficits in the 1990s, despite all manner of contrary opinion in the financial press and the threat of cuts in their credit rating

large institutional investors have for secure, liquid investments.[24] Yet governments themselves are under increasing pressure to put their fiscal house in order, most importantly by limiting social spending. Thus the very actors who are best able to acquire the credit necessary for investment to provide social infrastructure and fulfill basic needs are coming under pressure to curtail these expenditures.

This situation is ironic in that there appear to be enormous amounts of capital in the global financial system in search of investment-grade opportunities. Although difficult to measure, stocks of capital available for investment appear to have been larger than ever during the post-1972 period. Official liquidity among the five major monetary powers increased from $70 billion to $358 billion, while assets of the fifty largest banks headquartered in these same countries increased from $620 billion to $12172 billion. And as figure 4.1 shows, long-term capital flowed around the world in astronomical amounts. In terms of sheer amounts, then, there was more capital to be invested during this period than ever before. Yet, the requirements demanded by financial institutions, when coupled with the demands of producing for a world market, allowed orthodox financial discipline to limit investments in social infrastructure and meeting basic needs. Although most easily seen in the relationship between Third World governments and the IMF, this process was equally at work in the industrialized nations, who have sought ways of reducing social and infrastructure spending. The social and political record of the 1980s and 1990s, with the rise of neo-conservatism, market liberalization, deregulation, and the retreat of the Left, all attest to the growing power of conservative financial orthodoxy and its socio–political consequences.

Summary

The international organization of credit has undergone a profound structural transformation since 1972 which is still continuing. Begin-

(*Financial Times*, 20 May 1992: 22; *Economist*, 28 August 1993: 76; and *Financial Times*, 27 July 1995: 26).

[24] Walter (1993: 202) argues that the *institutionalization* of savings in pension funds and other large investor collectives has predisposed investment in safe issues of securities, amongst which government issues must be considered the safest. The concentration of investment decisions in fewer hands is thus the counterpart to the concentration of control over who can gain access to this surplus, both of which bias the investment of credit towards large public and private actors.

ning slowly in the 1970s, changes in the sources of international credit combined with a changing capital recycling mechanism to produce in the 1980s a structural transformation of the first order. While the changing sources of international credit have been the most visible aspect of this transformation, in the long run, the more important changes have taken place in the form of credit made available to the world-economy, in the networks of monetary agents which control access to this credit, and in the relationship between public monetary agents and private monetary agents within the global financial system. The international organization of credit has entered a new era best understood as one of "decentralized globalization."

The argument that the international organization of credit has undergone an important structural transformation in the 1980s helps to explain a number of interesting developments within the past decade. First, similar to periods of structural transformation in the past, new and untried systemic creditors were reckless in their lending practices, resulting in an explosion of available credit first after the OPEC oil price rise and then after the recession of 1980–2. These creditors, whether Euro-banks, Japanese banks or junk bond specialists, upset established lending practices and helped to fuel the credit bubble of the mid-1980s. Second, economic problems have been exacerbated by an unstable international organization of credit. The recession of the early 1990s coincided with a stock market slump in Japan and a withdrawal of Japanese capital from world markets. This recession was thus more protracted in Japan and in those areas especially reliant on Japanese capital for investment, such as North America and parts of Asia. Finally, because public monetary authorities are an important part of the changes underway in global finance, their halting role during this recession can in part be attributed to the new situation in which they find themselves. Public authorities, however, were strong partners in leading the way towards the deregulation of financial markets that has so effectively increased the authority of private monetary agents in the global financial system. The manner in which public authorities have both responded to the condition of "decentralized globalization" and been a part of its cause is therefore the subject of chapter 5.

5   Decentralized globalization and the exercise of public authority

Shortly after the demise of Bretton Woods, one of its original architects could still comment that "the key problem of the international monetary system is to maintain an appropriate pattern of exchange rates, particularly among the large industrial countries" (Bernstein, 1972: 52). The argument of this chapter is that, while clearly important, maintaining stable exchange rates can no longer be considered the key preoccupation of public authorities; they must also attend to the way in which credit is organized internationally. Two kinds of public agencies are primarily responsible for exercising public regulatory authority over financial institutions: central banks and treasuries.[1] While the relationship between the two kinds of agencies is complicated and overlapping,[2] treasuries have largely concentrated upon the long-term exchange rates of their currencies and issues of capital mobility, while central banks have attempted to control the availability of credit and liquidity in their national financial systems and manage currency parities on a daily basis.

The overlap between the operations of these two agencies can be demonstrated in several ways. On the one hand, the determination of proper exchange rate levels by treasuries has a powerful impact upon

---

[1] Third parties are also sometimes involved, such as the office of Comptroller of the Currency in the United States and the Federal Bank Supervisory Agency in Germany, but usually in a minor way. The Comptroller of the Currency, for example, primarily supervises banking regulations in the United States, and influences monetary policy in that country indirectly through the medium of banking policy. In Britain, conversely, the Bank of England is the sole supervisory agency for the banking system.

[2] For example, in the United States the relationship between the Federal Reserve Board Chairman and the Secretary of the Treasury, although circumscribed by formal statute, is also guided very much by institutional tradition and the personal relationship between the incumbents (Volcker and Gyohten, 1992: 232–5).

the movement of funds into and out of currencies, and hence on the immediate availability of credit and liquidity to national financial systems. Equally important, long-term investors resist public and private investments in areas with volatile currencies, simply because of the uncertainty involved. In the case of public investments, they may demand a risk premium that makes borrowing for public use prohibitively expensive. On the other hand, only treasuries are legally mandated to issue debt to finance public expenditures. The issuing of short- and long-term debt is an extremely powerful means of influencing the international organization of credit, for it helps in a direct way to create the secondary markets which alone make certain kinds of public credit policies possible. It can also have a dramatic effect on the international movement of capital by virtue of the scale of funding required.[3]

An even more important method by which treasuries influence the international organization of credit is through the regulation of international capital movements. By regulating the ability of capital to move across borders, treasuries can critically influence the allocation of wealth created by the domestic economy, helping to determine how much of it is invested at home and how much abroad. Conversely, the availability of foreign capital for domestic investment makes controlling the national money supply by central banks more complicated and uncertain, since this supply is then subject to arbitrary flows of credit from abroad. Just as important, the regulation of capital markets determines the extent to which a financial center becomes integrated within the global financial system and thus able to act as a supplier of capital to world markets. One of the hurdles Tokyo has had to overcome in order to act as a world PFC has been the strict control which the Ministry of Finance has wielded over Japanese discount markets: by restricting the development of secondary markets as a source of liquidity open to international users of yen-denominated financial instruments, the role of Tokyo in the global financial system has been deliberately restricted.

On a day-to-day basis, however, central banks are a more active

---

[3] For example, the US government's need for foreign capital to finance its deficit both pushed up the value of the dollar and drove American Treasury authorities to press for the liberalization of Japanese financial markets in the mid-1980s, precisely as a way of freeing Japanese institutions to purchase American government bonds (Destler and Henning, 1989: 29). Although analytically separated here, in practice there is an integral link between exchange rates and the organization of credit.

component of the international organization of credit due to their nearly continuous involvement with the internal workings of capital markets. The primary instruments which they use to influence the creation and allocation of credit are manipulating interest rates to control the cost of funds; engaging in open market operations to control the quantity of funds available to banks for lending; setting the level of reserve requirements for banks to ensure that the national financial system remains sound; and moral suasion, or "window guidance" as it was known in Japan, to guide the allocation of credit. These instruments have been effective in regulating the short-term availability of credit and liquidity, and even in influencing the cost of funds over the medium term. They have also helped to ensure that banks are adequately prepared for unexpected financial shocks, although banks still fail on a regular basis.

Where these policy instruments are decidedly less successful is in influencing the operation of the capital recycling mechanism. The first three instruments are essentially methods to control the capacity of banks to loan funds by making it more or less expensive to do so, and by influencing their liquidity position in the context of regulatory statutes. The fourth instrument, moral suasion, involves central banks to a greater degree in the actual way in which banks allocate credit among their customers. Most of these policy instruments thus work through private monetary agents without attempting to influence how those agents make credit available to others. In short, those public institutions which have as their principal goal the smooth operation of domestic financial systems have few policy instruments with which they can influence how private monetary agents go about the business of lending funds or obtaining access to capital markets. Furthermore, the one policy instrument which does allow this influence to be exercised – moral suasion – appears to have been progressively abandoned over the past twenty years even by its most stalwart defender, the Bank of Japan.[4] As public authorities have moved away from direct financial intermediation within capital markets over the past two decades, market forces have acted to structure the international organization of credit according to the criteria of market

---

[4] It is not clear, however, how far this supposed abandonment has proceeded. Murphy, for example, argues that the Ministry of Finance remains omnipresent in the workings of the Japanese financial system, where it continues to set rules, guide credit decisions, and provide senior executives for the major Japanese banks and securities firms (1996: 50–9).

pressures. Interest rate controls, open market operations and reserve requirements, which are now the primary instruments of central bank intervention in financial markets, all complement this process by leaving the final decisions over the allocation of credit in the hands of private monetary agents.

Several scholars have noted this shift from public to private responsibility for certain aspects of the IMS.[5] None, however, has examined this shift with respect to the international organization of credit. This chapter will do so by examining both the effects of financial regulation and the ability of central banks' chosen policy instruments to influence the capital recycling mechanism. Most importantly, it will examine how these instruments affect the ability of financial institutions to make international credit available to those who have a demand or a need for it. Over the postwar period, the effective exercise of public authority on an international basis has depended upon the global reach of individual states, yet that effectiveness can now be questioned because the instruments used by monetary authorities no longer carry the necessary global reach to ensure effective public control over the global financial system. Indeed, the continued reliance upon these instruments both confirms the diffusion of public authority among states and reinforces the dominance of private over public authority within the international organization of credit.

The policy instruments of public authorities
Three prior questions

Before exploring how public monetary authorities exercise direct influence within the international organization of credit, three prior questions must be considered. The first question concerns whether this influence should be considered in terms of informal networks or state institutions. The role of informal networks of influence are important to any comprehensive understanding of how public policy is made and carried out. Included in this notion would be informal, *ad hoc* organizations that serve as meeting places for policy-makers and other élites; more formal, private organizations that serve to forge connections between élites and policy-makers; and the general recep-

---

[5] These include Cohen (1981: 29), Llewellyn (1985: 227), Strange (1985: 256–7), Tsoukalis (1985: 289), and, in a slightly different vein, Zysman (1983: 15). It is also considered but ultimately rejected by two recent studies (Helleiner, 1994; Kapstein, 1994).

tivity of policy-makers to interconnected sets of ideas which shape approaches to problems and the parameters of their solutions.[6] As important as these social networks of influence are, however, they are no substitute for an examination of the ability and capacity of states to influence events through specific policy instruments. In the case of credit, it is important to know precisely how states attempt to influence monetary agents, because it is their practices which constitute the global financial system. In order to understand the extent to which states control the creation and allocation of credit, we need to know how effective they are in institutional terms. Such an examination can then be used to provide the basis for discussing the social and political implications of how public authority is exercised within the international organization of credit.

A second question concerns whether we should consider the influence of public authority in terms of direct state action, or in terms of international institutions. If the exercise of public authority were to be examined through the medium of international institutions, the IMF and BIS would be the most important institutions to study, as historically they have served as the most influential forums of inter-state coordination on monetary and financial issues. Yet there are problems with such a focus. The IMF, for example, has an ambiguous relevance to the financial and monetary policies of major creditor states, and has no autonomous decision-making capacity within the IMS except perhaps over the most impoverished and debt-laden countries. While this is significant from the perspective of these countries, it relegates the IMF to the decision-making sidelines in any examination of the broad ways in which public authority is exercised within the international organization of credit. Although the IMF can play a critical role in exceptional circumstances such as when countries are faced with a sudden liquidity crisis with systemic implications, such as happened with regard to Mexico in 1982 and 1994–5, its role in the overall evolution of the global financial system has much less significance.

The success that the BIS has had in formulating international banking regulations provides a stronger argument for examining this international institution as a source of public influence within the global credit system. Even here, however, it is useful to note that the BIS acts more as a forum within which decisions are made rather than as an

---

[6] The role of informal networks of influence is closely examined by Gill (1990).

independent decision-making entity in its own right.[7] The Basle Committee of Bank Supervisors, for example, which drafted the Basle Concordat, is composed of members drawn not from the BIS itself, but from the central banks of the G-10 countries (and Switzerland), and decisions within this committee are negotiated by national representatives rather than by BIS officials.[8] Indeed, as Kapstein argues, "banking supervision remains the province of national authorities. The committee is only as effective as member states want it to be" (1994: 128). Thus to concentrate on the workings of international monetary institutions such as the IMF and BIS without a prior knowledge of how states themselves approach particular problems would produce misleading conclusions about the way in which public authority is exercised. In the case of policy instruments designed to control credit, therefore, it is more helpful to begin by examining the authority and influence that states themselves exercise rather than privileging the kind of influence exercised by international monetary institutions.[9]

Finally, it is helpful to ask whether the influence of public authority should be examined collectively, as a product of international cooperation, or individually, as a product of individual state action. With respect to international banking supervision, for example, it might be argued that a BIS-centered regime has emerged through international cooperation that clarifies lines of supervisory responsibility, ensures a higher minimum level of soundness for banks operating across national borders, and levels the competitive playing field amongst internationally active banks.[10] Other attempts at international coop-

---

[7] This view is confirmed by senior BIS officials, who argue that their institution has a triple role as a forum for certain kinds of inter-state financial–regulatory negotiations, a source of technical expertise and a repository of independent thinking on financial matters, all of which are performed without an autonomous decision-making capacity. Interviews with senior officials at the BIS (Basle, November 23, 1994).

[8] For example, the role of US and UK regulators in the negotiations leading up to the 1987 Basle capital adequacy accords was critical, for they had first to convince their Japanese and German counterparts of the necessity and legitimacy of such a minimum level of bank capital before cooperation on this matter could proceed (Kapstein, 1989: 337–44).

[9] The influence which international institutions wield may also be considered in terms of the ideas which they foster and disseminate, or in other words as one aspect of informal networks of influence. While this approach clearly offers many insights into the role of international institutions, it is again no substitute for considered investigations of what states actually do in the domain of finance.

[10] For some of the details of this cooperation, see "Developments in co-operation among banking supervisory authorities" (*Bank of England Quarterly Bulletin*, June 1981), "Basle Concordat: lessons from Ambrosiano" (*The Banker*, September 1983),

eration in the field of monetary affairs, however, have been decidedly less successful. After the Nixon shocks in 1971, for example, several rounds of negotiations, taken under the umbrella of the IMF's "Committee of Twenty," sought to revise that organization's Articles of Agreement. The agreements at the Smithsonian Institute in 1971 and at Jamaica in 1976 were important not for what they accomplished – this was either irrelevant or subsequently ignored – but for what they demonstrated about the role of international institutions in the monetary relations of the most powerful states: that these institutions are in fact utterly dependent upon the political practices of the strongest states. Even considering the case of banking supervision, it appears that the effectiveness of international cooperation is dependent upon the interests and willingness of states to engage in negotiation with one another; thus the actions and motivations of individual states remain the first and most important focal point for understanding how public authority is exercised within the international organization of credit.[11]

The ability of states to engage in international monetary cooperation is made problematic by two important conditions. On one hand, cooperation is constrained by the very different interests which central bankers and treasury officials bring to the bargaining table, especially in terms of their relations as monetary officials who share authority *within* particular jurisdictions and cooperate *across* different jurisdictions. As Yoichi Funabashi has argued with respect to negotiating the 1985 Plaza Accord, this difference of interest cuts along national lines as well as along lines of accountability, producing odd alignments of solidarity between central bankers and treasury officials (1989: 60). On the other hand, central banks are reluctant not only to place whatever independence of action they possess in determining monetary policy in jeopardy through reliance on others, but they are also very sensitive to the institutional costs of cooperation. While there is a very clear sense of *ésprit de corps* amongst central bankers,

and the remarks to the 7th International Conference of Banking Supervisors in 1992 by E. Gerald Corrigan, then President of the Federal Reserve Bank of New York (Corrigan, 1992). For critical assessments see Strange (1988: 111–12), Kapstein (1994: 103–28), Porter (1993: 52–102), and Helleiner (1994: 187–91).

[11] This is certainly the case with respect to the views of Paul Volcker and Toyoo Gyohten as they reflected on their distinguished careers in international monetary affairs (1992: chapters 8 and 9).

they recognize that the costs of cooperation are complex, institutionally problematic, and unpredictable.

A close examination of the record of international monetary cooperation since 1972 indicates that such cooperation has been largely dependent upon the consequences of unilateral American actions regarding the value of the US dollar. American concern for the value of the dollar has oscillated between periods of almost complete nonintervention such as from 1972 to 1978 and 1980 to 1985, periods of massive intervention, such as from 1978 to 1980 and 1985 to 1987, and the present period of moderate intervention since 1987 (Pauls, 1990). Other governments have been forced to respond to changing American policy, either by engaging in defensive measures to insulate their currency or currencies from the results of American actions, or by cooperating with the United States in an attempt to manage the repercussions of American intervention.[12] This has led Richard Cooper to question whether during much of the 1980s there was any apparent international monetary cooperation at all (1987: 9).[13]

The institutional resistance to extensive international monetary cooperation in areas outside of exchange rates, where at least the goal of cooperation can be easily measured, has been reinforced by a lack of "objective" knowledge in the discipline of international economics about the effects of one country's national monetary policy on other economies. Not only is it unclear how the effects of monetary policy are transmitted abroad, there is no clear consensus on a proper analytical framework. This has led Ralph Bryant, one of the original architects of the Bretton Woods system, to argue that the lack of convergence "is an impediment sufficiently severe to preclude ambitious efforts to coordinate economic policies" (1987: 10). And, indeed, the fate of earlier international discussions about the proper level of liquidity in the international system (Cohen, 1970: 6–8) and of devising objective measures of indicators for adjustment needs

---

[12] Two examples of these strategies include the creation of the European Monetary System (EMS) in 1979 as part of the attempt to insulate European currencies from further declines in the value of the US dollar, and the coordinated interventions resulting from the 1985 Plaza Accord, itself a product of the Reagan Administration's unilateral decision to halt the appreciation of the US dollar.

[13] This opinion is not only shared by liberal economists. Aglietta concurs (1985: 199), noting that despite a "prodigious advance in private financial interdependence over the last 20 years, . . . international monetary cooperation between the governments of the main currency countries has considerably regressed, with the notable exception of the European Monetary System."

(Crockett, 1977: 229–30) indicate that such a lack of convergence is inevitable in a financial system marked by powerful asymmetrical relationships. While international cooperation clearly has a role to play in how public authority is exercised within the global financial system, it remains subordinate to the individual actions of states. Rather, the exercise of public authority within the international organization of credit is more appropriately understood to emanate from states engaging in particular practices that have their origins in asymmetrical positions of power and influence.

In fact, there are very few states with the capacity to influence the international organization of credit. The United States, Germany, Japan, and perhaps the United Kingdom are the only states with the necessary resources and authority to influence the overall movement of credit and capital throughout the global financial system. The overall context within which their policies apply is that of a progressively integrated and deregulated IMS. As chapter 4 noted, globally active private monetary agents have integrated the world's capital markets both horizontally, by becoming bigger transnational enterprises, and vertically, by moving into all aspects of the financial services industry. This capacity to move funds across borders and to expand into all kinds of financial services is driven by two kinds of pressures. The first pressure stems from the existence of strong incentives to engage in financial innovation based upon technological developments, which is driven in part by the rising structural power of finance. The second pressure is the market-driven ideological practices of American and British politicians and regulators, which have resulted in fewer barriers to capital mobility in the American and British financial systems. Since 1974, when the United States first liberalized its capital controls, these pressures have spread throughout the global financial system due to the central positions of these two markets. Changing regulations covering the flow of international credit therefore set the context within which other policy instruments are exercised.

Finance ministries and the regulation of credit

The ability of central banks to control domestic monetary policy is circumscribed to varying degrees by the openness and integration of national financial systems to the global financial system. The extent of the openness and integration of national financial systems is determined primarily by the regulatory environment which governs them. Financial regulation, the rules establishing how different monetary agents operate within a given financial market and how capital moves across national borders, therefore provides public authorities with a direct way of influencing the international organization of credit. There are two interconnected aspects to this policy instrument: the regulation of domestic financial markets, especially with respect to foreign operators, and the regulation of capital movements across borders. Unlike other policy instruments, financial regulation involves no direct role for public authorities to play beyond the determination of the proper regulatory laws. These regulations establish the type of market that private and indeed certain public authorities such as central banks must operate within: they represent the *design-capacity* of governments (Vipond, 1993: 187). Like other policy instruments, however, the global reach which financial regulation carries is asymmetrical in terms of both its implementation and the effects which it has on the global system.

In terms of the regulation of financial markets, the most important development over the past two decades has been a shift in the regulatory focus from the activities which financial institutions engage in to the basic soundness of the institutions themselves. In other words, rather than regulating markets, governments have increasingly turned to regulating institutions in terms of certain minimum prudential requirements; these institutions are then left free to engage in market-determined behavior as demand and supply for their products warrants. Usually cast as deregulation rather than as a shift in regulation, these changes gathered strength in the late 1970s under the Carter Administration in the United States.[14] They were originally applied to several industries besides finance, including trucking, telecommunication, and airline travel (Hammond and Knott, 1988: 5–8). Although largely driven by domestic considerations in the United States, these changes in the form of financial regulation had a powerful impact upon other world PFCs. From Tokyo to London, enhanced American competition and increased US capital exports had suddenly to be accommodated in some way.

In Tokyo, for example, the implementation of the 1980 Foreign

[14] The direct American antecedent to this "deregulation" was the abolition by presidential decree in 1974 of a series of capital controls. These included the Interest Equalization Tax, the Voluntary Foreign Credit Restraints Program, and the Foreign Direct Investment Program (Baker, 1978: 6).

Exchange and Foreign Trade Control Act responded to the appreciation of the yen, which had been gathering force since 1978 (Frankel, 1984: 19–20). This liberalization eased rules for the outflow of capital from Japan on the assumption that this would place downward pressure on the yen. Similarly, the 1984 Yen–Dollar Agreement further lowered Japanese barriers to capital inflows and outflows, on the assumption that increased liberalization of capital flows would increase the global availability of the yen, thereby slowing its rise in value.

British liberalization, begun in 1979 and culminating in 1986, was driven by somewhat different pressures, including the ideological predispositions of the newly elected Thatcher government and the clear desire to maintain London's position at the center of the Eurocurrency market and European finance more generally. By making financial activity as free of market restraints as possible, consistent with sound conventional financial practices, the London capital market was able to ensure its primacy as a world financial *entrepôt*, and therefore as a necessary business location for any firm with global aspirations (Hamilton, 1986: 152–4).

As a result of easing capital controls in 1974, net American long-term capital outflows doubled from $12 billion in 1974 to over $24 billion in 1975, inaugurating a period of outflows and then inflows without historical precedent. The same dramatic increase in capital movements occurred in Britain after 1979, when the Thatcher Government moved to deregulate the London market. The easing of capital controls thus began in the United States before spreading throughout the global financial system. The Japanese financial system was one of the last to liberalize, but here again the results were dramatic. The 1984 Yen–Dollar Agreement, which opened the Tokyo capital market to foreign operators on a sustained basis, helped to more than double the flow of long-term capital out of Japan, from $20 billion in 1983 to $51 billion in 1984. Net long-term capital exports from Japan hit $64 billion in 1985, and soared to $134 billion in 1986. Thus by freeing up or restricting the ability to move capital around the globe, capital controls exert a powerful influence on the scale and direction of capital movements within the world-economy.

The extent of capital controls also heavily influences the nature of financial intermediation. The cumulative effect of withdrawing public scrutiny over the movement of capital is to place more control over its dispersion into private hands. As chapter 4 demonstrated, the amount of long-term capital under private control began to increase dramatically after 1974, again after 1980 and then again after 1986. There can be little doubt as to the causal connection between the dismantling of capital controls, the increase in international capital movements and the increasingly private nature of these movements. Even though the 1974 oil price increases may have complicated those connections during the middle of the 1970s, they were neither consistent enough nor large enough to sustain these developments over the entire post-1972 period. International credit flows have entered a new era as a consequence of changes in the rules governing capital mobility.

In fact, the main effects of changing the way financial markets and capital movements are regulated lies in altering the capacity of different kinds of monetary agents to control not only access to credit but also the type of intermediation available within the global financial system. Liberalization of financial markets has substantially increased the ability of foreign operators and borrowers to establish a presence in previously closed markets, most importantly in Tokyo. This has improved the access of foreigners to Japanese capital, although it is still true that foreign firms are marginal players in the Tokyo market (Pauly, 1988: 66–95). In New York and above all in London, by contrast, foreign firms are increasingly important players. Easing capital controls has also, paradoxically, strengthened the Euro-currency markets by making even more expatriate capital available to monetary agents operating in them. Overall, changes in the nature of financial regulation have made more capital and credit available to private and public borrowers world-wide, improving their access to credit, however unevenly.

Easing capital controls has also contributed towards the privatization of the international organization of credit. While it has allowed firms and governments to raise capital where the conditions are most lenient, it has also encouraged the growth of private international monetary agents in order to service a more integrated global financial system. This world of increased capital mobility sets firmer limits to state intervention in the financial system, especially with regard to developing institutions or programs to mediate between savers and borrowers on a global scale. Public intermediation in the financial system thus has less scope for development where the free movement of capital is predominant. Indeed, in such a system public authorities face increased systemic pressures simply to maintain existing levels of expenditure, much less undertake new burdens.

When public authorities restrict their influence on the international organization of credit to financial regulation, the balance on what Susan Strange calls the authority–market seesaw becomes strongly tilted towards the market. It is tilted in two very important ways. First, the immediate balance between those who create and allocate credit shifts towards market forces, so that it is they who derive the fullest rewards from participating in the financial system. While public authorities may regulate and underwrite the functioning of the financial system, it is private authorities who control the allocation of credit, and therefore who extract the rewards. Second, and more important in the long run, by restricting its role as an intermediary in the financial system, public authority has compromised its ability to intervene in economic activities to shape the context within which both public and private authorities act. This has restricted not only the regulatory scope of public authorities, but also their ability to fashion responses to change which go beyond the ability of private actors to address. By ensuring that a privately structured capital recycling mechanism dominates the international organization of credit, public authorities ensure that the priorities of the world-economy will be associated with the private sector, to the disadvantage of an entire spectrum of social actors not advantaged by these priorities. It is yet another indication of the changing balance of social power within the world-economy.

Central banks and the control of credit

With New York, Tokyo, and London all experiencing financial regulatory change of varying degrees since the late 1970s, and especially since 1984, how have central banks responded to these changes, and what has been the impact of their response? Not surprisingly, they have moved towards what can be clearly identified as market-oriented strategies for controlling the creation and allocation of credit, most particularly in the short term. In Britain, for example, the Bank of England has moved almost entirely towards an interest rate monetary control system, where the manipulation of overnight, discount, and interbank rates are the principal instruments used to regulate the cost of money, supplemented by open market operations to adjust the daily flow of funds throughout the banking system (Kneeshaw and Van Den Burgh, 1989: 45; Deane and Pringle, 1994: 131–3). In Japan, by contrast, open market operations are being increasingly used now that secondary markets for government and commercial paper are developing.[15] The British and Japanese cases mark the extremes of central bank intervention philosophies among the monetary great powers, and correspond to the degree to which their respective financial markets are liberalized and integrated into the global financial system. Nevertheless, both the Bank of England and the Bank of Japan are alike in the increased scope they are giving to market forces, and to their use of market-oriented methods for implementing monetary policy.[16]

Reserve requirements

Of the three principal policy instruments available to central banks for controlling the creation and allocation of credit, the regulation of reserve requirements has the least direct impact upon the international organization of credit. This is so for two reasons, above and beyond the fact that the use of reserve requirements varies widely according to the practices of central banks.[17] First, and most important, the targets of such policies are domestically active banks and their domestic activities. The setting of reserve requirements directly affects the amount of funds banks can lend to their customers by controlling how much capital they must set aside for pay-out purposes. In national banking systems, however, the customers of these

[15] Prior to the first efforts at financial liberalization in the early 1970s, the main Japanese city banks were in a continual state of being "overloaned" due to the tremendous demand for corporate investment. Consequently, they required constant recourse to reserves at the Bank of Japan, and were easily subject to the strictures of its lending priorities. As domestic corporate investment has eased, and other sources of funds developed, this need for central bank funds has waned, and with it the direct influence which made "window guidance" so effective (Coulbeck, 1984: 221). Although "window guidance" persisted officially until 1991, its final years were largely consultative (Frankel and Morgan, 1992: 582).

[16] As a result of the shift towards market-oriented policy instruments, moral suasion has been more or less abandoned as a general policy instrument. It has rarely been used by the Bank of England and Banque de France over the past twenty years, almost never by the Bundesbank, only ineffectively by the Fed, and decreasingly by the Bank of Japan. Moral suasion can therefore be ignored as a credible policy instrument available to public authorities in an era of decentralized globalization. See Moran (1986) on the Bank of England, Goodman (1992) on the Bundesbank and Banque de France, Volcker and Gyohten (1992) on the few instances when the Fed Chairman has tried to curb bank lending, and Kasman and Rodrigues (1991) on the Bank of Japan.

[17] The Bank of England, for example, has largely dispensed with reserve requirements (like Canada and Switzerland), while both Germany and Japan continue to employ them, along with the United States (Feinman, 1993: 584–5).

banks are borrowing for domestic purposes: foreign customers do not borrow from foreign banks to invest in their home countries. They either borrow in their own country from a national bank or a foreign subsidiary, or they raise capital in foreign markets with bond offerings using investment banks. In either case reserve requirements will not directly influence where this capital is procured. It may indirectly influence it by raising the marginal cost of running a global financial services firm, but this is a very small component of the global cost structure of banks operating internationally.[18]

The exception to this indirect influence is when reserve requirements are used as a form of capital control. For example, in 1969 the German government, in a bid to stop the inflow of short-term funds seeking speculative gain, imposed reserve requirements on all foreign mark-denominated accounts of 50 percent, versus only 15 percent for resident accounts. This had the immediate effect of making such speculative capital flows more expensive to undertake, and in conjunction with other policies helped to slow down the inflow. These requirements were eased after the October 1969 revaluation of the deutschemark (Strange, 1976: 327–30). Similarly, Japanese authorities imposed restrictions of this kind on yen-denominated foreign accounts up until 1980, and have since retained the regulatory capacity both to raise these kinds of requirements and to enforce differential interest rates on foreign holdings of yen in Japan should a future need arise (Horne, 1985: 151). Usually, however, reserve requirements are not used in this way, and when they are it is done only by central banks whose economies are net capital exporters.

The second reason for the low impact of reserve requirements on the international organization of credit is the decreasing importance of commercial banks in the capital recycling mechanism. Reserve requirements apply only to banks which take time deposits, on the assumption that it is more difficult for them to match the maturities of deposits and loans when the structure of their deposit base is fluid and open. The increasing importance of bond markets, and therefore of investment and securities houses in the capital recycling mechanism, means that there is an entire array of financial actors over

---

[18] Another indirect influence of reserve requirements on the organization of credit might lie in the amount of credit which companies borrow from domestic banks for investment abroad. While this is difficult to measure, it is also attenuated by the increased tendency of companies, especially transnational ones, to raise the money they need for foreign investment abroad.

which the setting of reserve requirements carries no influence. Unlike with banks, the imposition of reserve requirements poses no additional marginal costs on their operations, and offers no additional safety mechanism should they experience liquidity problems. As Joan Spero has pointed out (1988/89: 122), the role of different financial intermediaries has changed over the past two decades, yet little has been done to clear up the regulatory ambiguity of who is responsible for whom in a time of crisis. Indeed, they are often governed not by central banks at all but by securities commissions, which have their own agenda to advance and regulatory problematic to consider (Porter, 1993: 103–47; Underhill, 1995).

Open market operations

Open market operations at least have the virtue of being potentially able to influence the entire spectrum of financial actors, whether banks, securities firms, or even non-financial actors. This is possible because the target of open market operations is the money supply in general rather than the type of funds held by a particular institution (such as reserve requirements), although of course these operations are primarily directed at those institutions which buy, hold, and sell government securities as part of their treasury operations.[19] In other words, wherever a secondary market of any significance exists, open market operations will be a key policy instrument through which central banks manage monetary policy. The condition which allows open market operations to be viable, therefore, is the demand for and supply of liquidity in the form of government paper. And if liquidity can be defined as a financial asset which can be easily and *certainly* converted into a useful medium of exchange (Aglietta, 1985: 173–4), then the single most liquid asset in the world is US government debt in the form of bills and bonds. This *primus inter pares* position in the liquidity sweepstakes for US government securities is itself dependent upon the reserve currency position of the US dollar and the ample volume of outstanding US government securities: there is both a large enough supply and the guarantee of a certain market for these securities to be used for liquidity instruments among a wide spectrum of commercial firms and governments. This provides the basis of the

---

[19] This is a wide net insofar as corporations increasingly engage in international or long-distance trade and manage their foreign currency and liquidity obligations with recourse to modern corporate treasury methods.

global influence of the Federal Reserve Board in the conduct of its open market operations.

The effectiveness of open market operations resides in their ability to expand the liquidity position of monetary agents or, conversely, to mop up excess credit capacity. If a central bank is concerned with an overly hasty expansion of the money supply, it sells government bonds from within its own portfolio, thereby reducing the immediately available funds which banks and other financial sector firms have to lend to their clients. To pump liquidity into the system, a central bank need only to buy discounted bonds offered on the market (or encourage them to be put up for sale), thereby increasing the availability of cash to monetary agents for lending and other uses. This last activity should not be confused with lender-of-last-resort responsibilities, which are carried out through a central bank's discount window, where private banks have access to a central bank's reserves at a penalty rate. Open market operations are carried out on the market, using the systemic influence wielded by public authorities to influence the immediate availability of credit.

For the central banks of Germany, Japan, and the United States, however, the reach of their systemic influence is powerful but clearly unequal. There are three reasons for this asymmetry in the international consequences of open market operations for these public authorities. First, the outstanding volume of US government securities easily outdistances the volume of either Japanese or German government securities. When the US Federal Open Market Investment Committee buys government bonds on secondary markets, for example, it increases the liquidity of the entire global financial system in two important ways: by adjusting the quantity of US dollars available for lending and by altering the value of the reserves held by financial institutions (and upon which they base their lending). In either case the credit position of any firm which uses US government securities in its treasury operations is affected. While the gains are small on an individual basis, the cumulative effect of such an increase on the availability of credit on a global scale is significant. The United States is the only public authority which has this genuine global reach because it has both of the prerequisites: an enormous secondary market for its bonds, which guarantees their liquidity (and, to a limited extent, their value), and a large outstanding volume of bonds, which guarantees the global influence of such actions. Neither the German nor Japanese central banks can influence the organization of

Table 5.1 *Outstanding American, German, and Japanese government debt, 1975–93, selected years, $US billion (rounded)*

Year	United States	Germany	Japan
1975	437	44	51
1980	658	128	263
1985	1,599	136	732
1990	2,548	371	1,657
1993	3,392	546	N/A

Note: N/A not available.
Source: International Financial Statistics and *Government Financial Statistics* (various issues).

credit to a similar extent, simply because they do not have the depth of markets or volume of bonds to work with.[20] Table 5.1 provides a comparison of outstanding levels of government debt for Germany, Japan, and the United States over the post-1972 period.

The second reason for the asymmetrical global reach of open market operations by the world's three major central banks lies in the degree of openness which their domestic financial systems have to the global credit system. "Openness" is often associated with reference to international capital movements, and this systemic dimension does capture part of the openness of domestic to global finance. Here it is important to note that the United States still retains a more open regime of capital controls than do either Germany or Japan. However, the term "openness" also has an institutional dimension to it above and beyond a systemic dimension, and which in fact can operate independently of the regime of capital controls. "Institutional openness" here refers to the willingness of monetary agents to operate on a global scale, where changes in their overall liquidity position directly affect their international operations. In this sense Fed open market activities, even when directed primarily at domestic financial

[20] As table 5.1 indicates, the Japanese have by far the second largest outstanding volume of government debt among the world's major monetary powers. This suggests that should the Japanese financial system become even more open in the systemic and institutional senses outlined below, the Bank of Japan will be in a better position to influence the international organization of credit than the Bundesbank by virtue of influencing a larger stock of government bills and bonds through its open market operations.

Table 5.2 *Outstanding government debt of the United States, United Kingdom, Germany, Japan, and Switzerland, 1975–93, selected years, $US billion (rounded)*

Year	United States	United Kingdom	Germany	Japan	Switz
1975	437	N/A	44	51	4
1980	658	N/A	128	263	12
1985	1,599	128	136	732	12
1990	2,548	104	371	1,657	29
1993	3,392	115	546	N/A	47

Note: N/A not available.
Source: International Financial Statistics and *Government Financial Statistics* (various issues).

institutions, spill out into the global credit system on a regular basis by virtue of the international operations of American financial institutions. The American financial system is more "open" in this institutional sense than either the German or Japanese system, precisely because American financial institutions are more internationally-oriented than their German and Japanese counterparts.[21] The Swiss and British financial systems are also very "open" in this institutional sense, but their levels of government debt are not high enough to produce similar global consequences when they exercise public authority.[22] For example, whereas in 1990 the US government had an outstanding debt of about $2548 billion, comparable figures for the UK and Swiss governments were only $104 and $29 billion respectively, as table 5.2 indicates.[23] The cumulative increase in the

[21] This is certainly the case with respect to German banks, of which there are only two among the world's largest forty banks with more than 25 percent of their assets overseas. There are five US banks in this category, with three of these among the top fifteen global banks. The Japanese case is more difficult to compare, as there are five Japanese banks with more than 25 percent of their assets held abroad, but none in the top twenty. Furthermore, a very large percentage of Japanese banks' overseas assets are domiciled in either Singapore or Hong Kong, rather than in the world PFCs of London and New York. See *The Banker*'s 1995 survey of global banking (February 1995: 68–73).

[22] Both the United Kingdom and Switzerland have three banks each in the top ten of the largest global banks, including the four banks with the highest percentage of business conducted overseas (*The Banker*, February 1995: 68–73).

[23] These figures have been converted into US dollar equivalents following the prevailing end-of-year exchange rate figures contained in these publications.

liquidity positions of British and Swiss banks consequent upon active open market operations by their central banks is of only marginal consideration to the provision of liquidity within the international organization of credit.

The use of the US dollar as the most important reserve currency provides the third reason for the asymmetrical global reach of the major central banks' open market operations. The role which the US dollar plays in international trade and payments means that individuals, firms, and governments have a liquidity preference for holding dollar-denominated assets, knowing that there is a steady demand for their use and a large enough volume of buying and selling to ensure their liquidity. As Harold van B. Cleveland noted with respect to the interwar period (1976: 18–22), this confers on the Federal Reserve Board an inordinate amount of power over the international monetary system. The more limited use of the deutschemark and yen as either a reserve or transactions currency means that secondary markets are more restricted in scope, which in turn lessens the impact of German and Japanese open market operations on the international organization of credit. Even the large-scale Japanese capital exports of the early and mid-1980s had a relatively benign impact on the increased use of the yen as a reserve currency, primarily because such a large proportion of these exports consisted of the purchase of foreign government bonds in local currencies. The result of these purchases increased demand for local currencies (especially the US dollar), depressed demand for the yen, and further inhibited the use of this currency as a reserve and transaction asset.[24] Were the US dollar to lose its reserve currency role, the global reach of the Fed would be adversely affected to the extent that US dollar-denominated financial instruments declined in use.

Such a decline might be influenced by three sets of factors. First, the reimposition of capital controls and the decoupling of the American capital market from the global financial system would circumscribe the liquidity of US dollar financial instruments, and hence reduce the

---

[24] There are many other factors which contribute to the emergence of a reserve and transaction currency. They include availability and demand of the currency, secondary markets, governmental cooperation, a significant trading presence in the world-economy, and a presence in world politics commensurate to the nation's economic role. Depending on how measurements are made, the role of the yen falls short in several categories.

role of the US dollar as a transaction vehicle. Second, increased use of other currencies, primarily the deutschemark and yen, might erode the primary position of the US dollar, as would the creation of a common European currency should European monetary union occur. Finally, a reduction in the American trade and capital account deficits, as well as the government deficit, might curtail the outflow of US dollars into the world-economy. This would limit the volume of US dollars in circulation beyond the shores of America and force other currencies to be more widely used for international transactions. It is unlikely, however, that any of these developments will fully materialize in the foreseeable future. On one hand, the American capital market remains central to the global financial system in terms of the network of monetary agents which constitutes its core, and these agents will continue to use the US dollar whatever its value and availability. While the cost of using this currency may fluctuate, the necessity of its use remains. On the other hand, the array of social forces reliant on both access to the American capital market and the continued integration of this market with the global financial system is formidable. These actors will vigorously oppose any attempt to alter the degree of integration of these two systems; thus the outward flow and ease of use of US dollar financial instruments will continue. On the face of it, therefore, the social and political conditions supporting the continued use of the US dollar as an important reserve currency are secure for the immediate future.[25] This will help to preserve the global reach of US open market operations, maintaining one of the key cornerstones of this asymmetry in the exercise of public authority within the international organization of credit.

Interest rates

Manipulating interest rates (whether discount, overnight, or other) is the final policy instrument used by central banks to control credit in domestic economies. This is the single most effective instrument for influencing the price of credit, being both instantaneous and wide-ranging in its effect. Domestic banks respond usually without delay to movements in central bank discount rates, and unlike reserve requirements which are restricted in their application to banks, interest rates

---

[25] One might also point to the continued reluctance of German and Japanese policy-makers to allow increased international use of their currencies, as well as the likely continuation of high American trade, capital, and governmental deficits as additional factors supporting this conclusion.

affect any institution involved in creating or allocating credit. Manipulating interest rates, therefore, influences every aspect of the capital recycling mechanism.

Interest rates also have the most visibly dramatic global reach of the three policy instruments considered here, albeit again to different degrees for the three major monetary powers. As with open market operations, the United States has since 1947 generally enjoyed the greatest global reach, and was able to make interest rate policy almost without regard to international considerations until the mid-1980s. American interest rates had an international ripple effect for several reasons. The American economy is and will remain into the next century the world's largest, and any change in its demand for imported goods produced by interest rate changes will affect the entire world-economy. The American capital market is also the world's largest source of mobile capital under a single national jurisdiction, so changes in the cost of that capital influence the cost of capital world-wide. The almost complete integration of the American capital market with Eurocurrency and other capital markets, together with its systemic and institutional openness, allows the effects of American interest rate policy to move outwards rapidly and effectively. Finally, the effects which interest rate changes have on the value of widely held American government bonds, and on its widely used currency, further reinforce the global impact of American interest rate changes. They are indeed the most watched interest rates in the industrialized world, not only for what they mean for the international cost of credit but also for how they will affect the demand of Americans for imported goods and services.

The phase of high interest rates inaugurated by Paul Volcker in 1979 is the classic case of the global reach of American interest rates. While there may be some debate concerning the mix of domestic and international motives behind this dramatic change in American monetary policy,[26] there can be little doubt as to the powerful global effects of this change. These included the intensification of the debt crisis, global recession, currency realignment, an absolute drop in world trade (the first recorded since the postwar period began), and the erosion of living standards commonly associated with economic stagnation and recession. High interest rates also increased the cost of

---

[26] For Volcker's own recollections, which stress domestic concerns with inflation, see Volcker and Gyohten (1992: 164–76).

capital globally, and by substantially raising the value of the US dollar they contributed to the massive changes in international capital movements detailed in chapter 4. A similar increase in either German or Japanese interest rates at that time could not have produced an equally dramatic result, simply because of the less central positions of their economies in world markets.

More than ten years of extraordinarily high fiscal deficits and inflows of foreign capital, however, have substantially eroded the ability of the American Federal Reserve Board to decisively influence global interest rates. In Europe, for example, the Bundesbank is now more influential both because of the role of the deutschemark in the European Monetary System (EMS) and the role of the German economy in the European Union. With German rates crucial to European rates, and Europe one of three key economic regions of the world-economy, the regional influence of German interest rates is now explicit. This has been clear in the course of German interest rates since unification, which have been diverging rather significantly from American and Japanese rates. Japanese rates have recently also become more generally influential beyond the borders of Japan, precisely because of the new position of Japanese capital exports in the international organization of credit. The cost of capital in Japan now has international repercussions in two ways. First, the relatively low cost of capital in Japan attracts foreign borrowers to Tokyo, thus helping to internationalize its financial practices: the world has come to Tokyo in search of cheap credit. Second, Japanese institutions have been encouraged to go abroad in search of higher rates of return. Partly in order to find higher rates of return, and partly to assist Japanese companies to do this, Japanese financial institutions have internationalized themselves prodigiously over the past fifteen years. Relatively low interest rates were a fact in Japan from the early 1970s to the late 1980s, and they provided an important incentive for Japanese companies to invest abroad. Since the bursting of the so-called "bubble economy" in the early 1990s, those rates have been absolutely as well as relatively low. With the Japanese economy now a major source of capital to the world-economy, its interest rates play a much more significant role within the international allocation of credit. It would appear, therefore, that a putative regionalization of interest rates within the world-economy is under way.

Of the three primary policy instruments available to central banks considered here, then, open market operations and interest rate manipulation have had the strongest influence upon the international organization of credit. This influence, however, has been largely of a structural nature, rippling outwards from domestic financial systems to the extent that these are integrated with or are principal suppliers of credit to the global financial system. The influence of international cooperation with regard to banking regulation has been a less important, although not insignificant, influence on the international organization of credit. Stricter banking regulations complement central bank policy instruments in one important respect, however: both have as a common focus the strengthening of those private monetary agents which lie at the heart of the capital recycling mechanism.[27] Whether it is using market-oriented policy instruments or tightening up the capital adequacy ratios by which internationally active banks must abide, the common goal is to confer greater scope in deciding who gains access to credit to market participants. In other words, regulating institutions rather than markets has become a policy priority for public monetary authorities, leading both to stronger financial institutions and to the consolidation of market priorities in determining the international allocation of credit. The exercise of public authority under conditions of decentralized globalization has thus been an integral part of the transformation in the contemporary international organization of credit.

Summary

This chapter has argued that there are four main policy instruments by which public authorities have attempted to manage the post-1972 condition of "decentralized globalization." These include central bank activities such as setting reserve requirements, engaging in open market operations and manipulating interest rates, and treasury policies regarding the regulation of domestic capital markets and international capital flows. In many ways the most influential policy instruments have been regulatory in nature, in particular the regulation of capital markets and capital flows. Both central bank and treasury policies have served to strengthen the role of market forces in

[27] This common focus is not without its own tensions, as Louis Pauly has argued. He points out (1990: 40–2) that international convergence on stricter banking requirements encouraged banks to abandon lending to heavily indebted Third World countries in the 1980s, thereby undercutting the efforts of public officials to respond to the international debt crisis through a call for new bank lending.

the global financial system, and therefore to tilt the balance of power towards private monetary agents. This has had an important effect upon the role of public authorities within the international organization of credit, primarily with regard to their ability to intervene as an intermediary in the allocation of credit on a global basis. Thus, even though capital is now more easily able to flow from areas of surplus to areas of demand or need, the criteria of private monetary agents intervene to shape the access which all actors have to this mobile pool of capital. In this sense the future context of financing growth and development within the world-economy is being shaped to reflect the priorities of the changing balance of social power among public and private authorities, a balance which has tilted heavily towards the interests of private authorities.

The actions of states have thus been an integral element of the emergence of the condition of "decentralized globalization" within the international organization of credit. The instruments which states use to influence the creation and allocation of credit empower market actors by making them the conduits of public authority: it is exercised through, by, and on behalf of markets and market participants. Equally important, the asymmetrical influence which American, German, and Japanese policy instruments have on international credit conditions further weakens the degree of control public authority wields: unlike under the London-centered or the New York-centered global credit systems, no single public authority today controls the commanding heights of global finance. While the global reach of the United States is evident in the consequences of its open market operations, interest rates are becoming increasingly regionalized throughout the world-economy, while reserve requirements are losing their efficacy due to the growing role of financial institutions other than commercial banks within the capital recycling mechanism. The transfer of authority from state to market is thus reinforced by the fragmentation of influence which any single monetary power is able to exercise within the international organization of credit. In the end, this changing balance of power between public and private authority must be considered one of the driving forces behind the reconstitution of international monetary order in the contemporary period.

6 Finance, power, and the world-economy approach: towards an historical–institutional international political economy

This chapter draws together the arguments of part 2 to explore the changing nature of power in the contemporary international organization of credit. In particular, it considers the implications which the shift towards market authority carries for the way in which finance is organized, and how it functions. The insights provided by the world-economy approach suggest that the international organization of credit will be unstable into the early years of the twenty-first century because of the changing balance of power within finance and the world-economy more broadly considered. With the sources of power now more diffuse than at any time in the twentieth century, the possibility of fashioning effective international leadership in financial matters remains highly circumscribed, although not impossible. The chapter then stands back to reflect upon the world-economy approach and the disciplinary future of IPE. It closes by arguing the case for what I call an historical–institutional future for IPE based upon the advantages offered by the ontology of the world-economy approach.

The changing nature of power in the international organization of credit

The balance of power between state and market authority has been transformed since the 1970s. States today are less involved in the creation and allocation of credit in terms of both the actual movement of funds across borders and the regulation of capital movements. They are also less involved in the determination of exchange rates, and have fewer resources at their disposal to influence these rates compared to either the volume of foreign exchange transactions or the asset base of internationally active banks. By reducing and transforming their role in the capital recycling mechanism, states have allowed private monetary agents, organized through markets, to dominate the decisions of who is granted access to credit and on what terms. The international organization of credit has been transformed in its essentials from a quasi-public to a nearly fully private one.

States, however, have not reduced their role in the capital recycling mechanism by making less credit available for international transactions, for the record shows that public sources of international credit have increased in absolute terms throughout the postwar period. Rather, their capacity to directly channel flows of international credit has been undermined by the precipitous decline in the proportion of internationally mobile credit provided by public authorities since the early 1970s. By virtue of the dramatic increase in the amount of international credit provided by private monetary authorities, the direction of international credit flows has become largely determined by these private authorities. Consequently, the international allocation of credit is today largely a private exercise. Similarly, the role of public authorities within the international financial system has been transformed from one of active intermediation to a more passive regulation. The establishment of regulatory frameworks which allow capital to move across borders relatively freely has become the preferred method of public involvement in the capital recycling mechanism. Moreover, the ability of states to influence the international organization of credit remains asymmetrical: the largest and most well integrated international capital markets such as those centered in New York, Tokyo, Frankfurt, and London empower their respective state authorities with a leadership capacity, while other states tend to follow the regulations established by these authorities. The direction of regulatory changes over the past several decades confirms this tendency, as it has spread outwards from the United States and United Kingdom to other financial systems. We may therefore say that the changing nature of public intervention in the financial system empowers private monetary authorities at the expense of public monetary authorities.

This transformation in the relationship between public and private authority, which became fully established only in the 1980s, will clearly erode some of the pillars of the Bretton Woods period. Most importantly, it compromises the "embedded" nature of postwar liberalism as identified by John Ruggie (1982: 393). The ability of states to maintain support for social welfare policies has been undermined, due primarily to their reliance upon debt to fund rising proportions of state expenses. With national debt increasing throughout the past two decades, and more being funded from large-scale domestic and foreign bond issues rather than from small-scale personal savings bonds, the ability of governments to raise funds at a reasonable cost has become increasingly dependent upon the willingness of private monetary agents to buy and hold public securities. In this way governments have become more susceptible to systemic pressure to control their deficits precisely because they have become more reliant upon private markets to fund their debt. This situation has allowed the interests which private monetary agents have in controlling public deficits to undermine the commitment which states have to welfare policies, one of the central pillars of the postwar order.

Market forces have also emerged relatively triumphant in the battle over the regulation of capital movements. With capital moving freely into and out of the American and British markets, the Eurocurrency markets, and increasingly also the German and Japanese markets, a significant victory has been scored for the interests of internationally mobile capital. A world market has opened up not only in foreign exchange trading, but in credit and finance as well. This world market goes well beyond the limited vision of capital mobility enshrined in the actual Bretton Woods agreements, and certainly beyond the regulatory network built up over the decade of the 1960s, when the United States imposed a number of restrictive rules and taxes on capital movements in an effort to control its deteriorating balance of payments position (Helleiner, 1993; Hawley, 1987). It has ushered in what Gill and Law have described as (1988: 174–6) the "brave new world of capital mobility," where financial interests represented by global monetary agents are most strategically placed to profit.

While the most important transformation in the contemporary international organization of credit has been in the nexus of authority between public and private monetary agents, much discussion centers on the status of the United States, which transformed itself from a mature creditor to a mature debtor economy in the space of less than a decade. The eclipse of the American economy as the principal source of international credit means that the ability of the United States to provide resources for the future political and economic development of the world-economy is being challenged in a number of ways. This is most apparent with regard to the availability of public resources, where the swollen American budget deficit limits the discretionary spending powers of the US government. The budget deficit, a magnet for domestic and foreign capital alike, limits the outflow of public credit from the United States even as it encourages an inflow of private credit. It therefore constrains the role of the most important monetary state in global financial intermediation.[1] Similarly, the reduced ability of the US government to transfer resources to the Third World means that the influence of the United States on development priorities will be reduced.[2] Other governments, notably Japan, are increasing their share of development assistance, and in the process altering the direction of regional economic development in important parts of the world such as east Asia. Another consequence of deficit reduction pressures is the US effort to reduce its military and bilateral aid commitments world-wide, which will further erode its ability to directly influence the political and economic development of its allies. The pressure to rectify American public finances is inclining the United States to engage in the same kind of retrenchment that imperial powers have been forced to undertake throughout history.

Even in the face of this retrenchment, however, the United States will wield formidable political and economic power into the indefinite future, a consequence of its still significant market power, its paramount military dominance, and the strong appeal of the ideology of liberal internationalism associated with its élites. The US economy remains the largest in the world, and its low rate of savings means that a higher proportion of income is spent on consumer goods than in most other advanced industrial economies. While this may have economically deleterious consequences for the growth in productivity of the American economy, it also means that foreign access to this market will continue to be an important source of power for American policy-makers to exploit as they attempt to fashion a world to their liking. Such market power is reinforced by the military superiority of the United States, which has not waned to any appreciable degree

---

[1] This conclusion must be qualified by acknowledging that the capacity to have others finance American public and private over-consumption might also be seen as a mark of American power in the global financial system. Here the ability of the US government to obtain foreign funding for its deficit flows from the central position of the US dollar, the American capital market and US dollar-denominated financial instruments in the global financial system. As chapter 5 observes, this has allowed the Federal Reserve Board to exercise an asymmetrical influence within that system.

[2] The nasty debate over the Reagan Administration's IMF quota increase in 1983 is indicative of a lowered commitment by many US political leaders to shaping the development of the Third World (Frieden, 1987: 181–90).

over the past two decades. In fact, it has been reinforced in the 1990s with the collapse of the Soviet Union and the successful waging of the Gulf War. The US military stands alone in its capacity to project force on a global basis. And finally, as Henry Nau and Joseph Nye have recently argued (Nau, 1990; Nye, 1990), American ideals have so informed international political and economic life that even though American material capabilities may have declined relative to the postwar zenith, the power of those ideas remains vibrant and strong. American leadership in political and economic affairs flows from these sources of power, to be used, misused, or abused depending upon the choices American policy-makers decide to make.

At the same time that certain aspects of American power remain intact, the consequences of prolonged high American budgetary, trade, and capital deficits have begun to shift the capacity to exercise power to other actors in the financial system. This can be seen most clearly in the changing direction of capital movements in the global financial system since the early 1980s, with long-term capital flowing into rather than out of the United States. For example, peripheral areas which in the 1970s were capital importers on the order of $30–50 billion per year suddenly found themselves after 1982 being forced to repatriate resources simply to meet their debt repayments: although the sum of repayments was small, the violent change from being a large-scale capital importer to a capital exporter stalled these economies and in fact enforced depression-era conditions on them for much of the 1980s (Lindert, 1989: 251, 263–4). Much of this reversal was directed back to the United States, as American banks were the prime lenders to Latin America and most repayments were directed towards commercial loans. To these repayments must be added the large sums moving from Japan to the United States during the 1980s, mostly due to Japanese purchases of US treasury notes. Since its postwar economic recovery, Japan has often been the second largest foreign investor in the United States, ranking behind the United Kingdom but ahead of Canada and Germany. The inflow of Japanese capital into the United States, however, increased markedly during the decade of the 1980s, moving from a low of US$805 million in 1982 to a high of over US$31 billion in 1988. Moreover, in four years – 1981, 1984, 1985, and 1988 – Japanese companies were the single largest foreign purchaser of US treasury notes and bonds, including a staggering US$21.8 billion worth in 1988 alone. Table 6.1 provides details of these inflows during the 1980s.

Table 6.1 *Long-term Japanese investment in the United States,*[a] *1981–90,*
$US million (rounded)

Year	Treasury bonds and notes	Other investments	Combined
1981[b,c]	−1,301	−123	−1,424
1982	−797	−8	−805
1983	−2,315	−945	−3,260
1984[b]	−6,289	−1,287	−7,576
1985[b]	−17,909	−5,725	−23,634
1986	+22	−12,916	−12,894
1987	−868	−12,986	−13,854
1988[b]	−21,750	−9,608	−31,358
1989	−1,681	−9,661	−11,342
1990	+14,784	+2,164	+16,948
Totals	−38,104	−51,095	−89,199

Notes: [a] These include investments in US treasury bonds and noted, US government and Federal Agency bonds, US corporate bonds, and US corporate stocks.
[b] Denotes those years in which the Japanese were the largest foreign purchasers of US treasury bonds and notes.
[c] In 1981 Japan is recorded as the largest single foreign purchaser of US treasury bonds and notes, surpassed only by the collectively totaled purchases of the oil-producing Gulf states, who bought just over $11 billion worth of treasury offerings.
− = Inflow to US.
+ − Outflow from US.
Source: Treasury Bulletin (various issues).

These changes are working to alter the exercise of what Susan Strange (1988: 24–9) calls "structural power" within the international organization of credit. As Japan, Britain, and Germany become key sources of credit for the world-economy, control over the regulation of credit conditions will slowly pass to their central banks and Treasuries. This can be seen most importantly in the realm of interest rate policy, where the Bank of Japan and the Bundesbank now chart their own independent interest rate policies within an integrated global financial system. This independence is in marked contrast to the 1960s when they could follow such policies precisely because of their relative insulation from the global financial system. Today German and Japanese interest rates weigh heavily upon interest rate levels in Europe and east Asia respectively, denying to the Federal Reserve Board the capacity to overly determine global interest rates.

This loss of one aspect of American structural power must be balanced with an appreciation of the centrality of both US interest rates and US dollar-denominated financial instruments to the global financial system. American interest rates remain an important factor in determining where funds are raised and in what direction they flow, especially in conditions of increasingly unfettered capital mobility. In this sense, interest rates around the world continue to reflect the pull of US rates, even if this pull is today partially circumscribed. More importantly, with the likelihood of large capital flows into and out of the United States continuing into the indefinite future, the volume of US dollar-denominated financial instruments flowing throughout the global financial system will remain high relative to those denominated in other major currencies. The continued liquidity and ease of transaction of US dollar financial instruments provide powerful incentives for non-US actors to use them, thus helping to maintain the Federal Reserve Board's influence over global short-term credit conditions. When combined with the central role of the US dollar and the central position of the American capital market within the global financial system, the volume of outstanding American debt will allow the United States to continue wielding an important form of structural power into the near-term future.[3]

Finally, the nature of financial intermediation has changed within the international organization of credit. A pendulum shift is moving the form of financial intermediation away from foreign direct investment (FDI) and bank loans and back again towards the issuing of securities and bonds. In technical terms it is away from indirect mediation and towards direct mediation of capital, or what many have called "disintermediation." This alters the relationship among financial actors in subtle but important ways. On one hand it means that a new type of monetary agent is gaining influence in the capital cycling mechanism, or more properly regaining influence. Whereas corporations and money-center or clearing banks once controlled the private international movement of funds by engaging in FDI and bank lending, it is now largely merchant banks and securities firms which are engaged in the movement of private funds across borders through

---

[3] In a different vein, both Susan Strange (1969) and Eric Helleiner (1989) have commented upon the ambiguity which creditor and debtor status holds for the ability of states to exercise influence in international finance and politics. The point which they stress, and which is argued here also, is that power and influence flow from the juxtaposition of many capabilities, and that to focus narrowly on only one aspect of power may be misleading.

share and securities issues. Banks, of course, maintain a strong presence in the securities and bond-writing industries, especially in the Eurocurrency markets, and there is some cross-ownership of banks with firms that offer these types of financial services. Indeed, it is possible to speculate that the involvement of banks in these activities may fundamentally change how they approach their core business of indirect financial mediation.[4] Nevertheless, "old" types of players are gaining a new clout, and helping to transform global finance in the process.

On the other hand, the enhanced role of near-bank monetary agents presents new problems for public regulation of the financial system. Traditional regulatory agencies for near-banks, such as securities commissions, do not have extensive inter-governmental links, and have not needed to develop expertise in the international regulation of financial transactions; their focus is squarely on the domestic activities of these firms (Porter, 1993; Underhill, 1995). Central banks do focus upon these factors in their capacity as guardians of national price stability, but do not have the statutory authority to regulate near-banks. An ambiguity thus emerges which treats near-banks as traditional economic (that is, non-financial) actors even though they now have a significant role in the global financial system.[5] The result is an uneven degree of public regulation over the financial system as a whole.[6]

Taken together, the re-emergence of "old" players and the enhanced regulatory ambiguity over responsibility for changing forms of capital flows ensures that the traditional mechanisms through which states have exercised financial power are changing. They are no longer as effective simply because the main institutional objects of state regulation – banks – no longer play the same kind of role within the financial

---

[4] It may be argued, for example, that banks are changing from institutions in which savers and borrowers meet to institutions that manage and sell risk measured in terms of financial products (*The Economist*, 10–16 April 1993: Survey of International Banking).

[5] For example, GE Financial Services, an American non-bank financial firm owned by General Electric, has assets surpassed only by the six largest American banks. It engages in all manner of financial operations through its main subsidiary GE Capital Corporation (and until recently Kidder Peabody, one of America's oldest and most respected investment banking and brokerage houses). Yet it is not a bank and is not subject to banking regulations. It is a non-bank monetary agent actively involved in the capital recycling mechanism (*Financial Times*, 20 May 1992: section III, v).

[6] Ethan Kapstein has also argued that a non-level commercial playing field has been created with regard to global banking regulations, in which near-bank monetary agents are favored (1989: 345).

system that they once did. This has implications most importantly for Japanese financial power, which is predicated upon close ties between the Ministry of Finance, the Bank of Japan, and the main city banks. Indeed, one recent critic has argued that the effects of the "bubble economy" and its collapse are partly related to the puncturing of these once-close ties (Murphy, 1996: chapter 9). Equally important, however, is the way in which the move to more direct financial mediation empowers capital markets to shape the demand and supply of credit. Direct mediation strengthens the market power of financial élites, subjecting those in need of capital to a stricter and more profit-oriented set of market criteria. Finally, to complete the circle, direct mediation, by strengthening the market power of financial élites, also reinforces the primacy of the largest and most open capital markets. It therefore reinforces the centrality of the New York and London markets despite the capital-richness of Tokyo and Frankfurt, because the former are the easiest and most lucrative markets to operate within. The shift towards direct mediation thus maintains in part the structural power of the American state even though the American economy is the world's largest debtor.

It is in this sense that the very nature of power in the international organization of credit is being profoundly transformed by these changes. At one level, asymmetries in the exercise of public power are being concentrated in the United States, Japan, Germany, and, more ambiguously, the United Kingdom. But the power available to these states is no longer undifferentiated in its scope. Rather, as we have seen, the ability of these states to exercise power in financial matters depends upon the mechanisms used, whether interest rates, open market operations, or capital regulations. The ability of the United States to decisively influence global interest rates is declining while the ability of Germany and Japan to influence the interest rates of their economic hinterlands is rising. In terms of open market operations or capital movements as determined by regulatory restrictions, the centrality of the New York capital market and the volume and liquidity of American government securities bestows upon the American state an unparalleled ability to influence the international organization of credit in certain respects. As German and Japanese secondary markets in government securities develop, however, this degree of structural power cannot be expected to last.[7]

---

[7] In this respect, the unexpectedly large German deficits needed to fund unification

At the same time, however, the very sources of structural power are now more ambiguous in their origin than at any time during the postwar period. No single center exists that is the source of both international credit and political/military power. London during the nineteenth century and New York during the Bretton Woods period functioned in this dual sense, also supported by the international role of their respective currencies. Today, however, not only are there three PFCs, but there is a sharp distinction between the major supplier of international military security and the major supplier of international credit. The capacity to exercise effective power over the financial system under such conditions is fragmented precisely because the sources of power are no longer concentrated in a single center as they have been historically.

In terms of the actual exercise of structural power, markets have been empowered to exercise increased authority within the international organization of credit. Power is thus exercised indirectly through market forces, where it is lodged in the multiple actions of commercial firms engaged in the competitive provision of access to stocks of internationally mobile capital. The structural power of the market is thus both collective in nature and fragmented in practice. It is collective in the sense that financial markets are led by a relatively small number of highly competitive firms; the homogeneity of their views towards the exercise of power over access to international credit largely flows from their collective understanding of how markets are in fact organized. Moreover, many credit decisions are made in the light of determinations of credit ratings which are collective in the sense of being provided to the entire financial industry. At the same time, the exercise of power is necessarily fragmented in practice because power is exercised through individual firms via their individuated decisions to grant access to credit. On these terms the accountability of power is becoming intensely private in nature, divided along the lines of both firm and nationality. This privatization of structural power within global finance strongly supports the critiques of markets as more than simply points of exchange between buyers and sellers of goods and services: they are systems of power in their own right and deserve to be studied as such.

Structural power is also more diffuse now because the ability of

ought to speed up this process by increasing the volume of mark-denominated financial instruments available in the German secondary market.

public authorities to exercise power is in a state of transition. Whereas the United States is still able to exercise a certain kind of structural power in the world credit system through open market operations and capital regulations, it is able to exercise less power via the netting of domestic interest rates. Global interest rates are no longer set by the Federal Reserve Board as they were in the early 1980s, but rather by the interaction of German, Japanese, and American central bank rates. The emergence of Germany and Japan as major international creditors is thus confirmed in their ability to exercise an increased degree of structural power over the cost of capital. At the same time the enormous quantity of American bills and bonds in financial markets ensures that the United States will have into the future an enormous degree of leverage in shaping the immediate credit and liquidity conditions of the global financial system. Structural power flows from both debt and credit under the contemporary international organization of credit, and it is likely to continue to do so into the twenty-first century.

The 1990s, therefore, ought to be the last decade in which the contemporary international organization of credit bears any resemblance to its Bretton Woods predecessor. Not only will the world's major international creditor no longer be the United States, but the very system through which credit moves will cease to bear much of a relationship to that which emerged and evolved over the Bretton Woods period. The only constant points of departure will be the importance of New York as a PFC of significant stature and the concomitant importance of the American economy to world demand. While America's paramount military position will also continue, this will have less of a direct impact upon the organization of credit and more of an indirect impact upon monetary order by virtue of expanding the political boundaries of the world-economy. In terms of historical epochs, the 1990s will confirm that global finance has indeed been structurally transformed and that this transformation crystalized most importantly during the middle of the 1980s.

On this reading, the role of the major monetary states over the next decade will be at once critical, fragile, and powerful. Their role will be critical by virtue of being one of the few sources of resources to which marginalized and less powerful actors have access through political mobilization. Many of the financial challenges facing the world-economy will be resolved only through state participation in the process of financial mediation. This role is at the same time fragile because the resources available to state actors within the contemporary social hierarchy are highly stretched. Worrisome public debt loads, the triumph of conservative free market forces, and the progressive abandonment of a public role in the international allocation of credit, all make more fragile the ability of states to meet these financial challenges. And yet, certain states retain a powerful position within a progressively integrated global capital market precisely because of the structural influence which their actions wield over the commanding heights of global finance. They have only to act, or to coordinate their actions, for the organization of credit to be shaped in ways desired by these states. Even though the balance of financial power between public and private authority has been redrawn during the contemporary period, there is much that states can still do to shape the international organization of credit. As many recent scholars have argued from within the IPE tradition, political decisions remain both severely constrained by the international organization of credit and central to its future development.

International political economy and the historical mode of thought

At the close of his epic investigation into the relationship between civilization and capitalism from the fifteenth to eighteenth centuries, Fernand Braudel (1979/1984: 619) felt "the need to throw open the doors and windows, to give the house a good airing, even to go outside it." The house, or model, he sought to step outside of was the specific understanding of the structure of the world-economy that had served him so well on his three-hundred-plus-year journey through the early modern world. By examining his model outside of its established boundaries, he was able to ask not how well it was able to navigate the waters for which it was constructed (we are entitled to arrive at our own conclusions about that), but how well it might work on those waters for which it was not constructed, namely the present. His final chapter, in this vein, was fittingly titled "By Way of Conclusion: Past *and* Present" (emphasis added). Past and present are central for this project as well, in terms of attempting both to construct an historically informed theoretical framework for understanding the international organization of credit, and to explore the insights yielded by such an approach for understanding contemporary developments. But as chapter 1 made clear, examining the changing international organization of credit also provides the avenue through which we can take part in a larger disciplinary debate. By stepping outside of the house constructed during the course of chapters 2–5, we can argue that the Braudelian inspired world-economy approach offers an important pathway to IPE. While it is not the only possible future pathway for IPE, it is one with which it is necessary to engage if IPE is to consolidate itself as a field of study in its own right.

Constructing the world-economy approach has demonstrated that a rich vein of scholarship exists out of which an IPE free of the imperial pretensions of economics and political science can be fashioned. More open to skepticism perhaps is the claim that the world-economy approach also provides IPE with an object of inquiry around which it can cohere as a discipline in its own right. Chief among such skeptical arguments may be the worry that the world-economy approach is at its core a structural approach, complete with all of the problems which such an approach entails.[8] Most importantly, an approach to IPE informed by a consideration of Braudel's work might fall prey to a deterministic structuralism reminiscent of either its Althusserian or neo-realist variants, in which people are the bearers rather than the builders of structure.[9] Although structural in terms of its origins, the world-economy approach need be neither reductionist in its logic nor deterministic in its application. It can escape both perils if it is understood to be historical in terms of its method and institutional in terms of its focus. The world-economy approach thus holds the promise of opening up an historical–institutional future for IPE.[10]

At the center of the world-economy approach is the historical mode of thought. This way of thinking is "historical" in two important senses. First, and most obviously, it looks to history for the raw materials out of which it is constructed and to which its method is

[8] Many historians have taken Braudel to task for his peculiar form of structuralism. See Hexter (1972) and Kinser (1981).

[9] Ashley (1984) and Thompson (1978) have issued the classic critiques of neo-realist and Althusserian structuralisms respectively. Wendt (1987) and Dessler (1989) have carried this debate forward in IR with a focus on questions of agency and structure, but considered from the perspectives of structuration theory and scientific realism.

[10] This future, however, is not an exclusionary one. No claims are being made here about the advantages of creating a discipline informed by a single dominant paradigm. Rather, what follows is the charting of an approach capable of providing one (but only one) of the future paths to IPE. The proper path to select depends upon a range of factors which can be determined only in conjunction with the selection of the problem to be explained. However, engagement between the paths will be necessary for the discipline to evolve.

applied. There are no ahistorical routes to constructing and verifying knowledge for this approach. Second, and more significantly, its ontology is historical in the dual sense of being transformative and self-referential: for the world-economy approach the historicity of knowledge denies that a single unchanging essence can be imputed to human beings and to the meanings which their actions represent; rather it legitimates the various meanings which we attach to human activity through reflection upon how they have become embedded in human practice. Knowledge about human acts, or *res gestae* (Collingwood, 1946: 1–10), is thus historical knowledge, and can be admitted as such only through a reflective three-way dialogue between historical evidence, an understanding of the motivations of historical subjects, and the historian or social scientist. And even though what constitutes "historical evidence" may be open to dispute, the elasticity inherent in this movement between evidence, object, and subject (to use a more common vocabulary) confers on this form of knowledge an ontology whose defining mark is its historicity.[11] Posed in these terms, the transformative potential of such an ontology resides in the intimate connection between knowledge and practice, and in the power of self-reflection, to change the parameters of human practice. On this basis the structuralism which the world-economy approach offers is an inherently non-deterministic one, distinguishable from both marxist and neo-realist structuralisms even as it builds on some of their more powerful insights.

The historical ontology of the world-economy approach encourages it to ask questions which have become identified with the tradition of critical theory. To follow Robert Cox's rendering of this tradition (1981: 129), it "stands apart from the prevailing order of the world and asks how that order came about. Critical theory . . . does not take institutions and social and power relations for granted but calls them into question by concerning itself with their origins and how and whether they might be in the process of changing." By being "genetic" in this sense, i.e., by asking how the prevailing order has come into being in terms of institutions (and therefore how prevailing social and power relations have become institutionalized), the world-economy approach escapes from the propensity towards reductionism so evident across the social sciences. Institutions are seen to be neither

---

[11] On the contestability of historical facts see Carr (1961: 7–30), and on the elasticity of the concepts at the heart of historical knowledge see Thompson (1978: 45–50, 109–11).

the functional by-product of larger social processes such as the world system nor the product only of purposive instrumental rationality. Rather, institutions are the basic organizational channels of human activity; the institutionalization of collective human activity is the means by which these activities become embedded into common-sense understandings and absorbed into the wider web of social, political, and economic practices that are bound up with a prevailing social order. The structuralism of the world-economy approach is thus set apart from other structuralisms not simply by its historicity, but also by its focus on institutions and the concrete practices through which the world-economy is constituted.

The historical and transformative ontology of the world-economy approach thus offers three key advantages to IPE theorizing. First, it focuses on concrete institutions as the key to understanding collective human activity, without at the same time severing these institutions from their wider social context. The institutional focus of the world-economy approach explores the historical practices associated with particular configurations of social and political power relations, but without making either institutions or context ontologically primitive. It escapes this tendency by considering the historicity of the practices involved. In the case of the international organization of credit, this involves looking directly at how financial institutions are organized, and at how they are responding to their environment even as they attempt to shape it. Beyond this, the focus on historical practice as channeled through concrete institutions guards against reducing the complexity of agency and structure to a question of abstract principles such as the profit motive or the balance of power. While motivations are a key determinant of human practice, they are for the world-economy approach always informed by institutional dynamics and shaped by common-sense understandings of what is proper, acceptable and possible. An institutional focus thus connects theory to the object under study by way of historical practice.

The second key advantage offered to IPE by the ontology of the world-economy approach is the recognition that state activity is only a sub-set of the institutional activities which constitute the world-economy. States are but one of the ways in which collective human practice is channeled. The world-economy approach thus undermines traditional dichotomies within IPE such as state and market, public and private, the economy and polity, by placing them on a continuum which distinguishes them according to a particular institutional form rather than according to their inherent qualities. More importantly, the state cannot serve as the only or even predominant focus of analysis. It is the continuum of institutional form itself, the ensemble of institutions in their relations with one another and with social and political power more generally, which ought to be the subject of inquiry. Here the world-economy approach joins with critical theory, and its Gramscian variant in particular, to demand that political society and the "extended" state always be seen in relation to civil society: the state and its institutions are part of the power structure of society rather than its defining dimension.[12] The state is neither ignored nor made the sole focus of inquiry; it is instead seen in its context as one of the key institutional forms of the world-economy.

But perhaps the most important advantage offered to IPE by the ontology of the world-economy approach is a clear core object of inquiry and a genuine openness to the insights of disciplines above and beyond those of politics and economics. The world-economy approach provides a clear core object of inquiry in terms of a bounded social totality which today is nearly global in scope. The aim of IPE, in this reading, is to increase our knowledge about this bounded social totality, understood in its historical and transformative sense. It is to acquire, in other words, what Collingwood (1946: 10) called "human self-knowledge." The object of inquiry for IPE is thus closely bound up with its ontological foundations: IPE seeks to inquire into the origins and practices of a bounded social totality that has come into being and which can be changed by institutionalized human practice. Neither comparative political economy, with its focus on specific geographical areas, nor foreign economic policy, with its focus on the policies of specific states, can serve to define such an IPE. Upholding the centrality of a wide-ranging bounded social totality as its key object of inquiry is therefore critical for the development of IPE as a field of study in its own right.

Advancing a clear conception of its core object of inquiry, however, will do little for IPE if it does not at the same time remain open to incursions from other disciplines. Not only politics and economics, but sociology, law, business studies, geography, organizational behavior, psychology, feminism, and cultural studies: these constitute the natural constituencies within which IPE can develop as a community

---

[12] The Gramscian variant of critical theory can be found in its clearest form in the writings of Cox (1983, 1987), Gill (1990, 1993), and Murphy (1994), all of which seek to associate changing forms of state with shifts in the social relations of civil society.

of scholarship, irrespective of disciplinary boundaries. To the extent that these scholarly endeavors can be enlisted as legitimate avenues of inquiry, IPE must embrace them in order to learn about the bounded social totality that marks it out as a specific discipline in its own right. And it is here where the final argument for the historical mode of thought can be employed, for it is one of the unique contributions of history that it can serve as a common point of contact for all of the social sciences. An historical–institutional future for IPE, therefore, involves a prior commitment of genuine openness to the insights of other disciplines in terms of what they can tell us of the world-economy as a bounded social totality. Such an approach offers a clear conception of the object of inquiry, a useful analytical focus, and a form of knowledge appropriate to the subject matter that is consistent with both its ontological foundations and the human practices which themselves produce *res gestae*. An historical–institutional future for IPE, in other words, confirms one important path to the creation of human self-knowledge, which after all is the starting point for all inquiry within the social sciences.

Appendix
Top merchant/investment banks, by city and era

I **Antwerp (sixteenth century)**
Fugger[1]
Welser
Hochstetter
Seiler
All of the above are South German banking houses

II **Amsterdam (seventeenth and eighteenth centuries)**
Hope & Co.[1]
Arend, Joseph (failed 1763)
Gebruder de Neufville (failed 1763)
Clifford & Son (failed 1772)
Andre Fels & Son
A. & S. Boas & Son
Couderc, Brants & Changuion
Horneca, Hogguer & Co.
Tepper & Co.

III **London (nineteenth and early twentieth centuries)**
N. M. Rothschilds & Sons[1]
Baring Brothers[1]
Mullens & Co.
Glyn, Mills & Co.
Currie & Co.
J. S. Morgan/J. P. Morgan/Morgan, Grenfell & Co.[1]
Brown, Shipley & Co.
Overend, Gurney (failed 1866)
Antony Gibbs & Sons

Speyer & Co.
C. J. Hambro & Son[1]
Frederick Huth & Co.[1]
Lazard Brothers
Kleinwort, Sons & Co.
J. Henry Schroder & Co.

Berlin (nineteenth century)
S. Bleichröder
Mendelssohn
Hansemann

IV   **New York (late nineteenth and early twentieth centuries)**
Drexel, Morgan/J. P. Morgan/Morgan, Stanley & Co.[1,2]
Kuhn, Loeb & Co.[1]
J. & W. Seligman & Co.[1]
Morton, Bliss & Co.[1]
August Belmont & Co.[1]
Moore & Schley
Brown Brothers & Co.
Dillon, Read & Co.
Harris, Forbes
Lee, Higginson & Co.

V   **London (contemporary period)**
S. G. Warburg[1] (SBC)
Morgan Grenfell[1] (Deutsche Bank)
Kleinwort Benson[1] (Dresdner Bank)
BZW (Barclay's Bank)
Hambros
Schroders
Baring Bank (ING Bank)

Plus all of the major US investment banks.

VI   **New York (contemporary period)**
J. P. Morgan[1]
Morgan Stanley[1]
Goldman Sachs[1]
Merrill Lynch[1]
Salomon Brothers[1]

Lehman Brothers[1]

The above are known collectively as the "bulge-bracket" firms.

Notes

1 Denotes firms of the highest calibre.
2 As a result of the legal barriers between different kinds of banking imposed by the 1932 Glass–Steagall Act, J. P. Morgan was forced to choose between being an investment bank or a deposit-taking institution. The result was the creation out of J. P. Morgan of a commercial bank (J. P. Morgan) and an investment bank (Morgan Stanley).

References

Abu-Lughod, Janet, 1989. *Before European Hegemony: The World System* AD *1250–1350*, Oxford: Oxford University Press

Acheson, A. L. K., Chant, J. F. and Prachowny, M. F. J. (eds.), 1972. *Bretton Woods Revisited*, Toronto: University of Toronto Press

Adler, John H. (ed.), 1967. *Capital Movements and Economic Development*, New York: St. Martin's Press, for the International Economic Association

Aglietta, Michel, 1985. "The creation of international liquidity," in Tsoukalis (1985)

Agnew, John and Corbridge, Stuart, 1995. *Mastering Space: Hegemony, Territory and International Political Economy*, London: Routledge

Albert, Michel, 1993/1991. *Capitalism Against Capitalism*, trans. Paul Haviland, London: Whurr Publishers

Andreff, Wladimir, 1984. "The international centralization of capital and the reordering of world capitalism," trans. Hugo Radice, *Capital & Class*, 22 (Spring): 58–80

Arrighi, Giovanni, 1994. *The Long Twentieth Century: Money, Power and the Origins of Our Times*, London: Verso

Ashley, Richard, 1984. "The poverty of neorealism," *International Organization*, 38 (2): 225–86

Bagehot, Walter, 1873/1917. *Lombard Street: A Description of the Money Market*, London: John Murray

Baker, James C., 1978. *International Bank Regulation*, New York: Praeger

Balance of Payments Yearbook, various issues. Washington, DC: International Monetary Fund

Balderston, Theo, 1989. "War finance and inflation in Britain and Germany, 1914–1918," *Economic History Review*, 2nd series, 42 (2): 222–44

Bank of England Quarterly Review, various issues

The Banker (London), various issues

Barraclough, Geoffrey, 1964/1967. *An Introduction to Contemporary History*, Harmondsworth: Penguin Books

Bell, Geoffery, 1973. *The Euro-dollar Market and the International Financial System*, London: Macmillan

Bernstein, Edward, 1972. "The evaluation of the International Monetary Fund," in Acheson, Chant and Prachowny (1972)

Block, Fred, 1977. *The Origins of International Economic Disorder*, Berkeley: University of California Press

Bloomfield, Arthur I., 1959. *Monetary Policy Under the International Gold Standard, 1880–1914*, New York: Federal Reserve Bank of New York

    1963. "Short-term capital movements under the pre-1914 gold standard," *Princeton Studies in International Finance*, 11, Princeton: International Finance Section, Princeton University

    1968. "Patterns of fluctuation in international investment before 1914," *Princeton Studies in International Finance*, 21, Princeton: International Finance Section, Princeton University

Born, Karl E., 1977/1983. *International Banking in the 19th and 20th Centuries*, trans. by V. R. Berghahn, Oxford: Berg

Braudel, Fernand, 1958/1980. "History and the social sciences. The longue durée," in *On History*, trans. S. Matthews, London: Weidenfeld & Nicolson

    1967/1973. *Capitalism and Material Life, 1400–1800*, trans. Miriam Kochan, New York: Harper & Row

    1977. *Afterthoughts on Material Civilization and Capitalism*, trans. P. M. Ranum, Baltimore, MD: Johns Hopkins University Press

    1979/1982. *Civilization and Capitalism, 15th to 18th Centuries, Vol. II, The Wheels of Commerce*, trans. Sian Reynolds, New York: Harper & Row

    1979/1984. *Civilization and Capitalism, 15th to 18th Centuries, Vol. III, The Perspective of the World*, trans. Sian Reynolds, London: Collins/Fontana

Brown, William A., 1940/1970. *The International Gold Standard Reinterpreted, 1914–1934*, 2 vols., New York: AMS Press

Bryant, Ralph C., 1987. "Intergovernmental coordination of economic policies: an interim stocktaking," in Volcker *et al.* (1987)

Burgess, Randolph P., 1927. *The Reserve Banks and the Money Market*, New York: Harper & Bros.

Cairncross, Alec K., 1953. *Home and Foreign Investment, 1870–1913*, Cambridge: Cambridge University Press

Calleo, David (ed.), 1976a. *Money and the Coming World Order*, New York: New York University Press, for the Lehrman Institute

    1976b. "The decline and rebuilding of an international economic system: some general considerations," in Calleo (1976a)

    1976c. "The historiography of the interwar period: reconsiderations," in Rowland (1976)

    1982. *The Imperious Economy*, Cambridge, MA: Harvard University Press

Calverly, John and O'Brien, Richard (eds.), 1987. *Finance and the International Economy*, Oxford: Oxford University Press, for the *AMEX Bank Review*

References

Cameron, Rondo, 1966. *France and the Historical Development of Europe: 1800–1914,* Chicago: Rand McNally

Carosso, Vincent P., 1987. *The Morgans: Private International Bankers, 1854–1913,* Cambridge, MA: Harvard University Press

Carr, Edward H., 1946. *The Twenty Years' Crisis: 1919–1939,* 2nd edn., London: Macmillan

1961. *What is History?,* Harmondsworth: Penguin

Cassis, Yousef, 1985. "Bankers in English society in the late nineteenth century," *Economic History Review,* 2nd series, 38 (2): 210–29

1987. *City Bankers, 1890–1914,* trans. Margaret Rocques, Cambridge: Cambridge University Press

1991. "Financial elites in three European centres: London, Paris, Berlin, 1880s-1930s," *Business History,* 33 (3): 53–71

de Cecco, Marcello, 1974. *Money and Empire: The International Gold Standard, 1890–1914,* Oxford: Blackwell

Cerny, Philip G. (ed.), 1993. *Finance and World Politics,* Aldershot: Edward Elgar

Chandler, Lester V., 1958. *Benjamin Strong, Central Banker,* Washington, DC: The Brookings Institution

Chase-Dunn, Christopher, 1989. *Global Formation: Structures of the World-Economy,* Oxford: Blackwell

Cipolla, Carlo M., 1956/1967. *Money, Prices, and Civilization in the Mediterranean World: 5th to 17th Century,* New York: Gordian Press

(ed.), 1976. *The Fontana Economic History of Europe: The Twentieth Century, Part Two,* London: Collins/Fontana

Clarke, Stephen V. O., 1967. *Central Bank Cooperation, 1924–1931,* New York: Federal Reserve Bank of New York

1973. "The reconstruction of the international monetary system: the attempts of 1922 and 1933," *Princeton Studies in International Finance,* 33, Princeton: International Finance Section, Princeton University

1977. "Exchange-rate stabilization in the mid-1930s: negotiating the tripartite agreement," *Princeton Studies in International Finance,* 41, Princeton: International Finance Section, Princeton University Press

1984. *American Banks in the International Interbank Market,* New York: New York University Press, for the Salomon Brothers Center for the Study of Financial Institutions

Clay, Henry, 1957. *Lord Norman,* London: Macmillan

Cleveland, Harold van B., 1976. "The international monetary system in the interwar period," in Rowland (1976)

Cohen, Benjamin J., 1977. *Organizing the World's Money: The Political Economy of International Monetary Relations,* New York: Basic Books

1981. *Banks and the Balance of Payments,* London: Croom Helm

1986. *In Whose Interest? International Banking and American Foreign Policy,* New Haven: Yale University Press for the Council on Foreign Relations

1996. "Phoenix risen: the resurrection of global finance," *World Politics,* 48 (1): 268–96

184

Cohen, Stephen D., 1970. *International Monetary Reform, 1964–69: The Political Dimension*, New York: Praeger

Collingwood, R. G., 1946. *The Idea of History*, Oxford: Clarendon Press

Cooper, Richard N., 1968. *The Economics of Interdependence*, New York: McGraw-Hill, for the Council on Foreign Relations

    1975. "Prolegomena to the choice of an international monetary system," *International Organization*, 29 (1): 63–97

    1985. "The gold standard: historical facts and future prospects," in Eichengreen (1985)

    1987. "Does the international financial system need reform?," in Kaushik (1987)

Corrigan, E. Gerald, 1992. "Challenges facing the international community of banking supervisors," *FRBNY Quarterly Review*, 17 (3): 1–9

Costigliola, Frank, 1977. "Anglo-American financial rivalry in the 1920s," *Journal of Economic History*, 37 (4): 911–34

Cottrell, P. L., 1975. *British Overseas Investment in the Nineteenth Century*, London: Macmillan

Coulbeck, Neil, 1984. *The Multinational Banking Industry*, New York: New York University Press

Cox, Robert W., 1981. "Social forces, states and world order: beyond international relations theory," *Millennium*, 10 (2): 126–55

    1983. "Gramsci, hegemony and international relations: an essay in method," *Millennium*, 12 (2): 162–75

    1987. *Production, Power and World Order*, New York: Columbia University Press

Crockett, Andrew, 1977. *International Money: Issues and Analysis*, New York: Academic Press

Crouch, Colin (ed.), 1979. *State and Economy in Contemporary Capitalism*, London: Croom Helm

Crough, G. J., 1979. *Transnational Banking and the World Economy*, Sydney: Transnational Corporations Research Project

Crouzet, François, 1964. "Wars, blockade, and economic change in Europe, 1792–1815," *Journal of Economic History*, 24 (December): 567–88

Deane, Marjorie and Pringle, Robert, 1994. *The Central Banks*, London: Hamish Hamilton

Dessler, David, 1989. "What's at stake in the agent–structure debate?," *International Organization*, 43 (3): 441–73

Destler, I. M. and Henning, C. Randall, 1989. *Dollar Politics: Exchange Rate Policymaking in the United States*, Washington: Institute for International Economics

Diaper, Stephanie, 1986. "Merchant banking in the inter-war period: the case of Kleinwort, Sons & Co," *Business History*, 28 (4): 55–76

Dickson, P. G. M., 1967. *The Financial Revolution in England: A Study in the Development of Public Credit, 1688–1756*, London: Macmillan

van Dormael, Armand, 1978. *Bretton Woods: Birth of a Monetary System*, London: Macmillan

References

Drucker, Peter F., 1986. "The changed world economy," *Foreign Affairs*, 64 (4): 768–91

Drummond, Ian M., 1979. "London, Washington, and the management of the franc, 1936–1939," *Princeton Studies in International Finance*, 45, Princeton: International Finance Section, Princeton University

  1981. *The Floating Pound and the Sterling Area: 1931–1939*, Cambridge: Cambridge University Press

Dufey, Gunter and Giddy, Ian H., 1978. *The International Money Market*, Engle-wood Cliffs: Prentice-Hall

The Economist (London), various issues

Ehrenberg, Richard, 1928/1963 (first published 1896). *Capital and Finance in the Age of the Renaissance*, trans. H. M. Lucas, New York: Augustus M. Kelley

Eichengreen, Barry (ed.), 1985. *The Gold Standard in Theory and History*, New York: Methuen

  1990. *Elusive Stability: Essays in the History of International Finance, 1919–1939*, Cambridge: Cambridge University Press

  1992. *Golden Fetters: The Gold Standard and the Great Depression, 1919–1939*, Oxford: Oxford University Press

  1993. *Reconstructing Europe's Trade and Payments: The European Payments Union*, Manchester: Manchester University Press

Feinman, Joshua N., 1993. "Reserve requirements: history, current practice, and potential reform," *Federal Reserve Bulletin* (June): 569–90

Feis, Herbert, 1930/1964. *Europe, the World's Banker, 1870–1914*, New York: Augustus M. Kelley

Financial Times (London), various issues

Ford, A. G., 1960/1985. "Notes on the working of the gold standard before 1914," in Eichengreen (1985)

Frankel, Allen and Morgan, Paul, 1992. "Deregulation and competition in Japanese banking," *Federal Reserve Bulletin* (August): 579–93

Frankel, Jeffrey A., 1984. *The Yen/Dollar Agreement: Liberalizing Japanese Capital Markets*, Washington, DC: Institute for International Economics

Frankel, Jeffrey A. and Kahler, Miles (eds.), 1993. *Regionalism and Rivalry: Japan and the United States in Pacific Asia*, Chicago: University of Chicago Press

Frey, Bruno, 1984. "The public choice view of international political economy," *International Organization*, 38 (2): 199–223

Frey, Bruno and Serna, Angela, 1995. "What economics journals should political scientists read?," *Political Studies*, 43 (2): 343–48

Frieden, Jeffry, 1981. "Third World indebted industrialization: international finance and state capitalism in Mexico, Brazil, Algeria and South Korea," *International Organization*, 35 (3): 407–31

  1987. *Banking on the World: The Politics of American International Finance*, New York: Harper & Row

Funabashi, Yoichi, 1989. *Managing the Dollar: From the Plaza to the Louvre*, 2nd edn., Washington, DC: Institute for International Economics

Gardner, Richard N., 1969. *Sterling–Dollar Diplomacy*, 2nd edn., New York: McGraw-Hill

1972. "The political setting," in Acheson, Chant and Prachowny (1972)

Germain, Randall D., 1996a. "The worlds of finance: a Braudelian perspective on IPE," *European Journal of International Relations*, 2 (2): 201–30

1996b. "Free trade and finance in North America: a Braudellian view," *New Political Economy*, 1 (2): 185–207

1996c. "Regionalism and finance: a conceptual approach," *Competition and Change*, 1 (4): 357–78

Gilbert, Charles, 1970. *American Financing of World War I*, Westport, CT: Greenwood

Gilbert, Milton, 1980. *The Quest for Monetary Order: The Gold Dollar Standard and its Aftermath*, New York: John Wiley, for the Twentieth Century Fund

Gill, Stephen, 1990. *American Hegemony and the Trilateral Commission*, Cambridge: Cambridge University Press

1993 (ed.). *Gramsci, Historical Materialism and International Relations*, Cambridge: Cambridge University Press

Gill, Stephen and Law, David, 1988. *The Global Political Economy*, Baltimore, MD: Johns Hopkins University Press

1989. "Global hegemony and the structural power of capital," *International Studies Quarterly*, 33 (4): 475–99

Gilpin, Robert, 1981. *War and Change in World Politics*, Cambridge: Cambridge University Press

1987. *The Political Economy of International Relations*, Princeton: Princeton University Press

1989. "Where does Japan fit in?," *Millennium*, 18 (3): 329–42

Globe & Mail, various issues

Goldman, Eric F., 1956. *The Crucial Decade: America, 1945–1955*, New York: Alfred A. Knopf

Goldthorpe, John (ed.), 1984a. *Order and Conflict in Contemporary Capitalism*, Oxford: Oxford University Press

1984b. "The end of convergence: corporatist and dualist tendencies in modern western societies," in Goldthorpe (1984a)

Goodman, John B., 1992. *Monetary Sovereignty: The Politics of Central Banking in Western Europe*, Ithaca: Cornell University Press

Goodman, John B. and Pauly, Louis W., 1993. "The obsolescence of capital controls? Economic management in an age of global markets," *World Politics*, 46 (1): 50–82

Gourevitch, Peter, 1978. "The second image reversed: the international sources of domestic politics," *International Organization*, 32 (4): 881–911

Government Financial Statistics, Washington, DC: International Monetary Fund

Gowa, Joanne, 1983. *Closing the Gold Window*, Ithaca: Cornell University Press

Grubel, Herbert G., 1981. *International Economics*, Homewood, IL: Richard D. Irwin

References

Guttmann, Robert, 1994. *How Credit-Money Shapes the Economy: The United States in a Global System*, Armonk, NY: M. E. Sharpe

Halliday, Fred, 1986. *The Making of the Second Cold War*, 2nd edn., London: Verso

Hamada, Koichi, 1985. *The Political Economy of International Monetary Interdependence*, trans. Charles Yuji Horioka and Chi-Hung Kwan, Cambridge, MA: MIT Press

Hamilton, Adrian, 1986. *The Financial Revolution*, New York: Free Press

Hammond, Bray, 1957. *Banks and Politics in America: From the Revolution to the Civil War*, Princeton: Princeton University Press

Hammond, Thomas H. and Knott, Jack H., 1988. "The deregulatory snowball: explaining deregulation in the financial industry," *Journal of Politics*, 50 (1): 3–30

Harrod, Roy, 1951. *The Life of John Maynard Keynes*, New York: W. W. Norton

Hawley, James P., 1987. *Dollars and Borders*, Armonk, NY: M. E. Sharpe

Hawtrey, Ralph G., 1962. *A Century of Bank Rate*, London: Frank Cass

Helleiner, Eric, 1989. "Money and influence: Japanese power in the international monetary and financial system," *Millennium*, 18 (3): 343–58

    1990. "Fernand Braudel and international political economy," *International Studies Notes*, 15 (3): 73–8

    1992. "Japan and the changing global financial order," *International Journal*, 47 (2): 420–44

    1993. "When finance was the servant: international capital movements in the Bretton Woods order," in Cerny (1993)

    1994. *States and the Reemergence of Global Finance*, Ithaca: Cornell University Press

Henderson, David, 1994. "Putting 'trade blocs' into perspective," in Vincent Cable and David Henderson (eds.), *Trade Blocs? The Future of Regional Integration*, London: The Royal Institute of International Affairs

Hexter, J. H., 1972. "Fernand Braudel and the *Monde Braudellien . . .*," *Journal of Modern History*, 44 (4): 480–539

Higgott, Richard and Stone, Diane, 1994. "The limits of influence: foreign policy think tanks in Britain and the USA," *Review of International Studies*, 20 (1): 15–34

Hirsch, Fred, 1967. *Money International*, Harmondsworth: Penguin Books

Hirsch, Fred and Doyle, Michael, 1977. "Politicization in the world economy: necessary conditions for an international economic order," in Hirsch, Doyle and Morse (1977)

Hirsch, Fred, Doyle, Michael and Morse, Edward, 1977. *Alternatives to Monetary Disorder*, New York: McGraw-Hill, for the Council on Foreign Relations

Hoffman, Mark, 1987. "Critical theory and the inter-paradigm debate," *Millennium*, 16 (2): 231–49

Horne, James, 1985. *Japan's Financial Markets: Conflict and Consensus in Policymaking*, London: George Allen & Unwin

Imlah, Albert H., 1958/1969. *Economic Elements in the Pax Britannica*, New York: Russell & Russell

Ingham, Geoffrey, 1984. *Capitalism Divided? The City and Industry in British Social Development*, London: Macmillan

Inoguchi, Takashi and Okimoto, Daniel I. (eds.), 1988. *The Political Economy of Japan, Vol. 2: The Changing International Context*, Stanford: Stanford University Press

International Financial Statistics, Washington, DC: International Monetary Fund

Kapstein, Ethan B., 1989. "Resolving the regulator's dilemma: international coordination of banking regulations," *International Organization*, 43 (2): 323–47

1994. *Governing the Global Economy*, Cambridge, MA: Harvard University Press

Kasman, Bruce and Rodrigues, Anthony P., 1991. "Financial liberalization and monetary control in Japan," *FRBNY Quarterly Review*, 16 (3): 28–46

Katzenstein, Peter J. (ed.), 1978. *Between Power and Plenty*, Madison: University of Wisconsin Press

Kaushik, S. K. (ed.), 1987. *International Banking and World Economic Growth*, New York: Praeger

Kennedy, Paul, 1987. *The Rise and Fall of the Great Powers*, New York: Random House

Keohane, Robert, 1980. "The theory of hegemonic stability and changes in international economic regimes, 1967–1977," in Ole R. Holsti, Randolph M. Siverson and Alexander L. George (eds.), *Change in the International System*, Boulder: Westview Press

1984a. *After Hegemony: Cooperation and Discord in the World Political Economy*, Princeton: Princeton University Press

1984b. "The world political economy and the crisis of embedded liberalism," in Goldthorpe (1984a)

Kindleberger, Charles P., 1967/1981. "The politics of international money and world language," in Kindleberger (1981)

1969/1981. "The Eurodollar and the internationalization of United States monetary policy," in Kindleberger (1981)

1973/1986. *The World in Depression, 1929–1939*, 2nd edn., Berkeley: University of California Press

1974. "The formation of financial centers: a study in comparative economic history," *Princeton Studies in International Finance*, 36, Princeton: International Finance Section, Princeton University

1976/1981. "The international monetary system," in Kindleberger (1981)

1978a. *Manias, Panics, and Crashes: A History of Financial Crises*, New York: Basic Books

1978b. *Economic Response: Comparative Studies in Trade, Finance, and Growth*, Cambridge, MA: Harvard University Press

1981. *International Money: A Collection of Essays*, London: George Allen & Unwin

References

1984/1993. *A Financial History of Western Europe*, 2nd edn., London: George Allen & Unwin

Kindleberger, Charles *et al.*, 1966/1981. "The dollar and world liquidity: a minority view," in Kindleberger (1981)

Kinser, Samuel, 1981. "*Annaliste* paradigm? The geohistorical structuralism of Fernand Braudel," *American Historical Review*, 86 (1): 63–105

Kirshner, Jonathan, 1995. *Currency and Coercion: The Political Economy of International Monetary Power*, Princeton: Princeton University Press

Kisch, Cecil H. and Elkin, W. A., 1932. *Central Banks*, 4th edn., London: Macmillan

Kneeshaw, J. T. and Van Den Burgh, P., 1989. "Changes in central bank money market operating procedures in the 1980s," *BIS Economic Papers*, 23, Basle: Bank for International Settlements, Monetary and Economic Department

Kooker, Judith L., 1976. "French financial diplomacy: the interwar years," in Rowland (1976)

Krasner, Stephen D., 1976. "State power and the structure of international trade," *World Politics*, 28 (3): 317–47

LaFeber, Walter, 1963. *The New Empire: An Interpretation of American Expansion, 1860–1898*, Ithaca: Cornell University Press, for the American Historical Association

Lake, David A., 1984. "Beneath the commerce of nations: a theory of international economic structures," *International Studies Quarterly*, 28 (2): 143–70

Lapid, Yosef, 1987. "The third debate: on the prospects of international theory in a post-positivist era," *International Studies Quarterly*, 33 (3): 235–54

Lary, Hal B., 1943. *The United States in the World Economy*, Washington, DC: Government Printing Office

Lincoln, Edward J., 1988. *Japan: Facing Economic Maturity*, Washington, DC: The Brookings Institution

Lindberg, Leon and Maier, Charles (eds.), 1985. *The Politics of Inflation and Economic Stagnation*, Washington, DC: The Brookings Institution

Lindert, Peter H., 1969. "Key currencies and gold, 1900–1913," *Princeton Studies in International Finance*, 24, Princeton: International Finance Section, Princeton University

1989. "Response to debt crisis: what is different about the 1980s?" in Barry Eichengreen and Peter H. Lindert (eds.), *The International Debt Crisis in Historical Perspective*, Cambridge, MA: MIT Press

Lipietz, Alain, 1986. *Mirages and Miracles: The Crisis of Global Fordism*, London: Verso

Llewellyn, David, 1985. "The role of international banking," in Tsoukalis (1985)

Lomax, David and Gutmann, P. T. G., 1981. *The Euromarkets and Financial Policies*, New York: John Wiley

Lombra, Raymond and Witte, William (eds.), 1982. *The Political Economy of International and Domestic Monetary Relations*, Ames: Iowa State University Press

Maddison, Angus, 1976. "Economic policy and performance in Europe: 1913–1970," in Cipolla (1976)

Madeuf, Bernadette and Michalet, Charles-Albert, 1978. "Global forces: a new approach to international economics," *International Social Science Journal*, 30 (2): 253–83

Mattione, Richard P., 1985. *OPEC's Investments and the International Financial System*, Washington, DC: The Brookings Institution

McNeil, William C., 1986. *American Money and the Weimar Republic*, New York: Columbia University Press

Meyer, Richard H., 1970. *Banker's Diplomacy: Monetary Stabilization in the Twenties*, New York: Columbia University Press

Michalet, Charles Albert, 1982. "From international trade to world economy," in Harry Makler *et al.* (eds.), *The New International Economy*, Beverley Hills: Sage

Milward, Alan S., 1984. *The Reconstruction of Western Europe: 1945–1951*, New York: Methuen

Moffitt, Michael, 1983. *The World's Money: International Banking from Bretton Woods to the Brink of Insolvency*, London: Michael Joseph

Moggridge, Donald E., 1972. *British Monetary Policy: 1924–1931*, Cambridge: Cambridge University Press

Moran, Michael, 1986. *The Politics of Banking*, 2nd edn., London: Macmillan

Morse, Edward, 1977. "Political choice and alternative monetary regimes," in Hirsch, Doyle and Morse (1977)

Murphy, Craig N., 1994. *International Organization and Industrial Change*, Cambridge: Polity Press

Murphy, R. Taggert, 1989. "Power without purpose: the crisis of Japan's global financial dominance," *Harvard Business Review*, 67 (2): 71–83

1996. *The Real Price of Japanese Money*, London: Weidenfeld & Nicolson

Nau, Henry R., 1990. *The Myth of America's Decline: Leading the World Economy into the 1990s*, Oxford: Oxford University Press

Neal, Larry, 1990. *The Rise of Financial Capitalism*, Cambridge: Cambridge University Press

Neufeld, Mark, 1995. *The Restructuring of International Relations Theory*, Cambridge: Cambridge University Press

Nye, Joseph S., 1990. *Bound to Lead: The Changing Nature of American Power*, New York: Basic Books

O'Brien, Richard, 1992. *Global Financial Integration: The End of Geography*, London: Pinter

Odell, John S., 1982. *US International Monetary Policy: Markets, Power and Ideas as Sources of Change*, Princeton: Princeton University Press

Overbeek, Henk, 1988. *Global Capitalism and Britain's Decline*, Amsterdam: University of Amsterdam Press

Palloix, Christian, 1975. "The internationalization of capital and the circuit of social capital," trans. Judith White, in Hugo Radice (ed.), *International Firms and Modern Imperialism*, Harmondsworth: Penguin Books

References

Pardee, Scott E., 1990. "Japanese financial markets," in Stoll (1990)
Parry, J. H., 1966. *The Establishment of the European Hegemony: 1415–1715*, New York: Harper & Row
Paterson, Thomas G., 1973. *Soviet–American Confrontation: Postwar Reconstruction and the Origins of the Cold War*, Baltimore, MD: Johns Hopkins University Press
Pauls, B. Dianne, 1990. "US exchange rate policy: Bretton Woods to present," *Federal Reserve Bulletin* (November): 891–908
Pauly, Louis W., 1988. *Opening Financial Markets: Banking Politics on the Pacific Rim*, Ithaca: Cornell University Press
  1990. "Institutionalizing a stalemate: national financial policies and the international debt crisis," *Journal of Public Policy*, 10 (1): 23–43
Pirenne, Henri, 1936. *Economic and Social History of Europe*, trans. I. E. Clegg, New York: Harcourt, Brace & World
Platt, D. C. M., 1968. *Finance, Trade, and Politics in British Foreign Policy: 1815–1914*, Oxford: Clarendon Press
Polanyi, Karl, 1944/1957. *The Great Transformation*, Boston: Beacon Press
Porter, Tony, 1993. *States, Markets and Regimes in Global Finance*, New York: St. Martin's Press
Reed, Howard Curtis, 1981. *The Preeminence of International Financial Centers*, New York: Praeger
Ridley, William P., 1987. "Japan: an uneasy transition to a rentier society," in Calverly and O'Brien (1987)
Riley, James C., 1980. *International Government Finance and the Amsterdam Capital Market, 1740–1815*, Cambridge: Cambridge University Press
Roberts, Richard, 1993. "What's in a name? Merchants, merchant bankers, accepting houses, issuing houses, industrial bankers and investment bankers," *Business History*, 35 (3): 22–38
Rolfe, Sidney and Burtle, James, 1973. *The Great Wheel: The World Monetary System, A Reinterpretation*, New York: Quadrangle/The New York Times Book Co.
de Roover, Raymond, 1963. *The Rise and Decline of the Medici Bank, 1397–1494*, Cambridge, MA: Harvard University Press
Rosecrance, Richard, 1986. *The Rise of the Trading State*, New York: Basic Books
Rowland, Benjamin (ed.), 1976. *Balance of Power or Hegemony: The Interwar Monetary System*, New York: New York University Press
Ruggie, John, 1982. "International regimes, transactions, and change: embedded liberalism in the postwar order," *International Organization*, 36 (2): 379–405
  1983 (ed.). *The Antinomies of Interdependence*, New York: Columbia University Press
Ruggie, John and Kratochwil, F., 1986. "International organization: a state of the art on an art of the state," *International Organization*, 40 (4): 753–75
Scammell, W. M., 1965/1985. "The working of the gold standard," in Eichengreen (1985)

1968. *The London Discount Market*, London: Elek Books

1987. *The Stability of the International Monetary System*, London: Macmillan

Schubert, Eric S., 1988. "Innovations, debts, and bubbles: international integration of financial markets in western Europe, 1688–1720," *Journal of Economic History*, 48 (2): 299–306

Schuker, Stephen A., 1988. "American 'reparations' to Germany, 1919–33: implications for the Third-World debt crisis," *Princeton Studies in International Finance*, 61, Princeton: International Finance Section, Princeton University

Schwartz, Herman M., 1994. *States Versus Markets: History, Geography, and the Development of the International Political Economy*, New York: St. Martins Press

Shinkai, Yoichi, 1988. "The internationalization of finance in Japan," in Inoguchi and Okimoto (1988)

Simon, Matthew, 1967. "The pattern of new British portfolio investment, 1865–1914," in Adler (1967)

Sinclair, Timothy J., 1994. "Passing judgement: credit rating processes as regulatory mechanisms of governance in the emerging world order," *Review of International Political Economy*, 1 (1): 133–59

Smith, Alan K., 1991. *Creating a World Economy: Merchant Capital, Colonialism and World Trade, 1400–1825*, Boulder: Westview Press

Smith, Woodruff D., 1984. "The function of commercial centres in the modernization of European capitalism: Amsterdam as an information exchange in the seventeenth century," *Journal of Economic History*, 44 (4): 985–1005

Sobel, Andrew C., 1994. *Domestic Choices, International Markets*, Ann Arbor: University of Michigan Press

Spero, Joan E., 1988/89. "Guiding global finance," *Foreign Policy* (Winter): 114–34

1977/1990. *The Politics of International Relations*, 4th edn., New York: St. Martin's Press

Spindler, J. Andrew, 1984. *The Politics of International Credit*, Washington, DC: The Brookings Institution

Stern, Fritz, 1984. *Gold and Iron: Bismarck, Bleichröder, and the Building of the German Empire*, New York: Alfred A. Knopf

Stoll, Hans R. (ed.), 1990. *International Finance and Financial Policies*, New York: Quorum Books

Stopford, John and Strange, Susan, 1991. *Rival States, Rival Firms*, Cambridge: Cambridge University Press

Strange, Susan, 1969. "The meaning of multilateral surveillance," in Robert W. Cox (ed.), *International Organization: World Politics*, London: Macmillan

1971. *Sterling and British Policy*, London: Oxford University Press, for the Royal Institute of International Affairs

1976. *International Economic Relations of the Western World: 1959–1971, Vol. 2, International Monetary Relations*, London: Oxford University Press

References

1982. "Still an extraordinary power: America's role in a global monetary system," in Lombra and Witte (1982)

(ed.), 1984. *Paths to International Political Economy*, London: George Allen & Unwin

1985. "Protectionism and world politics," *International Organization*, 39 (?) 233–59

1987. "The persistent myth of lost hegemony," *International Organization*, 41 (4): 551–74

1988. *States and Markets*, London: Pinter

1986/1989. *Casino Capitalism*, 2nd edn., Oxford: Basil Blackwell

1990. "Finance, information and power," *Review of International Studies*, 16 (3): 259–74

Strange, Susan and Calleo, David, 1984. "Money and world politics," in Strange (1984)

Swoboda, Alexander K., 1980. "Credit creation in the Euromarket: alternative theories and implications for control," *Group of Thirty Occasional Paper*, 2, New York

Taylor, Peter J., 1996. *The Way the Modern World Works: World Hegemony to World Impasse*, Chichester: John Wiley

Tew, Brian, 1982. *Evolution of the International Monetary System, 1945–1976*, London: Hutchinson

Thomas, Brinley, 1967. "The historical record of international capital movements to 1913," in Adler (1967)

Thomas, Woodlief, 1947. "Monetary aspects of public debt: the heritage of war finance," *American Economic Review*, 37 (2): 205–15

Thompson, E. P., 1978. *The Poverty of Theory and Other Essays*, London: Monthly Review Press

Tilly, Charles, 1992. *Coercion, Capital and European States, AD 990–1992*, Oxford: Blackwell

Tooze, Roger, 1988. "The unwritten preface: 'international political economy' and epistemology," *Millennium*, 17 (2): 285–93

Treasury Bulletin, various issues. Washington, DC: US Treasury Department

Triffin, Robert, 1960. *Gold and the Dollar Crisis: The Future of Convertibility*, New Haven: Yale University Press

1987a. "The paper exchange standard: 1971–19??," in Volker *et al.* (1987)

1987b. "WMS: the world monetary system or scandal?," in Kaushik (1987)

Tsoukalis, Loukas (ed.), 1985. *The Political Economy of International Money: In Search of a New Order*, London: Sage

Underhill, Geoffrey R. D., 1995. "Keeping governments out of politics: transnational securities markets, regulatory cooperation and political legitimacy," *Review of International Studies*, 21 (3): 251–78

United Nations (UN), 1949. *International Capital Movements During The Inter-War Period*, Lake Placid, NY: Department of Economic Affairs

Vernon, Raymond, 1966. "International investment and international trade in the product cycle," *Quarterly Journal of Economics*, 80 (2): 190–207

Vipond, Peter A., 1993. "The European Financial Area in the 1990s: Europe and the transnationalization of finance," in Cerny (1993)

Volcker, Paul A. *et al.*, 1987. "International monetary cooperation: essays in honor of Henry C. Wallich," *Essays in International Finance*, 169, Princeton: International Finance Section, Princeton University

Volcker, Paul A. and Gyohten, Toyoo, 1992. *Changing Fortunes: The World's Money and the Threat to American Leadership*, New York: Times Books

Walker, R. B. J., 1987. "Realism, change and international political theory," *International Studies Quarterly*, 31 (1): 65–86

Wallerstein, Immanuel, 1974. *The Modern World-System I*, New York: Academic Press

Walter, Andrew, 1993. *World Power and World Money*, 2nd edn., London: Harvester Wheatsheaf

Wendt, Alexander E., 1987. "The agent–structure problem in international relations theory," *International Organization*, 41 (3): 335–70

Whale, P. B., 1937/1985. "The working of the prewar gold standard," in Eichengreen (1985)

Wicker, Elmus, 1966. *Federal Reserve Monetary Policy, 1917–1933*, New York: Random House

Williams, David, 1963. "London and the 1931 financial crisis," *Economic History Review*, 2nd series, 15 (3): 513–28

Williams, Eric, 1944/1964. *Capitalism and Slavery*, London: André Deutsch

Woolley, John, 1985. "Central banks and inflation," in Lindberg and Maier (1985)

Zysman, John, 1983. *Governments, Markets and Growth*, Ithaca: Cornell University Press

Index

CAMBRIDGE STUDIES IN INTERNATIONAL RELATIONS